Post-Conviction Relief: C.O.A. in the Supreme Court

Kelly Patrick Riggs

Freebird Publishers

www.FreebirdPublishers.com

Freebird Publishers

221 Pearl St., Ste. 541, North Dighton, MA 02764
Info@FreebirdPublishers.com
www.FreebirdPublishers.com

Copyright © 2019
Post-Conviction Relief: C.O.A. in the Supreme Court
By Kelly Patrick Riggs

All Freebird Publishers titles, imprints, and distributed lines are available at special quantity discounts for bulk purchases for sales promotions, premiums, fundraising educational or institutional use.

ISBN-13: 978-1-7332826-2-8
ISBN-10: 1-7332826-2-9

Printed in the United States of America

SCOPE AND PURPOSE

My goal, as I write this book, is to provide an understanding of how The Supreme Court of the United States works and its function as it pertains to Certificates of Appealability. This book is my effort to teach you how to put your best foot forward as you petition the highest Court in the land. In this book, you will learn what the true function of the Supreme Court is, what it has the power to do, where it comes from, and how you can benefit from this knowledge in your own case.

TABLE OF CONTENTS

INTRODUCTION

This installment to the Post-Conviction Relief series is written as a layman's guidance to petition the Supreme Court after you have been denied by the Court of Appeals in your circuit. To be clear, there is no specific science that guarantees review in the Supreme Court of the United States. If you consider the numbers alone, you will see that the odds of getting relief in the Supreme Court are against you. It is for that reason that you must present your best when asking the Supreme Court to review a case.

One of the most important things to remember is that there is a lot more to the Supreme Court than just filing a petition for a writ of certiorari. In my own experience, I have prepared over 100 petitions to the Supreme Court on behalf of prisoners. To date, I have not been granted certiorari in any case. I have, however, received orders from lower courts, had Constitutional questions certified, and influenced many district courts. The secret to invoking the power of the Supreme Court is asking the right questions, asking the age-old questions that are never asked.

In this book, I'm going to teach you how to improve your chances of getting the truth out of your district court. Two of the most important questions laid before the Supreme Court are, "What does that really mean," and "Is that legal under the Constitution?"

CHAPTER ONE

FIRST THING FIRST

The first and most important thing to know about the Supreme Court is how strict they will hold you to the rules. One of those rules, Rule thirteen, requires that a petitioner file for a writ of certiorari within 90 days of being denied relief in the United States Court of Appeals. Rule thirteen states in pertinent part that:

> "*1. Unless otherwise provided by law, a petition for a writ of certiorari to review a judgement in any case, civil or criminal, entered by state court of last resort or a United States Court of Appeals (including the United States Court of Appeals for the Armed Forces) is timely when it is filed with the clerk of the Court within 90 days after entry of judgment.*
>
> *2. The clerk will not file any petition for writ of certiorari that is jurisdictionally out of time, see, e.g. 28 U.S.C. § 2101(c)."*

This is *not* a full reading of Rule thirteen. This is only a sample of the rule found in the next chapter of this book. I share it here because of its importance. To be clear you have 90 days from the ''entry of the judgment or order sought to be reviewed ...'' In other words, you have 90 days from the date the court files its decision on its own docket.

- *not* from the day you receive it;
- *not* from the "issuance date of the mandate ...";
- *not* from the day it's recorded in the digest; and
- *not* three months after the judgment.

When the court says 90 days from the "entry of the judgment" that's exactly what they mean. Thus, because of this time limit it's time to get some things out of the way now. Later in this book I'll be recommending that you use a particular form. So let's send out a request to get the form now.

With a simple letter to the clerk's office of the Supreme Court of the United States the clerk will gladly send you a short guide that can be helpful to inmates who wish to file petitions in the high court, along with a form for filing. In this chapter you will find a sample letter that you can personalize and send to the clerk of the Supreme Court of the United States at:

Supreme Court of The United States
1 First Street, N.E.
Washington, D.C. 20543

You may also refer your family to:

Clerk of Court
(202) 479-3011
http://www.supremecourt.gov

SAMPLE LETTER

FROM: Kelly Patrick Riggs
           Reg #
           Federal Correctional Institution
           P.O. Box 9000
           Seagoville, TX 75159

TO: Supreme Court of the United States
           1 First Street, N.E.
           Washington, D.C. 20543

RE: BLANK FORMS

Dear Clerk of Court:

I have recently been denied a certificate of appealability in the United States Court of Appeals. I wish to file a petition for a writ of certiorari in The Supreme Court of The United States. I request that you send me the blank forms that are made available by your office for prospective indigent petitioners to the above-listed address.

Thank you in advance for your assistance.

Respectfully,

X_____

Kelly Patrick Riggs   Pro Se

These final pages of Chapter One are copies of what you will receive in about thirty (30) days. This copy is used as an example only, do not try to use it for filing in the Supreme Court.

October 2018

OFFICE OF THE CLERK
SUPREME COURT OF THE UNITED STATES
WASHINGTON, D. C. 20543

GUIDE FOR PROSPECTIVE INDIGENT PETITIONERS FOR WRITS OF CERTIORARI

I. Introduction

These instructions and forms are designed to assist petitioners who are proceeding *in forma pauperis* and without the assistance of counsel. A copy of the Rules of the Supreme Court, which establish the procedures that must be followed, is also enclosed. Be sure to read the following Rules carefully:

Rules 10-14 (Petitioning for certiorari)
Rule 29 (Filing and service on opposing party or counsel)
Rule 30 (Computation and extension of time)
Rules 33.2 and 34 (Preparing pleadings on 8½ x 11 inch paper)
Rule 39 (Proceedings *in forma pauperis*)

II. Nature of Supreme Court Review

It is important to note that review in this Court by means of a writ of certiorari is not a matter of right, but of judicial discretion. The primary concern of the Supreme Court is not to correct errors in lower court decisions, but to decide cases presenting issues of importance beyond the particular facts and parties involved. The Court grants and hears argument in only about 1% of the cases that are filed each Term. The vast majority of petitions are simply denied by the Court without comment or explanation. The denial of a petition for a writ of certiorari signifies only that the Court has chosen not to accept the case for review and does not express the Court's view of the merits of the case.

Every petitioner for a writ of certiorari is advised to read carefully the *Considerations Governing Review on Certiorari* set forth in Rule 10. Important considerations for accepting a case for review include the existence of a conflict between the decision of which review is sought and a decision of another appellate court on the same issue. An important function of the Supreme Court is to resolve disagreements among lower courts about specific legal questions. Another consideration is the importance to the public of the issue.

III. The Time for Filing

You must file your petition for a writ of certiorari within 90 days from the date of the entry of the final judgment in the United States court of appeals or highest state appellate court or 90 days from the denial of a timely filed petition for rehearing. The issuance of a mandate or remittitur after judgment has been entered has no bearing on the computation of time and does not extend the time for filing. See Rules 13.1 and

13.3.   Filing in the Supreme Court means the actual receipt of paper documents by the Clerk; or their deposit in the United States mail, with first-class postage prepaid, on or before the final date allowed for filing; or their delivery to a third-party commercial carrier, on or before the final date allowed for filing, for delivery to the Clerk within 3 calendar days.   See Rule 29.2.

IV.   What To File

Unless you are an inmate confined in an institution and not represented by counsel, file:

—An original and ten copies of a motion for leave to proceed *in forma pauperis* and an original and 10 copies of an affidavit or declaration in support thereof.   See Rule 39.

—An original and 10 copies of a petition for a writ of certiorari with an appendix consisting of a copy of the judgment or decree you are asking this Court to review including any order on rehearing, and copies of any opinions or orders by any courts or administrative agencies that have previously considered your case.   See Rule 14.1(i).

—One affidavit or declaration showing that all opposing parties or their counsel have been served with a copy of the papers filed in this Court.   See Rule 29.

If you are an inmate confined in an institution and not represented by counsel, you need file only the original of the motion for leave to proceed *in forma pauperis*, affidavit or declaration when needed in support of the motion for leave to proceed *in forma pauperis*, the petition for a writ of certiorari, and proof of service.

If the court below appointed counsel in the current proceeding, no affidavit or declaration is required, but the motion should cite the provision of law under which counsel was appointed, or a copy of the order of appointment should be appended to the motion. See Rule 39.1.

The attached forms may be used for the original motion, affidavit or declaration, and petition, and should be stapled together in that order.   The proof of service should be included as a detached sheet, and the form provided may be used.

The Court's practice is to scan and make available on its website most filings submitted by litigants representing themselves.   The Court scans petitions, motions to proceed *in forma pauperis*, proofs of service, and the portion of an appendix that includes relevant lower court opinions and rulings.   While the Court does not scan other portions of an appendix from a *pro se* litigant, the entire appendix is fully a part of the Court's record and is available to the Justices.

V. Page Limitation

The petition for a writ of certiorari may not exceed 40 pages excluding the pages that precede Page 1 of the form. The documents required to be contained in the appendix to the petition do not count toward the page limit. See Rule 33.2(b).

VI. Redaction of Personal Information

Pursuant to Rule 34.6, certain types of personal information should not be included in filings. For example, social security numbers and taxpayer identification numbers should be redacted so that only the last four digits of the number are included, and the names of minor children should be redacted so that only initials are included. In general, Rule 34.6 adopts the redaction practices that are applicable to cases in the lower federal courts. See, e.g., Federal Rule of Civil Procedure 5.2.

VII. Method of Filing

All documents to be filed in this Court must be addressed to the Clerk, Supreme Court of the United States, Washington, D. C. 20543 and must be served on opposing parties or their counsel in accordance with Rule 29.

INSTRUCTIONS FOR COMPLETING FORMS

I. Motion for Leave to Proceed *In Forma Pauperis* - Rule 39

A. On the form provided for the motion for leave to proceed *in forma pauperis*, leave the case number blank. The number will be assigned by the Clerk when the case is docketed.

B. On the line in the case caption for "petitioner", type your name. As a *pro se* petitioner, you may represent only yourself. On the line for "respondent", type the name of the opposing party in the lower court. If there are multiple respondents, enter the first respondent, as the name appeared on the lower court decision, followed by "et al." to indicate that there are other respondents. The additional parties must be listed in the LIST OF PARTIES section of the petition.

C. If the lower courts in your case granted you leave to proceed *in forma pauperis*, check the appropriate space and indicate the court or courts that allowed you to proceed *in forma pauperis*. If none of the lower courts granted you leave to proceed *in forma pauperis*, check the block that so indicates.

D. Sign the motion on the signature line.

II. Affidavit or Declaration in Support of Motion for Leave to Proceed *In Forma Pauperis*

On the form provided, answer fully each of the questions. If the answer to a question is "0," "none," or "not applicable (N/A)," enter that response. If you need more space to answer a question or to explain your answer, attach a separate sheet of paper, identified with your name and the question number. Unless each question is fully answered, the Clerk will not accept the petition. The form must either be notarized or be in the form of a declaration. See 28 U. S. C. § 1746.

III. Cover Page - Rule 34

When you complete the form for the cover page:

A. Leave case number blank. The number will be assigned by the Clerk when the case is docketed.

B. Complete the case caption as you did on the motion for leave to proceed *in forma pauperis*.

C. List the court from which the action is brought on the line following the words "on petition for a writ of certiorari to." If your case is from a state court, enter the name of the court that last addressed the merits of the case. For example, if the highest state court denied discretionary review, and the state court of appeals affirmed the decision of the trial court, the state court of appeals should be listed. If your case is federal, the United States court of appeals that decided your case will always be listed here.

D. Enter your name, address, and telephone number in the appropriate spaces.

IV. Question(s) Presented

On the page provided, enter the question or questions that you wish the Court to review. The questions must be concise. Questions presented in cases accepted for review are usually no longer than two or three sentences. The purpose of the question presented is to assist the Court in selecting cases. State the issue you wish the Court to decide clearly and without unnecessary detail.

V. List of Parties

On the page provided, check either the box indicating that the names of all parties appear in the caption of the case on the cover page or the box indicating that there are additional parties. If there are additional parties, list them. Rule 12.6 states that all parties to the proceeding whose judgment is sought to be reviewed shall be deemed parties in this Court, and that all parties other than petitioner shall be respondents. The court whose judgment you seek to have this Court review is **not** a party.

VI. Table of Contents

On the page provided, list the page numbers on which the required portions of the petition appear. Number the pages consecutively, beginning with the "Opinions Below" page as page 1.

VII. Index of Appendices

List the description of each document that is included in the appendix beside the appropriate appendix letter. Mark the bottom of the first page of each appendix with the appropriate designation, *e.g.*, "Appendix A." See Rule 14.1 pertaining to the items to be included in the appendix.

A. Federal Courts

If you are asking the Court to review a decision of a federal court, the decision of the United States court of appeals should be designated Appendix A. Appendix A should be followed by the decision of the United States District Court and the findings and recommendations of the United States magistrate judge, if there were any. If the United States court of appeals denied a timely filed petition for rehearing, a copy of that order should be appended next. If you are seeking review of a decision in a habeas corpus case, and the decision of either the United States District Court or the United States Court of Appeals makes reference to a state court decision in which you were a party, a copy of the state court decision must be included in the appendix.

B. State Courts

If you are asking the Court to review a decision of a state court, the decision of which review is sought should be designated Appendix A. Appendix A should be followed by the decision of the lower court or agency that was reviewed in the decision designated Appendix A. If the highest court of the state in which a decision could be had denied discretionary review, a copy of that order should follow. If an order denying a timely filed petition for rehearing starts the running of the time for filing a petition for a writ of certiorari pursuant to Rule 13.3, a copy of the order should be appended next.

As an example, if the state trial court ruled against you, the intermediate court of appeals affirmed the decision of the trial court, the state supreme court denied discretionary review and then denied a timely petition for rehearing, the appendices should appear in the following order:

Appendix A   Decision of State Court of Appeals

Appendix B   Decision of State Trial Court

Appendix C   Decision of State Supreme Court Denying Review

Appendix D   Order of State Supreme Court Denying Rehearing

VIII. Table of Authorities

On the page provided, list the cases, statutes, treatises, and articles that you reference in your petition, and the page number of your petition where each authority appears.

IX. Opinions Below

In the space provided, indicate whether the opinions of the lower courts in your case have been published, and if so, the citation for the opinion below. For example, opinions of the United States courts of appeals are published in the Federal Reporter. If the opinion in your case appears at page 100 of volume 30 of the Federal Reporter, Third Series, indicate that the opinion is reported at 30 F. 3d 100. If the opinion has been designated for publication but has not yet been published, check the appropriate space. Also indicate where in the appendix each decision, reported or unreported, appears.

X. Jurisdiction

The purpose of the jurisdiction section of the petition is to establish the statutory source for the Court's jurisdiction and the dates that determine whether the petition is timely filed. The form sets out the pertinent statutes for federal and state cases. You need provide only the dates of the lower court decisions that establish the timeliness of the petition for a writ of certiorari. If an extension of time within which to file the petition for a writ of certiorari was granted, you must provide the requested information pertaining to the extension. If you seek to have the Court review a decision of a state court, you must provide the date the highest state court decided your case, either by ruling on the merits or denying discretionary review.

XI. Constitutional and Statutory Provisions Involved

Set out verbatim the constitutional provisions, treaties, statutes, ordinances and regulations involved in the case. If the provisions involved are lengthy, provide their citation and indicate where in the Appendix to the petition the text of the provisions appears.

XII. Statement of the Case

Provide a **concise** statement of the case containing the facts material to the consideration of the question(s) presented; you should summarize the relevant facts of the case and the proceedings that took place in the lower courts. You may need to attach additional pages, but the statement should be concise and limited to the relevant facts of the case.

XIII. Reasons for Granting the Petition

The purpose of this section of the petition is to explain to the Court why it should grant certiorari. It is important to read Rule 10 and address what compelling reasons exist for the exercise of the Court's discretionary jurisdiction. Try to show not only why the decision of the lower court may be erroneous, but the national importance of having the Supreme Court decide the question involved. It is important to show whether the decision of the court that decided your case is in conflict with the decisions of another appellate court; the importance of the case not only to you but to others similarly situated; and the ways the decision of the lower court in your case was erroneous. You will need to attach additional pages, but the reasons should be as concise as possible, consistent with the purpose of this section of the petition.

XIV. Conclusion

Enter your name and the date that you submit the petition.

XV. Proof of Service

You must serve a copy of your petition on counsel for respondent(s) as required by Rule 29. If you serve the petition by first-class mail or by third-party commercial carrier, you may use the enclosed proof of service form. If the United States or any department, office, agency, officer, or employee thereof is a party, you must serve the Solicitor General of the United States, Room 5614, Department of Justice, 950 Pennsylvania Ave., N.W., Washington, D. C. 20530–0001. The lower courts that ruled on your case are not parties and need not be served with a copy of the petition. The proof of service may be in the form of a declaration pursuant to 28 U. S. C. § 1746.

KELLY PATRICK RIGGS

No. _____

_____

IN THE

SUPREME COURT OF THE UNITED STATES

_____

_____ — PETITIONER
(Your Name)

VS.

_____ — RESPONDENT(S)

MOTION FOR LEAVE TO PROCEED *IN FORMA PAUPERIS*

The petitioner asks leave to file the attached petition for a writ of certiorari without prepayment of costs and to proceed *in forma pauperis*.

Please check the appropriate boxes:

☐ Petitioner has previously been granted leave to proceed *in forma pauperis* in the following court(s):

_____

_____

☐ Petitioner has **not** previously been granted leave to proceed *in forma pauperis* in any other court.

☐ Petitioner's affidavit or declaration in support of this motion is attached hereto.

☐ Petitioner's affidavit or declaration is **not** attached because the court below appointed counsel in the current proceeding, and:

☐ The appointment was made under the following provision of law: _____

_____, or

☐ a copy of the order of appointment is appended.

_____
(Signature)

AFFIDAVIT OR DECLARATION
IN SUPPORT OF MOTION FOR LEAVE TO PROCEED *IN FORMA PAUPERIS*

I, _____ , am the petitioner in the above-entitled case.   In support of my motion to proceed *in forma pauperis*, I state that because of my poverty I am unable to pay the costs of this case or to give security therefor; and I believe I am entitled to redress.

1. For both you and your spouse estimate the average amount of money received from each of the following sources during the past 12 months.   Adjust any amount that was received weekly, biweekly, quarterly, semiannually, or annually to show the monthly rate.   Use gross amounts, that is, amounts before any deductions for taxes or otherwise.

Income source	Average monthly amount during the past 12 months		Amount expected next month	
	You	Spouse	You	Spouse
Employment	$_____	$_____	$_____	$_____
Self-employment	$_____	$_____	$_____	$_____
Income from real property (such as rental income)	$_____	$_____	$_____	$_____
Interest and dividends	$_____	$_____	$_____	$_____
Gifts	$_____	$_____	$_____	$_____
Alimony	$_____	$_____	$_____	$_____
Child Support	$_____	$_____	$_____	$_____
Retirement (such as social security, pensions, annuities, insurance)	$_____	$_____	$_____	$_____
Disability (such as social security, insurance payments)	$_____	$_____	$_____	$_____
Unemployment payments	$_____	$_____	$_____	$_____
Public-assistance (such as welfare)	$_____	$_____	$_____	$_____
Other (specify): _____	$_____	$_____	$_____	$_____
Total monthly income:	$_____	$_____	$_____	$_____

2. List your employment history for the past two years, most recent first. (Gross monthly pay is before taxes or other deductions.)

Employer	Address	Dates of Employment	Gross monthly pay
_____	_____	_____	$_____
_____	_____	_____	$_____
_____	_____	_____	$_____

3. List your spouse's employment history for the past two years, most recent employer first. (Gross monthly pay is before taxes or other deductions.)

Employer	Address	Dates of Employment	Gross monthly pay
_____	_____	_____	$_____
_____	_____	_____	$_____
_____	_____	_____	$_____

4. How much cash do you and your spouse have? $_____
Below, state any money you or your spouse have in bank accounts or in any other financial institution.

Type of account (e.g., checking or savings)	Amount you have	Amount your spouse has
_____	$_____	$_____
_____	$_____	$_____
_____	$_____	$_____

5. List the assets, and their values, which you own or your spouse owns. Do not list clothing and ordinary household furnishings.

☐ Home
 Value _____

☐ Other real estate
 Value _____

☐ Motor Vehicle #1
 Year, make & model _____
 Value _____

☐ Motor Vehicle #2
 Year, make & model _____
 Value _____

☐ Other assets
 Description _____
 Value _____

6. State every person, business, or organization owing you or your spouse money, and the amount owed.

Person owing you or your spouse money	Amount owed to you	Amount owed to your spouse
_____	$_____	$_____
_____	$_____	$_____
_____	$_____	$_____

7. State the persons who rely on you or your spouse for support. For minor children, list initials instead of names (e.g. "J.S." instead of "John Smith").

Name	Relationship	Age
_____	_____	_____
_____	_____	_____
_____	_____	_____

8. Estimate the average monthly expenses of you and your family. Show separately the amounts paid by your spouse. Adjust any payments that are made weekly, biweekly, quarterly, or annually to show the monthly rate.

	You	Your spouse
Rent or home-mortgage payment (include lot rented for mobile home)	$_____	$_____
Are real estate taxes included? ☐ Yes ☐ No		
Is property insurance included? ☐ Yes ☐ No		
Utilities (electricity, heating fuel, water, sewer, and telephone)	$_____	$_____
Home maintenance (repairs and upkeep)	$_____	$_____
Food	$_____	$_____
Clothing	$_____	$_____
Laundry and dry-cleaning	$_____	$_____
Medical and dental expenses	$_____	$_____

	You	Your spouse
Transportation (not including motor vehicle payments)	$_____	$_____
Recreation, entertainment, newspapers, magazines, etc.	$_____	$_____

Insurance (not deducted from wages or included in mortgage payments)

	You	Your spouse
Homeowner's or renter's	$_____	$_____
Life	$_____	$_____
Health	$_____	$_____
Motor Vehicle	$_____	$_____
Other: _____	$_____	$_____

Taxes (not deducted from wages or included in mortgage payments)

	You	Your spouse
(specify): _____	$_____	$_____

Installment payments

	You	Your spouse
Motor Vehicle	$_____	$_____
Credit card(s)	$_____	$_____
Department store(s)	$_____	$_____
Other: _____	$_____	$_____
Alimony, maintenance, and support paid to others	$_____	$_____
Regular expenses for operation of business, profession, or farm (attach detailed statement)	$_____	$_____
Other (specify): _____	$_____	$_____
Total monthly expenses:	$_____	$_____

9. Do you expect any major changes to your monthly income or expenses or in your assets or liabilities during the next 12 months?

   ☐ Yes   ☐ No   If yes, describe on an attached sheet.

10. Have you paid – or will you be paying – an attorney any money for services in connection with this case, including the completion of this form?   ☐ Yes   ☐ No

    If yes, how much? _____

    If yes, state the attorney's name, address, and telephone number:

11. Have you paid—or will you be paying—anyone other than an attorney (such as a paralegal or a typist) any money for services in connection with this case, including the completion of this form?

    ☐ Yes   ☐ No

    If yes, how much? _____

If yes, state the person's name, address, and telephone number:

12. Provide any other information that will help explain why you cannot pay the costs of this case.

I declare under penalty of perjury that the foregoing is true and correct.

Executed on: _____ , 20____

_____
(Signature)

No. _____

_____

IN THE

SUPREME COURT OF THE UNITED STATES

_____

_____ — PETITIONER

(Your Name)

vs.

_____ — RESPONDENT(S)

ON PETITION FOR A WRIT OF CERTIORARI TO

_____

(NAME OF COURT THAT LAST RULED ON MERITS OF YOUR CASE)

PETITION FOR WRIT OF CERTIORARI

_____

(Your Name)

_____

(Address)

_____

(City, State, Zip Code)

_____

(Phone Number)

QUESTION(S) PRESENTED

LIST OF PARTIES

[ ] All parties appear in the caption of the case on the cover page.

[ ] All parties **do not** appear in the caption of the case on the cover page. A list of all parties to the proceeding in the court whose judgment is the subject of this petition is as follows:

TABLE OF CONTENTS

INDEX TO APPENDICES

TABLE OF AUTHORITIES CITED

CASES   PAGE NUMBER

STATUTES AND RULES

OTHER

IN THE

SUPREME COURT OF THE UNITED STATES

PETITION FOR WRIT OF CERTIORARI

Petitioner respectfully prays that a writ of certiorari issue to review the judgment below.

OPINIONS BELOW

[ ] For cases from **federal courts**:

The opinion of the United States court of appeals appears at Appendix _____ to the petition and is

[ ] reported at _____; or,
[ ] has been designated for publication but is not yet reported; or,
[ ] is unpublished.

The opinion of the United States district court appears at Appendix _____ to the petition and is

[ ] reported at _____; or,
[ ] has been designated for publication but is not yet reported; or,
[ ] is unpublished.

[ ] For cases from **state courts**:

The opinion of the highest state court to review the merits appears at Appendix _____ to the petition and is

[ ] reported at _____; or,
[ ] has been designated for publication but is not yet reported; or,
[ ] is unpublished.

The opinion of the _____ court appears at Appendix _____ to the petition and is

[ ] reported at _____; or,
[ ] has been designated for publication but is not yet reported; or,
[ ] is unpublished.

1.

JURISDICTION

[ ] For cases from **federal courts**:

The date on which the United States Court of Appeals decided my case
was _____.

[ ] No petition for rehearing was timely filed in my case.

[ ] A timely petition for rehearing was denied by the United States Court of
Appeals on the following date: _____, and a copy of the
order denying rehearing appears at Appendix _____.

[ ] An extension of time to file the petition for a writ of certiorari was granted
to and including _____ (date) on _____ (date)
in Application No. ___ A _____.

The jurisdiction of this Court is invoked under 28 U. S. C. § 1254(1).

[ ] For cases from **state courts**:

The date on which the highest state court decided my case was _____.
A copy of that decision appears at Appendix _____.

[ ] A timely petition for rehearing was thereafter denied on the following date:
_____, and a copy of the order denying rehearing
appears at Appendix _____.

[ ] An extension of time to file the petition for a writ of certiorari was granted
to and including _____ (date) on _____ (date) in
Application No. ___ A _____.

The jurisdiction of this Court is invoked under 28 U. S. C. § 1257(a).

CONSTITUTIONAL AND STATUTORY PROVISIONS INVOLVED

STATEMENT OF THE CASE

REASONS FOR GRANTING THE PETITION

CONCLUSION

The petition for a writ of certiorari should be granted.

Respectfully submitted,

_____

Date: _____

POST-CONVICTION RELIEF: C.O.A. IN THE SUPREME COURT

No. _____

_____

IN THE

SUPREME COURT OF THE UNITED STATES

_____

_____ — PETITIONER
(Your Name)

VS.

_____ — RESPONDENT(S)

PROOF OF SERVICE

I, _____, do swear or declare that on this date,
_____, 20 ___, as required by Supreme Court Rule 29 I have
served the enclosed MOTION FOR LEAVE TO PROCEED *IN FORMA PAUPERIS*
and PETITION FOR A WRIT OF CERTIORARI on each party to the above proceeding
or that party's counsel, and on every other person required to be served, by depositing
an envelope containing the above documents in the United States mail properly addressed
to each of them and with first-class postage prepaid, or by delivery to a third-party
commercial carrier for delivery within 3 calendar days.

The names and addresses of those served are as follows:

_____

_____

_____

I declare under penalty of perjury that the foregoing is true and correct.

Executed on _____, 20___

_____
(Signature)

SUPREME COURT OF THE UNITED STATES
OFFICE OF THE CLERK
WASHINGTON, D. C. 20543–0001

October 2018

SCOTT S. HARRIS
CLERK OF THE COURT

AREA CODE 202
479–3011

MEMORANDUM TO THOSE INTENDING TO PREPARE A PETITION FOR A WRIT OF CERTIORARI IN BOOKLET FORMAT AND PAY THE $300 DOCKET FEE.

This memorandum is directed to those who intend to prepare a petition for a writ of certiorari in booklet format pursuant to Rule 33.1 and pay the $300 docket fee required by Rule 38(a). It highlights the most common mistakes observed by the Clerk's Office. By following these guidelines you may help to expedite the processing of your petition. If you have questions, they should be directed to a case analyst in the Clerk's Office. This memorandum is useful also for those preparing appeals under Rule 18. The Rules of the Supreme Court, including amendments to those Rules that went into effect on November 13, 2017, are available at the Filing and Rules section of the Court's website.

In November 2017, the Court began requiring attorneys to submit petitions and other documents through its electronic filing system. At this time, paper remains the official means of filing, and the electronic filing requirements are in addition to the existing requirements for paper filings. Attorneys must register through the electronic filing system prior to submitting their documents; it may take 1–2 days for an application to be approved, so attorneys should apply well in advance of a filing deadline. Documents should be submitted through the electronic filing system contemporaneously with the submission of the paper version. Certain types of filings—including those containing sealed material and those in cases that were governed below by Fed. R. Civ. P. 5.2(c)—should not be submitted electronically. Personal identifying information contained in filings must be redacted pursuant to Rule 34.6. More detailed information can be found in the Court's Rules, in the Guidelines for the Submission of

Documents to the Supreme Court's Electronic Filing System, and in other guidance available at the Electronic Filing section of the Court's website.

1. PAGE AND TYPE SIZE:

The petition and the appendix required by Rule 14 must be presented on paper that is 6⅛ by 9¼ inches and not less than 60 pounds in weight as stated in Rule 33.1(a) and (c). The color of the cover must be white. Rule 33.1(g)(i). The petition shall be typeset in a Century family (*e.g.*, Century Expanded, New Century Schoolbook, or Century Schoolbook) 12-point type with 2-point or more leading between lines. Footnotes must be 10-point with 2-point or more leading between lines. Any type that does not measure on a typesize finder to be 12-point for the body and 10-point for footnotes will not be accepted. Attached are sample copies of correct and incorrect type.

Petitions produced on a personal computer using word processing, electronic publishing, or image setting are considered typeset and are acceptable. Petitions produced on a typewriter are not acceptable. Quotations exceeding 50 words shall be indented. The text of the petition and the appendix thereto must appear on both sides of the page. Rule 33.1(b).

2. COVER and COVER PAGE INFORMATION:

The front and back covers of the petition shall consist of 65-pound weight white paper. Rule 33.1(e). Items on the cover of the petition shall be in the order set forth in Rule 34.1(a) through (f). The caption of the case must list the petitioner(s) in this Court on the topside of the *versus* with your real opponent(s) on the bottom side. You should not copy the caption of the case as it appeared in the lower court unless it accurately identifies who the petitioner(s) and who the respondent(s) are in this Court. Counsel of record shall be a member of the Bar of this Court at the time the petition is presented for filing. Rule 34.1(f). Names of other attorneys who are members of the Bars of the several states may be listed on the cover, but names of non-lawyers such as research assistants, law students, and advisors may not appear on the cover under any circumstances; nor are they to be credited with having contributed to the preparation of the petition either in the text, in a footnote, or at the conclusion of the petition. If you are representing yourself, your name, address, and telephone number shall appear on the cover. If the names of the parties are too lengthy to be fully included on the cover of the petition, a short caption may be used. The complete listing of the parties to the proceeding in this Court shall be placed on the page following Questions Presented for Review. Rule 14.1(b). No text of the petition is to appear on the inside of the front or back covers. Do not list the October Term of the Court on the cover of the petition. A sample cover that may be followed as to form only is attached to this memo.

3. QUESTIONS PRESENTED:

The first page of the petition, not the back of the front cover, must contain **Questions Presented for Review.** Rule 14.1(a). The caption of the petition is not to be repeated on this page. The question(s) may be prefaced by a very brief introductory statement to set the scene, so that the question(s) may be understood. The question(s) should be short and concise and may not be argumentative or repetitious. If the petitioner or respondent is under a death sentence that may be affected by the disposition of the petition, the notation **"CAPITAL CASE"** shall precede the words "Questions Presented." No other information is to be included on this page. Rule 14.1(a).

4. PARTIES TO PROCEEDING:

The next page shall list the parties to the proceeding in this Court if all their names do not appear on the cover. Rule 14.1(b). This listing must be precise. Should a corporate entity be a petitioner, the Rule 29.6 corporate disclosure statement is to appear on this page. If there is no parent or publicly held company owning 10% or more of the corporation's stock, a statement to that effect shall be included on this page. Rule 29.6.

5. NUMBERING OF PAGES:

The pages containing questions presented for review, the list of parties and corporate disclosure statement, table of contents, and table of authorities should be numbered (i), (ii), (iii), etc. The table of contents and the table of authorities are followed by the text of the petition.   Rule 14.1(c).   There should be no second cover page prior to beginning the text of the petition.   The pages of the text of the petition should be numbered 1, 2, 3, etc., and not a continuation of (i), (ii), (iii), etc.   In no event may the text of the petition exceed 9000 words.   Rule 33.1(d) and Rule 33.1(g)(i).

6.   CONTENTS OF APPENDIX:

The appendix to the petition must contain all items required by Rule 14.1(i).   If you are seeking review of a state court judgment and an intermediate state appellate court was the last court to act on the merits, you shall include in the appendix any order regarding a petition for rehearing that may have been acted upon by that court as well as any orders denying discretionary review that may have been issued by higher state courts.   Any order denying rehearing that starts the running of the time for filing the petition must also be contained in the appendix.   Those orders shall include the caption showing the name of the issuing court, the title and number of the case, and the date of entry.   Rule 14.1(i)(i) through (iv).   If you are seeking review of a judgment from a United States Court of Appeals, you must, on that document, include the names of the judges who acted on the appeal.   Any published and unpublished opinions issued with respect to the judgment sought to be reviewed shall be included in the appendix.   Should the appendix become too voluminous, it may be presented in a separate volume or volumes with white covers bearing the appropriate caption.

The Court's practice is to scan and make available on its website most filings submitted by litigants representing themselves.   The Court scans petitions, motions to proceed *in forma pauperis*, proofs of service, and the portion of an appendix that includes relevant lower court opinions and rulings.   While the Court does not scan other portions of an appendix from a *pro se* litigant, the entire appendix is fully a part of the Court's record and is available to the Justices.

7.   REPRODUCING DOCUMENTS IN APPENDIX:

Material contained in the appendix as required by Rule 14.1(i) must also comply in all respects with the type size and page size requirements contained in Rule 33.1.   Lower court orders and opinions issued on paper larger than 6⅛ by 9¼ inches *may not be photo-*

reduced. Rule 33.1(b). These items must be reformatted to comply with Rule 33.1 and they must contain the caption showing the name of the issuing court or agency, the title and number of the case, and the date of entry. Rule 14.1(i). If a signature is contained on the original, reproduce the name by using "s/". The seal of the lower court and the file stamp may be reproduced by typesetting the information verbatim. Photo reproductions from Federal Supplement, Federal 2nd and 3rd Reporters, and regional reporters are not acceptable under Rule 33.1. Such materials must be reformatted to comply with the type size requirements of Rule 33.1. Items in the appendix are to be arranged as required by Rule 14.1(i)(i) through (vi).

8.   BINDING:

The petition and appendix shall be bound firmly in at least two places along the left margin so as to make an easily opened volume. No part of the text may be obscured by the binding. Saddle stitching or perfect binding is preferred. Staples may be used, with at least two along the left margin, covered with tape. Under no circumstances may spiral, plastic, metal, or string bindings be used. Rule 33.1(c).

9.   DOCKET FEE:

The $300 docket fee and the certificate of service shall accompany the petition. These items should not be sent under separate cover. The $300 docket fee may be paid by personal check, cashiers check, money order, or certified check made out to "Clerk, U. S. Supreme Court." Rule 38(a). **Do not send cash.**

10.   CERTIFICATE OF SERVICE:

The certificate of service of the petition shall be on a separate piece of paper apart from the petition. Rule 29.5. The certificate of service shall identify who was served with three copies of the petition and list the names, addresses, and telephone numbers of counsel indicating the name of the party or parties each counsel represents. Rule 29.5. If the proof of service is signed by a member of the Bar of this Court, notarization is not needed. If it is executed by one who is not a member of the Bar of this Court, the signature shall be either notarized or be accompanied by a declaration in compliance with 28 U. S. C. § 1746. Rule 29.5(c). The certificate of service is not to be included in the bound petition.

11. CERTIFICATE OF COMPLIANCE:

The petition for a writ of certiorari must be accompanied by a certificate signed by the attorney, the unrepresented party, or the preparer of the document stating that the petition complies with the word limitation. The person preparing the certificate may rely on the word count of the word-processing system used to prepare the petition. The word-processing system must be set to include footnotes in the word count. The certificate must state the number of words in the petition. The certificate shall accompany the petition when it is presented to the Clerk for filing and shall be separate from it. If the certificate is signed by a person other than a member of the Bar of this Court, the counsel of record, or the unrepresented party, it must contain a notarized affidavit or declaration in compliance with 28 U. S. C. § 1746. A sample certificate of compliance that may be followed as to form is attached to this memo.

12. TIME FOR FILING:

You have ninety calendar days, not three months, from the date of entry of judgment, order or opinion, or the date a timely filed petition for rehearing is denied, or a subsequent judgment based on the grant of the petition for rehearing, within which to file with the Clerk a petition for a writ of certiorari. Rule 13.1 and .3. The time to file does not begin to run when the mandate, remittitur, rescript, or similar document issues or is filed in the lower court. Rule 13.3. In order for the petition to be timely filed, it shall either be received by the Clerk of the Court within those ninety days or be sent to the Clerk by first-class United States Postal Service, including express and priority mail, postage pre-paid, and bearing a postmark, other than a commercial postage meter label, showing that the document was mailed on or before the last day for filing; or if it is delivered on or before the last day for filing to a third-party commercial carrier for delivery to the Clerk within 3 calendar days.

CORRECT TYPE

by allowing defenses based on school misconduct in situations in which the school's involvement in the lending relationship was not unusually extensive.

For the same reason, petitioner errs in contending (Pet. 18–19) that the decision of the court of appeals conflicts with this Court's cases allowing state law to impose liability greater than the liability imposed by federal law. Such cases, including *English* v. *General Electric Co.,* 496 U. S. 72 (1990), and *California* v. *ARC America Corp.,* 490 U. S. 93 (1989), address situations in which there is no conflict between the State's imposition of greater liability and federal law. Here, as in *Hines,* there is a conflict, because the federal scheme did not simply permit state-law school-based defenses in specified circumstances but *limited* state-law school-based defenses to those circumstances.[5]

3. There is no conflict among the courts of appeals on the question presented by petitioner, as petitioner herself admits. Pet. 21, 24. Petitioner nonetheless urges this Court to grant review on the basis of "divergent decisions emerging from the lower courts." Pet 21. In fact, the lower courts have uniformly found state laws comparable to the one at issue here to be preempted. This Court's review is not warranted based on petitioner's assertion that those courts apply different rationales in reaching their uniform results.

---

[5] Petitioner's reliance (Pet. 20–21) on *United States* v. *Kimbell Foods, Inc.,* 440 U. S. 715 (1979), *Wallis* v. *Pan American Petroleum Corp.,* 384 U. S. 63 (1966), and *United States* v. *Yazell,* 382 U. S. 341 (1966), is also misplaced. Those decisions concern the issue whether a court should rely on state law or fashion a federal common law rule when the court must fill in the interstices of a federal program. They do not concern the question presented here—under what circumstances federal law preempts conflicting state law.

SAMPLE COVER TO FOLLOW AS TO FORM

No.

IN THE

Supreme Court of the United States

MY CLIENT(S),

Petitioner(s)

v.

MY OPPONENT(S)

Respondent(s)

On Petition For Writ Of Certiorari
To The (court whose judgment you seek to review)

PETITION FOR WRIT OF CERTIORARI

MY NAME
Counsel of Record
MY FIRM
MY STREET ADDRESS
CITY, STATE, ZIP CODE
MY TELEPHONE NUMBER

INCORRECT TYPE

ing whether an agency's statement is what the APA calls a "rule" can be a difficult exercise. We need not conduct that exercise in this case, however. For even assuming that a statement terminating the Program would qualify as a "rule" within the meaning of the APA, it would be exempt from the notice-and-comment requirement of § 553.[7] Termination of the Program might be seen as affecting the Service's organization, but "rules of agency organization" are exempt from notice-and-comment requirements under § 553(b)(A). Moreover, § 553(b)(A) also exempts "general statements of policy," which we have previously described as " 'statements issued by an agency to advise the public prospectively of the manner in which the agency proposes to exercise a discretionary power.' " *Chrysler Corp., supra,* at 302, n. 31 (quoting Attorney General's Manual on the Administrative Procedure Act 30, n. 3 (1947)). Whatever else may be considered a "general statemen[t] of policy," the term surely includes an announcement like the one before us, that an agency will discontinue a discretionary allocation of unrestricted funds from a lump-sum appropriation.

Our decision in *Citizens to Preserve Overton Park, Inc.* v. *Volpe,* 401 U. S. 402 (1971), confirms our conclusion that the Service was not required to follow the notice-and-comment procedures of § 553 before terminating the Program. *Overton Park* dealt with the Secretary of Transportation's decision to authorize the use of federal funds to construct an interstate highway through a public park in Memphis, Tennessee. Private citizens and conservation organizations

---

the organization, procedure, or practice requirements of an agency and includes the approval or prescription for the future of rates, wages, corporate or financial structures or reorganizations thereof, prices, facilities, appliances, services or allowances therefor or of valuations, costs, or accounting, or practices bearing on any of the foregoing."

[7]We express no view on the application of the publication requirements of § 552, or on the propriety of the relief granted by the District Court. The Court of Appeals did not address these issues. See, *supra,* at 190.

SAMPLE CERTIFICATE OF COMPLIANCE WITH WORD COUNT

CERTIFICATE OF COMPLIANCE

No. 07-

MY CLIENT(S),

Petitioner(s)

v.

MY OPPONENT(S)

Respondent(s)

As required by Supreme Court Rule 33.1(h), I certify that the petition for a writ of certiorari contains _____ words, excluding the parts of the petition that are exempted by Supreme Court Rule 33.1(d).

I declare under penalty of perjury that the foregoing is true and correct.

Executed on _____, 20__

_____

KELLY PATRICK RIGGS

40

CHAPTER TWO

RULES OF THE SUPREME COURT

You can expect to receive a large yellow envelope from the Supreme Court in about thirty days. In that envelope, you will find the universal packet that they send to everyone: Prisoners, indigent citizens, and those who wish to pay the cost and file in booklet format. The packet will include a copy of, The Rules of the Supreme Court of the United States, a Guide For Prospective Indigent Petitioners For Writs Of Certiorari, a Motion For Leave To Proceed *in forma pauperis*, and a Memorandum. At the end of Chapter One is a copy of the forms you will receive, which will be referred to for study only; do not file anything prematurely.

Again, you have, on average, at least thirty days to wait for the necessary forms, so let's use this time wisely. Although you will receive a copy of the Rules of the Supreme Court in the mail, you will find a full copy at the end of this chapter to help you become acquainted with them now.

The rules in this book, however, are a bit different from the ones you will receive. In this set of rules, I have italicized sections that are of critical interest to Pro Se litigants who are incarcerated. This is not to say that the italicized portions are all you will need, I'm only saying that these sections should not be neglected.

For the next thirty or so days, continue through this book to get an understanding of how an indigent prisoner may improve his chances of being heard by the Supreme Court of the United States. You may do well to become acquainted with the Court rules that follow; welcome to the *Rules* of the *Supreme Court of the United States:*

RULES OF THE SUPREME COURT OF THE UNITED STATES

PART I. THE COURT

Rule 1. Clerk

1. *The Clerk receives documents for filing with the Court and has the authority to reject any submitted filing that does not comply with these Rules.*

2. The Clerk maintains the Court's records and will not permit any of them to be removed from the Court building except as authorized by the Court. Any document filed with the Clerk and made a part of the Court's records may not thereafter be withdrawn from the official Court files. After the conclusion of proceedings in this Court, original records and documents transmitted to this Court by any other court will be returned to the court from which they were received.

3. Unless the Court or the Chief Justice orders otherwise, the Clerk's office is open from 9 a.m. to 5 p.m., Monday through Friday, except on federal holidays listed in 5 U.S.C. §6103.

Rule 2. Library

1. The Court's library is available for use by appropriate personnel of this Court, members of the Bar of this Court, Members of Congress and their legal staffs, and attorneys for the United States and for federal departments and agencies.

2. The library's hours are governed by regulations made by the Librarian with the approval of the Chief Justice or the Court.

3. Library books may not be removed from the Court building except by a Justice or a member of a Justice's staff.

Rule 3. Term

The Court holds a continuous annual Term commencing on the first Monday in October and ending on the day before the first Monday in October of the following year, see 28 U.S.C. §2. At the end of each Term, all cases pending on the docket are continued to the next Term.

Rule 4. Sessions and Quorum

1. Open sessions of the Court are held beginning at 10 a.m. on the first Monday in October of each year and thereafter as announced by the Court. Unless it orders otherwise, the Court sits to hear arguments from 10 a.m. until noon and from 1 p.m. until 3 p.m.

2. Six Members of the Court constitute a quorum, see 28 U.S.C. §1. In the absence of a quorum on any day appointed for holding a session of the Court, the Justices attending - or if no Justice is present, the Clerk or a Deputy Clerk - may announce that the Court will not meet until there is a quorum.

3. When appropriate, the Court will direct the Clerk or the Marshal to announce recesses.

PART II. ATTORNEYS AND COUNSELORS

Rule 5. Admission to the Bar

1. To qualify for admission to the Bar of this Court, an applicant must have been admitted to practice in the highest court of a State, Commonwealth, Territory or Possession, or the District of Columbia for a period of at least three years immediately before the date of application; must not have been subject to any adverse disciplinary action pronounced or in effect during that 3-year period; and must appear to the Court to be of good moral and professional character.

2. Each applicant shall file with the Clerk (1) a certificate from the presiding judge, clerk, or other authorized official of that court evidencing the applicant's admission to practice there and the applicant's current good standing and (2) a completely executed copy of the form approved by this Court and furnished by the Clerk containing (a) the applicant's personal statement, and (b) the statement of two sponsors endorsing the correctness of the applicant's statement, stating that the applicant possess all the qualifications required for admission, and affirming that the applicant is of good moral and professional character. Both sponsors must be members of the Bar of this Court who personally know but are not related to, the applicant.

3. If the documents submitted demonstrate that the applicant possesses the necessary qualifications, and if the applicant has signed the oath or affirmation and paid the required fee, the Clerk will notify the applicant of acceptance by the Court as a member of the Bar and issue a certificate of admission. An applicant who so wishes may be admitted in open court on oral motion by a member of the Bar of this Court provided that all other requirements for admission have been satisfied.

4. Each applicant shall sign the following oath or affirmation: I, _____, do solemnly swear (or affirm) that as an attorney and as a counselor of this Court, I will conduct myself uprightly and according to law, and that I will support the Constitution of the United States.

5. The fee for admission to the Bar and a certificate bearing the seal of the Court is $200, payable to the United States Supreme Court. The Marshal will deposit such fees in a separate fund to be

disbursed by the Marshal at the direction of the Chief Justice for the costs of admissions, for the benefit of the Court and its Bar, and for related purposes.

6. The fee for a duplicate certificate of admission to the Bar bearing the seal of the Court is $15, and the fee for a certificate of good standing is $10, payable to the United States Supreme Court. The proceeds will be maintained by the Marshal as provided in paragraph 5 of this Rule.

Rule 6. Argument *Pro Hac Vice*

1. An attorney not admitted to practice in the highest court of a State, Commonwealth, Territory or Possession, or the District of Columbia for the requisite three years but otherwise eligible for admission to practice in this Court under Rule 5.1 may be permitted to argue *pro hac vice*.

2. An attorney qualified to practice in the courts for a foreign state may be permitted to argue *pro hac vice*.

3. Oral argument *pro hac vice* is allowed only on motion of the counsel of record for the party on whose behalf leave is requested. The motion shall state concisely the qualifications of the attorney who is to argue *pro hac vice*. It shall be filed with the Clerk, in the form required by Rule 21, no later than the date on which the respondent's or appellee's brief on the merits is due to be filed, and it shall be accompanied by proof of service as required by Rule 29.

Rule 7. Prohibition Against Practice

No employee of this Court shall practice as an attorney or counselor in any court or before any agency of government while employed by the Court; nor shall any person after leaving such employment participate in any professional capacity, in any case, pending before this Court or in any case being considered for filing in this Court until two years have elapsed after separation; nor shall a former employee ever participate in any professional capacity in any case that was pending in this Court during the employee's tenure.

Rule 8. Disbarment and Disciplinary Action

1. Whenever a member of the Bar of this Court has been disbarred or suspended from practice in any court of record or has engaged in conduct unbecoming a member of the Bar of this Court, the Court will enter an order suspending that member from practice before this Court and affording the member an opportunity to show cause, within 40 days, why a disbarment order should not be entered. Upon response, or if no response is timely filed, the Court will enter an appropriate order.

2. After reasonable notice and an opportunity to show cause why disciplinary action should not be taken, and after a hearing, if material facts are in dispute, the Court may take any appropriate disciplinary action against any attorney who is admitted to practice before it for conduct unbecoming a member of the Bar or for failure to comply with these Rules or any Rule or order of the Court.

Rule 9. Appearance of Counsel

1. An attorney seeking to file a document in this court in a representative capacity must first be admitted to practice before this Court as provided in Rule 5, except that admission to the Bar of this Court is not required for an attorney appointed under the Criminal Justice Act of 1964, see 18 U.S.C. §3006A(d)(6), or under any other applicable federal statute. The attorney whose name, address, and telephone number appear on the cover of a document presented for filing is

considered counsel of record. If the name of more than one attorney is shown on the cover of the document, the attorney who is counsel of record shall be clearly identified, see Rule 34.1(f).

2. An attorney representing a party who will not be filing a document shall enter a separate notice of appearance as counsel of record indicating the name of the party represented. A separate notice of appearance shall also be entered whenever an attorney is substituted as counsel of record in a particular case.

PART III. JURISDICTION ON WRIT OF CERTIORARI

Rule 10. Considerations Governing Review on Certiorari

Review on a writ of certiorari is not a matter of right but of judicial discretion. A petition for a writ of certiorari will be granted only for compelling reasons. The following, although neither controlling nor fully measuring the Court's discretion, indicate the character of the reasons the Court considers:

(a) *a United States Court of Appeals has entered a decision in conflict with the decision of another United States Court of Appeals on the same important matter; has decided an important federal question in a way that conflicts with a decision by a state court of last resort; or has so far departed from the accepted and usual course of judicial proceedings, or sanctioned such a departure by a lower court, as to call for an exercise of this Court's supervisory power;*

(b) *a state court of last resort has decided an important federal question in a way that conflicts with the decision of another state court of last resort or of a United States court of appeals;*

(c) *a state court or a United States court of appeals has decided an important question of federal law that has not been, but should be, settled by this Court, or has decided an important federal question in a way that conflicts with relevant decisions of this Court.*

A petition for a writ of certiorari is rarely granted when the asserted error consists of erroneous factual findings or the misapplication of a properly stated rule of law.

Rule 11. Certiorari to a United States Court of Appeals Before Judgement

A petition for a writ of certiorari to review a case pending in a United States Court of Appeals before judgment is entered in that court will be granted only upon a showing that the case is of such imperative public importance as to justify deviation from normal appellate practice and to require immediate determination in this Court, see 28 U. S. C. § 2101(e).

Rule 12. Review on Certiorari: How Sought; Parties

1. Except as provided in paragraph 2 of this Rule, the petitioner shall file 40 copies of a petition for a writ of certiorari, prepared as required by Rule 33.1, and shall pay the Rule 38(a) docket fee.

2. A petitioner proceeding *in forma pauperis* under Rule 39 shall file an original and 10 copies of a petition for a writ of certiorari prepared as required by Rule 33.2, together with an original and 10 copies of the motion for leave to proceed *in forma pauperis*. A copy of the motion shall precede and be attached to each copy of the petition. *An inmate confined in an institution, if proceeding* in forma pauperis *and not represented by counsel, need file only an original petition and motion.*

3. *Whether prepared under Rule 33.1 or Rule 33.2, the petition shall comply in all respects with Rule 14 and shall be submitted with proof of service as required by Rule 29. The case then will be placed on the docket. It is the petitioner's duty to notify all respondents promptly, on a form*

supplied by the Clerk, of the date of filing, the date the case was placed on the docket and the docket number of the case. The notice shall be served as required by Rule 29.

4. *Parties interested jointly, severally, or otherwise in a judgment may petition separately for a writ of certiorari, or any two or more may join in a petition. A party not shown on the petition as joined therein at the time the petition is filed may not later join in that petition. When two or more judgments are sought to be reviewed on a writ of certiorari to the same court and involve identical or closely related questions, a single petition for a writ of certiorari covering all the judgments suffices. A petition for a writ of certiorari may not be joined with any other pleading, except that any motion for leave to proceed in forma pauperis shall be attached.*

5. No more than 30 days after a case has been placed on the docket, a respondent seeking to file a conditional cross-petition (i.e., a cross-petition that otherwise would be untimely) shall file, with proof of service as required by Rule 29, 40 copies of the cross-petition prepared as required by Rule 33.1, except that a cross-petitioner proceeding *in forma pauperis* under Rule 39 shall comply with Rule 12.2. The cross-petition shall comply in all respects with this Rule and Rule 14, except that material already reproduced in the appendix to the opening petition need not be reproduced ' again. A cross-petitioning respondent shall pay the Rule 38(a) docket fee or submit a motion for leave to proceed *in forma pauperis*. The cover of the cross-petition shall indicate clearly that it is a conditional cross-petition. The cross-petition then will be placed on the docket, subject to the provisions of Rule 13.4. It is the cross-petitioner's duty to notify all cross-respondents promptly, on a form supplied by the Clerk, of the date of filing, the date the cross-petition was placed on the docket and the docket number of the cross-petition. The notice shall be served as required by Rule 29. A cross-petition for a writ of certiorari may not be joined with any other pleading except that any motion for leave to proceed *in forma pauperis* shall be attached. The time to file a conditional cross-petition will not be extended.

6. *All parties to the proceeding in the court whose judgment is sought to be reviewed are deemed parties entitled to file documents in this Court unless the petitioner notifies the Clerk of this Court in writing of the petitioner's belief that one or more of the parties below have no interest in the outcome of the petition. A copy of such notice shall be served as required by Rule 29 on all parties to the proceeding below. A party noted as no longer interested may remain a party by notifying the Clerk promptly, with service on the other parties, of an intention to remain a party. All parties other than the petitioner are considered respondents, but any respondent who supports the position of a petitioner shall meet the petitioner's time schedule for filing documents, with the following exception: A response of a party aligned with petitioner below who supports granting the petition shall be filed within 30 days after the case is placed on the docket, and that time will not be extended. Counsel for such respondent shall ensure that counsel of record for all parties receive notice of its intention to file a brief in support within 20 days after the case is placed on the docket. A respondent not aligned with petitioner below who supports granting the petition, or a respondent aligned with petitioner below who takes the position that the petition should be denied, is not subject to the notice requirement and may file a response within the time otherwise provided by Rule 15.3. Parties who file no document will not qualify for any relief from this Court.*

7. The clerk of the court having possession of the record shall keep it until notified by the Clerk of this Court to certify and transmit it. In any document filed with this court, a party may cite or quote from the record, even if it has not been transmitted to this Court. When requested by the Clerk of this Court to certify and transmit the record, or any part of it, the clerk of the court having possession of the record shall number the documents to be certified and shall transmit

therewith a numbered list specifically identifying each document transmitted. If the record, or stipulated portions, have been printed for the use of the court below, that printed record, plus the proceedings in the court below, may be certified as the record unless one of the parties or the Clerk of this Court requests otherwise. The record may consist of certified copies, but if the lower court is of the view that original documents of any kind should be seen by this Court, that court may provide by order for the transport, safekeeping, and return of such originals.

Rule 13. Review on Certiorari: Time for Petitioning

1. *Unless otherwise provided by law, a petition for a writ of certiorari to review a judgment in any case, civil or criminal, entered by a state court of last resort or a United States Court of Appeals (including the United States Court of Appeals for the Armed Forces) is timely when it is filed with the Clerk of this Court within 90 days after entry of the judgment. A petition for a writ of certiorari seeking review of a judgment of a lower state court that is subject to discretionary review by the state court of last resort is timely when it is filed with the Clerk within 90 days after entry of the order denying discretionary review.*

2. *The Clerk will not file any petition for a writ of certiorari that is jurisdictionally out of time, see, e. g.,28 U. S. C. § 2101(c).*

3. *The time to file a petition for a writ of certiorari runs from the date of entry of the judgment or order sought to be reviewed, and not from the issuance date of the mandate (or its equivalent under local practice). But if a petition for rehearing is timely filed in the lower court by any party, or if the lower court appropriately entertains an untimely petition for rehearing or sua sponte considers rehearing, the time to file the petition for a writ of certiorari for all parties (whether or not they requested rehearing or joined in the petition for rehearing) runs from the date of the denial of rehearing or if rehearing is granted, the subsequent entry of judgment.*

4. *A cross-petition for a writ of certiorari is timely when it is filed with the Clerk as provided in paragraphs 1, 3, and 5 of this Rule, or Rule 12.5. However, a conditional cross-petition (which except for Rule 12.5 would be untimely) will not be granted unless another party's timely petition for a writ of certiorari is granted.*

5. *For good cause, a Justice may extend the time to file a petition for a writ of certiorari for a period not exceeding 60 days. An application to extend the time to file shall set out the basis for jurisdiction in this Court, identify the judgment sought to be reviewed, include a copy of the opinion and any order respecting rehearing, and set out specific reasons why an extension of time is justified. The application must be filed with the Clerk at least 10 days before the date the petition is due, except in extraordinary circumstances. The application must clearly identify each party for whom an extension is being sought, as any extension that might be granted would apply solely to the party or parties named in the application. For the time and manner of presenting the application, see Rules 21, 22, 30, and 33.2. An application to extend the time to file a petition for a writ of certiorari is not favored.*

Rule 14. Content of a Petition for a Writ of Certiorari

1. *A petition for a writ of certiorari shall contain, in the order indicated:*

   (a) *The questions presented for review are expressed concisely in relation to the circumstances of the case, without unnecessary detail. The questions should be short and should not be argumentative or repetitive. If the petitioner or respondent is under a death sentence that may be affected by the disposition of the petition, the notation "capital case" shall precede the questions presented. The questions shall be set out on the first page following the cover, and no other information may appear on that page. The statement of any question presented is deemed to comprise every subsidiary question fairly included therein. Only the questions set out in the petition, or fairly included therein, will be considered by the Court.*

(b) (i) *A list of all parties to the proceeding in the court whose judgment is sought to be reviewed (unless the caption of the case contains the names of all the parties);*

(ii) *a corporate disclosure statement as required by Rule 29.6; and*

(iii) *a list of all proceedings in state and federal trial and appellate courts, including proceedings in this Court, that are directly related to the case in this Court. For each such proceeding, the list should include the court in question, the docket number and case caption for the proceeding, and the date of entry of the judgment. For the purposes of this rule, a case is "directly related" if it arises from the same trial court case as the case in this Court (including the proceedings directly on review in this case) or if it challenges the same criminal conviction or sentence as is challenged in this Court, whether on direct appeal or through state or federal collateral proceedings.*

(c) *If the petition prepared under Rule 33.1 exceeds 1,500 words or exceeds five pages if prepared under Rule 33.2, a table of contents and a table of cited authorities. The table of contents shall include the items contained in the appendix.*

(d) *Citations of the official and unofficial reports of the opinions and orders entered in the case by courts or administrative agencies.*

(e) *A concise statement of the basis for jurisdiction in this Court, showing:*

(i) *the date the judgment or order sought to be reviewed was entered (and, if applicable, a statement that the petition is filed under this Court's Rule 11);*

(ii) *the date of any order respecting rehearing and the date and terms of any order granting an extension of time to file the petition for a writ of certiorari;*

(iii) *express reliance on Rule 12.5, when a cross-petition for a writ of certiorari is filed under that Rule, and the date of docketing of the petition for a writ of certiorari in connection with which the cross-petition is filed;*

(iv) *the statutory provision believed to confer on this Court jurisdiction to review on a writ of certiorari the judgment or order in question; and*

(v) *if applicable, a statement that the notifications required by Rule 29.4(b) or (c) have been made.*

(f) *The constitutional provisions, treaties, statutes, ordinances, and regulations involved in the case, set out verbatim with appropriate citation. If the provisions involved are lengthy, their citation alone suffices at this point, and their pertinent text shall be set out in the appendix referred to in subparagraph 1(i).*

(g) *A concise statement of the case setting out the facts material to consideration of the questions presented, and also containing the following:*

(i) *If review of a state-court judgment is sought, specification of the stage in the proceedings, both in the court of first instance and in the appellate courts, when the federal questions sought to be reviewed were raised; the method or manner of raising them and the way in which they were passed on by those courts; and pertinent quotations of specific portions of the record or summary thereof, with specific reference to the places in the record where the matter appears (e. g., court opinion, ruling on exception, portion of court's charge and exception thereto, assignment of error), so as to show that the federal question was timely and properly raised and that this Court has jurisdiction to review the judgment on a writ of certiorari. When the portions of the record relied on under this subparagraph are voluminous, they shall be included in the appendix referred to in subparagraph 1(i).*

    (ii) *If review of a judgment of a United States court of appeals is sought, the basis for federal jurisdiction in the court of first instance.*

(h) *A direct and concise argument amplifying the reasons relied on for allowance of the writ, see Rule 10.*

(i) *An appendix containing, in the order indicated:*

    (i) *the opinions, orders, findings of fact, and conclusions of law, whether written or orally given and transcribed, entered in conjunction with the judgment sought to be reviewed;*

    (ii) *any other relevant opinions, orders, findings of fact, and conclusions of law entered in the case by courts or administrative agencies, and, if reference thereto is necessary to ascertain the grounds of the judgment, of those in companion cases (each document shall include the caption showing the name of the issuing court or agency, the title and number of the case, and the date of entry);*

    (iii) *any order on rehearing, including the caption showing the name of the issuing court, the title and number of the case, and the date of entry;*

    (iv) *the judgment sought to be reviewed if the date of its entry is different from the date of the opinion or order required in sub-subparagraph (i) of this subparagraph;*

    (v) *material required by subparagraphs 1(f) or 1(g)(i); and*

    (vi) *any other material the petitioner believes essential to understand the petition. If the material required by this subparagraph is voluminous, it may be presented in a separate volume or volumes with appropriate covers.*

2. *All contentions in support of a petition for a writ of certiorari shall be set out in the body of the petition, as provided in subparagraph 1(h) of this Rule. No separate brief in support of a petition for a writ of certiorari may be filed, and the Clerk will not file any petition for a writ of certiorari to which any supporting brief is annexed or appended.*

3. *A petition for a writ of certiorari should be stated briefly and in plain terms and may not exceed the word or page limitations specified in Rule 33.*

4. *The failure of a petitioner to present with accuracy, brevity, and clarity whatever is essential to ready and adequate understanding of the points requiring consideration is sufficient reason for the Court to deny a petition.*

5. *If the Clerk determines that a petition submitted timely and in good faith is in a form that does not comply with this Rule or with Rule 33 or Rule 34, the Clerk will return it with a letter*

indicating the deficiency. A corrected petition submitted in accordance with Rule 29.2 no more than 60 days after the date of the Clerk's letter will be deemed timely.

Rule 15. Briefs in Opposition; Reply Briefs; Supplemental Briefs

1. *A brief in opposition to a petition for a writ of certiorari may be filed by the respondent in any case, but is not mandatory except in a capital case, see Rule 14.1(a), or when ordered by the Court.*

2. *A brief in opposition should be stated briefly and in plain terms and may not exceed the word or page limitations specified in Rule 33. In addition to presenting other arguments for denying the petition, the brief in opposition should address any perceived misstatement of fact or law in the petition that bears on what issues properly would be before the Court if certiorari were granted. Counsel are admonished that they have an obligation to the Court to point out in the brief in opposition, and not later, any perceived misstatement made in the petition. Any objection to consideration of a question presented based on what occurred in the proceedings below, if the objection does not go to jurisdiction, may be deemed waived unless called to the Court's attention in the brief in opposition. A brief in opposition should identify any directly related cases that were not identified in the petition under Rule 14.1(b)(iii), including for each such case the information called for by Rule 14.1(b)(iii).*

3. *Any brief in opposition shall be filed within 30 days after the case is placed on the docket unless the time is extended by the Court or a Justice or by the Clerk under Rule 30.4. Forty copies shall be filed, except that a respondent proceeding in forma pauperis under Rule 39, including an inmate of an institution, shall file the number of copies required for a petition by such a person under Rule 12.2, together with a motion for leave to proceed in forma pauperis, a copy of which shall precede and be attached to each copy of the brief in opposition. If the petitioner is proceeding in forma pauperis, the respondent shall prepare its brief in opposition, if any, as required by Rule 33.2, and shall file an original and 10 copies of that brief. Whether prepared under Rule 33.1 or Rule 33.2, the brief in opposition shall comply with the requirements of Rule 24 governing a respondent's brief, except that no summary of the argument is required. A brief in opposition may not be joined with any other pleading, except that any motion for leave to proceed in forma pauperis shall be attached. The brief in opposition shall be served as required by Rule 29.*

4. *No motion by a respondent to dismiss a petition for a writ of certiorari may be filed. Any objections to the jurisdiction of the Court to grant a petition for a writ of certiorari shall be included in the brief in opposition.*

5. *The Clerk will distribute the petition to the Court for its consideration upon receiving an express waiver of the right to file a brief in opposition, or, if no waiver or brief in opposition is filed, upon the expiration of the time allowed for filing. If a brief in opposition is timely filed, the Clerk will distribute the petition, brief in opposition, and any reply brief to the Court for its consideration no less than 14 days after the brief in opposition is filed, unless the petitioner expressly waives the 14-day waiting period.*

6. *Any petitioner may file a reply brief addressed to new points raised in the brief in opposition, but distribution and consideration by the Court under paragraph 5 of this Rule will not be deferred pending its receipt. Forty copies shall be filed, except that a petitioner proceeding in forma pauperis under Rule 39, including an inmate of an institution, shall file the number of*

copies required for a petition by such a person under Rule 12.2. The reply brief shall be served as required by Rule 29.

7. *If a cross-petition for a writ of certiorari has been docketed, distribution of both petitions will be deferred until the cross-petition is due for distribution under this Rule.*

8. *Any party may file a supplemental brief at any time while a petition for a writ of certiorari is pending, calling attention to new cases, new legislation, or other intervening matter not available at the time of the party's last filing. A supplemental brief shall be restricted to new matter and shall follow, insofar as applicable, the form for a brief in opposition prescribed by this Rule. Forty copies shall be filed, except that a party proceeding in forma pauperis under Rule 39, including an inmate of an institution, shall file the number of copies required for a petition by such a person under Rule 12.2. The supplemental brief shall be served as required by Rule 29.*

Rule 16. Disposition of a Petition for a Writ of Certiorari

1. After considering the documents distributed under Rule 15, the Court will enter an appropriate order. The order may be a summary disposition on the merits.

2. Whenever the Court grants a petition for a writ of certiorari, the Clerk will prepare, sign and enter an order to that effect and will notify forthwith counsel of record and the court whose judgement is to be reviewed. The case then will be scheduled for briefing and oral argument. If the record has not previously been filed in this Court, the Clerk will request the Clerk of the court having possession of the record to clarify and transmit it. A formal writ will not issue unless specially directed.

3. Whenever the Court denies a petition for a writ of certiorari, the Clerk will prepare, sign and enter an order to that effect and will notify forthwith counsel of record and the court whose judgement was sought to be reviewed. The order of denial will not be suspended pending disposition of a petition for rehearing except by order of the Court or a Justice.

PART IV. OTHER JURISDICTION

Rule 17. Procedure in an Original Action

1. *This Rule applies only to an action invoking the Court's original jurisdiction under Article III of the Constitution of the United States, see also 28 U. S. C. § 1251 and U. S. Const., Amdt. 11. A petition for an extraordinary writ in aid of the Court's appellate jurisdiction shall be filed as provided in Rule 20.*

2. *The form of pleadings and motions prescribed by the Federal Rules of Civil Procedure is followed. In other respects, those Rules and the Federal Rules of Evidence may be taken as guides.*

3. *The initial pleading shall be preceded by a motion for leave to file, and may be accompanied by a brief in support of the motion. Forty copies of each document shall be filed, with proof of service. Service shall be as required by Rule 29, except that when an adverse party is a State, service shall be made on both the Governor and the Attorney General of that State.*

4. *The case will be placed on the docket when the motion for leave to file and the initial pleading are filed with the Clerk. The Rule 38(a) docket fee shall be paid at that time.*

5. *No more than 60 days after receiving the motion for leave to file and the initial pleading, an adverse party shall file 40 copies of any brief in opposition to the motion, with proof of service*

as required by Rule 29. The Clerk will distribute the filed documents to the Court for its consideration upon receiving an express waiver of the right to file a brief in opposition, or, if no waiver or brief is filed, upon the expiration of the time allowed for filing. If a brief in opposition is timely filed, the Clerk will distribute the filed documents to the Court for its consideration no less than 10 days after the brief in opposition is filed. A reply brief may be filed, but consideration of the case will not be deferred pending its receipt. The Court thereafter may grant or deny the motion, set it for oral argument, direct that additional documents be filed, or require that other proceedings be conducted.

6. *A summons issued out of this Court shall be served on the defendant 60 days before the return day specified therein. If the defendant does not respond by the return day, the plaintiff may proceed ex parte.*

7. *Process against a State issued out of this Court shall be served on both the Governor and the Attorney General of that State.*

Rule 18. Appeal from a United States District Court

1. When a direct appeal from a decision of a United States district court is authorized by law, the appeal is commenced by filing a notice of appeal with the clerk of the district court within the time provided by law after entry of the judgment sought to be reviewed. The time to file may not be extended. The notice of appeal shall specify the parties taking the appeal, designate the judgment, or part thereof, appealed from and the date of its entry, and specify the statute or statutes under which the appeal is taken. A copy of the notice of appeal shall be served on all parties to the proceeding as required by Rule 29, and proof of service shall be filed in the district court together with the notice of appeal.

2. All parties to the proceeding in the district court are deemed parties entitled to file documents in this Court, but a party having no interest in the outcome of the appeal may so notify the Clerk of this Court and shall serve a copy of the notice on all other parties. Parties interested jointly, severally, or otherwise in the judgment may appeal separately, or any two or more may join in an appeal. When two or more judgments involving identical or closely related questions are sought to be revised on appeal from the same court, a notice of appeal for each judgment shall be filed with the clerk of the district court, but a single jurisdictional statement covering all the judgments suffices. Parties who file no document will not qualify for any relief from this Court.

3. No more than 60 days after filing the notice of appeal in the district court, the appellant shall file 40 copies of a jurisdictional statement and shall pay the Rule 38 docket fee, except that an appellant proceeding *in forma pauperis* under Rule 39, including an inmate of an institution, shall file the number of copies required for a petition by such a person under Rule 12.2, together with a motion for leave to proceed *in forma pauperis*, a copy of which shall precede and be attached to each copy of the jurisdictional statement. The jurisdictional statement shall follow, insofar as applicable, the form for a petition for a writ of certiorari prescribed by Rule 14, and shall be served as required by Rule 29. The case will then be placed on the docket. It is the appellant's duty to notify all appellees promptly, on a form supplied by the Clerk, of the date of filing, the date the case was placed on the docket and the docket number of the case. The notice shall be served as required by Rule 29. The appendix shall include a copy of the notice of appeal showing the date it was filed in the district court. For good cause, a Justice may extend the time to file a jurisdictional statement for a period not exceeding 60 days. An application to extend the time to file a jurisdictional statement shall set out the basis for jurisdiction in this Court; identify the judgment sought to be reviewed; include a copy of the opinion, any order respecting

rehearing, and the notice of appeal; and set out specific reasons why an extension of time is justified. For the time and manner of presenting the application, see Rule 21, 22, and 30. An application to extend the time to file a jurisdictional statement is not favored.

4. No more than 30 days after a case has been placed on the docket, an appellee seeking to file a conditional cross-appeal (i.e., a cross-appeal that otherwise would be untimely) shall file, with proof of service as required by rule 29, a jurisdictional statement that complies in all respects (including number of copies filed) with paragraph 3 of this Rule, except that material already reproduced in the appendix to the opening jurisdictional statement need not be reproduced again. A cross-appealing appellee shall pay the Rule 38 docket fee or submit a motion for leave to proceed *in forma pauperis*. The cover of the cross-appeal shall indicate clearly that it is a conditional cross-appeal. The cross-appeal will then be placed on the docket. It is the cross-appellant's duty to notify all cross-appellees promptly, on a form supplied by the Clerk, of the date of filing, the date the cross-appeal was placed on the docket and the docket number of the cross-appeal. The notice shall be served as required by Rule 29. A cross-appeal may not he joined with any other pleading, except that any motion for leave to proceed *in forma pauperis* shall be attached. The time to file a cross-appeal will not be extended.

5. After a notice of appeal has been filed in the district court but before the case is placed on this Court's docket, the parties may dismiss the appeal by stipulation filed in the district court, or the district court may dismiss the appeal on the appellant's motion, with notice to all parties. If a notice of appeal has been filed, but the case has not been placed on this Court's docket within the time prescribed for docketing, the district court may dismiss the appeal on the appellee's motion, with notice to all parties, and may make any just order with respect to costs. If the district court has denied the appellee's motion to dismiss the appeal, the appellee may move this Court to docket and dismiss the appeal by filing an original and 10 copies of a motion presented in conformity with Rules 21 and 33.2. The motion shall be accompanied by proof of service as required by Rule 29, and by a certificate from the clerk of the district court, certifying that a notice of appeal was filed and that the appellee's motion to dismiss was denied. The appellant may not thereafter file a jurisdictional statement without special leave of the Court, and the Court may allow costs against the appellant.

6. Within 30 days after the case is placed on this Court's docket, the appellee may file a motion to dismiss, to affirm, or in the alternative to affirm or dismiss. Forty copies of the motion shall be filed, except that an appellee proceeding *in forma pauperis* under Rule 39, including an inmate of an institution, shall file the number of copies required for a petition by such a person under Rule 12.2, together with a motion for leave to proceed *in forma pauperis*, a copy of which shall precede and be attached to each copy of the motion to dismiss, to affirm, or in the alternative to affirm or dismiss. The motion shall follow, to the extent applicable, the form for a brief in opposition prescribed by Rule 15 and shall comply with all requirements of Rule 21.

7. The Clerk will distribute the jurisdictional statement to the Court for its consideration upon receiving an express waiver of the right to file a motion to dismiss or to affirm or, if a waiver or motion is filed, upon the expiration of the time allowed for filing. If a motion to dismiss or to affirm is timely filed, the Clerk will distribute the jurisdictional statement, motion, and any brief opposing the motion to the court for its consideration no less than 14 days after the motion is filed, unless the appellant expressly waives the 14-day waiting period.

8. Any appellant may file a brief opposing a motion to dismiss or to affirm, but distribution and consideration by the Court under paragraph 7 of this Rule will not be deferred pending its receipt, forty copies shall be filed, except that an appellant proceeding *in forma pauperis* under Rule 39,

including an inmate of an institution, shall file the number of copies required for a petition by such a person under Rule 12.2. The brief shall be served as required by Rule 29.

9. If a cross-appeal has been docketed, distribution of both jurisdictional statements will be deferred until the cross-appeal is due for distribution under this Rule.

10. Any party may file a supplemental brief at any time while a jurisdictional statement is pending, calling attention to new cases, new legislation, or other intervening matters not available at the time of the party's last filing. A supplemental brief shall be restricted to new matters and shall follow, insofar as applicable, the form for a brief in opposition prescribed by Rule 15. Forty copies shall be filed, except that a party proceeding *in forma pauperis* under Rule 39, including an inmate of an institution, shall file the number of copies required for a petition by such a person under Rule 12.2. The supplemental brief shall be served as required by Rule 29.

11. The clerk of the district court shall retain possession of the record until notified by the Clerk of this Court to certify and transmit it, see Rule 12.7.

12. After considering the documents distributed under this Rule, the Court may dispose summarily of the appeal on the merits, note probable jurisdiction, or postpone consideration of jurisdiction until a hearing of the case on the merits. If not disposed of summarily, the case stands for briefing and oral argument on the merits. If consideration of jurisdiction is postponed, counsel, at the outset of their briefs and at oral argument, shall address the question of jurisdiction. If the record has not previously been filed in this Court, the Clerk of this Court will request the clerk of the court in possession of the record to certify and transmit it.

13. If the Clerk determines that a jurisdictional statement submitted timely and in good faith is in a form that does not comply with this Rule or with Rule 33 or Rule 34, the Clerk will return it with a letter indicating the deficiency. If a corrected jurisdictional statement is submitted in accordance with Rule 29.2 no more than 60 days after the date of the Clerk's letter, it will be deemed timely.

Rule 19. Procedure on a Certified Question

1. *A United States Court of Appeals may certify to this Court a question or proposition of law on which it seeks instruction for the proper decision of a case. The certificate shall contain a statement of the nature of the case and the facts on which the question or proposition of law arises. Only questions or propositions of law may be certified, and they shall be stated separately and with precision. The certificate shall be prepared as required by Rule 33.2 and shall be signed by the Clerk of the Court of Appeals.*

2. *When a question is certified by a United States Court of Appeals, this Court, on its own motion or that of a party, may consider and decide the entire matter in controversy, see 28 U. S. C. § 1254(2).*

3. *When a question is certified, the Clerk will notify the parties and docket the case. Counsel shall then enter their appearances. After docketing, the Clerk will submit the certificate to the Court for a preliminary examination to determine whether the case should be briefed, set for argument, or dismissed. No brief may be filed until the preliminary examination of the certificate is completed.*

4. *If the Court orders the case briefed or set for argument, the parties will be notified and permitted to file briefs. The Clerk of this Court then will request the clerk of the court in possession of the record to certify and transmit it. Any portion of the record to which the parties*

wish to direct the Court's particular attention should be printed in a joint appendix, prepared in conformity with Rule 26 by the appellant or petitioner in the court of appeals, but the fact that any part of the record has not been printed does not prevent the parties or the Court from relying on it.

5. *A brief on the merits in a case involving a certified question shall comply with Rules 24, 25, and 33.1, except that the brief for the party who is the appellant or petitioner below shall be filed within 45 days of the order requiring briefs or setting the case for argument.*

Rule 20. Procedure on a Petition for an Extraordinary Writ

1. *Issuance by the Court of an extraordinary writ authorized by 28 U. S. C. § 1651(a) is not a matter of right but of discretion sparingly exercised. To justify the granting of any such writ, the petition must show that the writ will be in aid of the Court's appellate jurisdiction, that exceptional circumstances warrant the exercise of the Court's discretionary powers, and that adequate relief cannot be obtained in any other form or from any other court.*

2. *A petition seeking a writ authorized by 28 U. S. C. § 1651(a), § 2241, or § 2254(a) shall be prepared in all respects as required by Rules 33 and 34. The petition shall be captioned "In re [name of petitioner]" and shall follow, insofar as applicable, the form of a petition for a writ of certiorari prescribed by Rule 14. All contentions in support of the petition shall be included in the petition. The case will be placed on the docket when 40 copies of the petition are filed with the Clerk, and the docket fee is paid, except that a petitioner proceeding in forma pauperis under Rule 39, including an inmate of an institution, shall file the number of copies required for a petition by such a person under Rule 12.2, together with a motion for leave to proceed in forma pauperis, a copy of which shall precede and be attached to each copy of the petition. The petition shall be served as required by Rule 29 (subject to subparagraph 4(b) of this Rule).*

3. *(a) A petition seeking a writ of prohibition, a writ of mandamus, or both in the alternative shall state the name and office or function of every person against whom relief is sought and shall set out with particularity why the relief sought is not available in any other court. A copy of the judgment with respect to which the writ is sought, including any related opinion, shall be appended to the petition together with any other document essential to understanding the petition.*

   (b) The petition shall be served on every party to the proceeding with respect to which relief is sought. Within 30 days after the petition is placed on the docket, a party shall file 40 copies of any brief or briefs in opposition thereto, which shall comply fully with Rule 15. If a party named as a respondent does not wish to respond to the petition, that party may so advise the Clerk and all other parties by letter. All persons served are deemed respondents for all purposes in the proceedings in this Court.

4. *(a) A petition seeking a writ of habeas corpus shall comply with the requirements of 28 U. S. C. §§ 2241 and 2242, and in particular with the provision in the last paragraph of § 2242, which requires a statement of the "reasons for not making application to the district court of the district in which the applicant is held." If the relief sought is from the judgment of a state court, the petition shall set out specifically how and where the petitioner has exhausted available remedies in the state courts or otherwise comes within the provisions of 28 U. S. C. § 2254(b). To justify the granting of a writ of habeas corpus, the petitioner must show that exceptional circumstances warrant the exercise of the Court's discretionary powers and that adequate relief cannot be obtained in any other form or from any other court. This writ is rarely granted.*

(b) *Habeas corpus proceedings, except in capital cases, are ex parte, unless the Court requires the respondent to show cause why the petition for a writ of habeas corpus should not be granted. A response, if ordered or in a capital case, shall comply fully with Rule 15. Neither the denial of the petition, without more, nor an order of transfer to a district court under the authority of 28 U. S. C. § 2241(b) is an adjudication on the merits and, therefore, does not preclude further application to another court for the relief sought.*

5. *The Clerk will distribute the documents to the Court for its consideration when a brief in opposition under subparagraph 3(b) of this Rule has been filed when a response under subparagraph 4(b) has been ordered and filed, when the time to file has expired, or when the right to file has been expressly waived.*

6. *If the Court orders the case set for argument, the Clerk will notify the parties whether additional briefs are required, when they shall be filed, and, if the case involves a petition for a common-law writ of certiorari, that the parties shall prepare a joint appendix in accordance with Rule 26.*

PART V. MOTIONS AND APPLICATIONS

Rule 21. Motions to the Court

1. *Every motion to the Court shall clearly state its purpose and the facts on which it is based and may present a legal argument in support thereof. No separate brief may be filed. A motion should be concise and shall comply with any applicable page limits. Non-dispositive motions and applications in cases in which certiorari has been granted, probable jurisdiction noted, or consideration of jurisdiction postponed shall state the position on the disposition of the motion or application of the other party or parties to the case. Rule 22 governs an application addressed to a single Justice.*

2. (a) *A motion in any action within the Court's original jurisdiction shall comply with Rule 17.3.*

   (b) *A motion to dismiss as moot (or a suggestion of mootness), a motion for leave to file a brief as amicus curiae, and any motion the granting of which would dispose of the entire case or would affect the final judgment to be entered (other than a motion to docket and dismiss under Rule 18.5 or a motion for voluntary dismissal under Rule 46) shall be prepared as required by Rule 33.1, and 40 copies shall be filed, except that a movant proceeding in forma pauperis under Rule 39, including an inmate of an institution, shall file a motion prepared as required by Rule 33.2, and shall file the number of copies required for a petition by such a person under Rule 12.2. The motion shall be served as required by Rule 29.*

   (c) *Any other motion to the Court shall be prepared as required by Rule 33.2; the moving party shall file an original and 10 copies. The Court subsequently may order the moving party to prepare the motion as required by Rule 33.1; in that event, the party shall file 40 copies.*

3. *A motion to the Court shall be filed with the Clerk and shall be accompanied by proof of service as required by Rule 29. No motion may be presented in open Court other than a motion for admission to the Bar, except when the proceeding to which it refers is being argued. Oral argument on a motion will not be permitted unless the Court so directs.*

4. *Any response to a motion shall be filed as promptly as possible considering the nature of the relief sought and any asserted need for emergency action, and, in any event, within 10 days of receipt, unless the Court or a Justice, or the Clerk under Rule 30.4, orders otherwise. A response to a motion prepared as required by Rule 33.1, except a response to a motion for leave*

to file an amicus curiae brief (see Rule 37.5), shall be prepared in the same manner if time permits. In an appropriate case, the Court may act on a motion without waiting for a response.

Rule 22. Applications to Individual Justices

1. An application addressed to an individual Justice shall be filed with the Clerk, who will transmit it promptly to the Justice concerned if an individual Justice has authority to grant the sought relief.

2. The original and two copies of any application addressed to an individual Justice shall be prepared as required by Rule 33.2 and shall be accompanied by proof of service as required by Rule 29.

3. An application shall be addressed to the Justice allotted to the Circuit from which the case arises. An application arising from the United States Court of Appeals for the Armed Forces shall be addressed to the Chief Justice. When the Circuit Justice is unavailable for any reason, the application addressed to that Justice will be distributed to the Justice then available who is next junior to the circuit Justice; the turn of the Chief Justice follows that of the most junior Justice.

4. A Justice denying an application will note the denial thereon. Thereafter, unless action therein is restricted by law to the Circuit Justice or is untimely under Rule 30.2, the party making an application, except in the case of an application for an extension of time., may renew it to any other Justice, subject to the provisions of this Rule. Except when the denial is without prejudice, a renewed application is not favored. Renewed application is made by a letter to the Clerk, designating the Justice to whom the application is to be directed, and accompanied by 10 copies of the original application and proof of service as required by Rule 29.

5. A Justice to whom an application for a stay or for bail is submitted may refer it to the Court for determination.

6. The Clerk will advise all parties concerned, by appropriately speedy means, of the disposition made of an application.

Rule 23. Stays

1. A stay may be granted by a Justice as permitted by law.

2. A party to a judgment sought to be reviewed may present to a Justice an application to stay the enforcement of that judgment, see 28 U.S.C.§2101(f).

3. An application for a stay shall set out with particularity why the relief sought is not available from any other court or judge. Except in the most extraordinary circumstances, an application for a stay will not be entertained unless the relief requested was first sought in the appropriate court or courts below or from a judge or judges thereof. An application for a stay shall identify the judgment sought to be reviewed and have appended thereto a copy of the order and opinion, if any, and a copy of the order, if any, of the court opinion, if any, and a copy of the order, if any of the court or judge below denying the relief sought, and shall set out specific reasons why a stay is justified. The form and content of an application for a stay are governed by Rules 22 and 33.2

4. A judge, court, or Justice granting an application for a stay pending review by this Court may condition the stay on the filing of a supersedes bond having an approved surety or sureties. The bond will be conditioned on the satisfaction of the judgment in full, together with any costs,

interest, and damages for delay that may be awarded. If a part of the judgment sought to be reviewed has already been satisfied or is otherwise secured, the bond may be conditioned on the satisfaction of the part of the judgment not otherwise secured or satisfied, together with costs, interest, and damages.

PART VI. BRIEFS ON THE MERITS AND ORAL ARGUMENTS

Rule 24. Briefs on the Merits: In General

1. *A brief on the merits of a petitioner or an appellant shall comply in all respects with Rules 33.1 and 34 and shall contain in the order here indicated:*

   (a) *The questions presented for review under Rule 14.1(a). The questions shall be set out on the first page following the cover, and no other information may appear on that page. The phrasing of the questions presented need not be identical to that in the petition for a writ of certiorari or the jurisdictional statement, but the brief may not raise additional questions or change the substance of the questions already presented in those documents. At its option, however, the Court may consider a plain error not among the questions presented but evident from the record and otherwise within its jurisdiction to decide.*

   (b) *A list of all parties to the proceeding in the court whose judgment is under review (unless the caption of the case in this Court contains the names of all parties). Any amended corporate disclosure statement, as required by Rule 29.6, shall be placed here.*

   (c) *If the brief exceeds 1,500 words, a table of contents and a table of cited authorities.*

   (d) *Citations of the official and unofficial reports of the opinions and orders entered in the case by courts and administrative agencies.*

   (e) *A concise statement of the basis for jurisdiction in this Court, including the statutory provisions and time factors on which jurisdiction rests.*

   (f) *The constitutional provisions, treaties, statutes, ordinances, and regulations involved in the case, set out verbatim with appropriate citation. If the provisions involved are lengthy, their citation alone suffices at this point, and their pertinent text, if not already set out in the petition for a writ of certiorari, jurisdictional statement, or an appendix to either document, shall be set out in an appendix to the brief.*

   (g) *A concise statement of the case, setting out the facts material to the consideration of the questions presented, with appropriate references to the joint appendix, e. g., App. 12, or to the record, e. g., Record 12.*

   (h) *A summary of the argument, suitably paragraphed. The summary should be a clear and concise condensation of the argument made in the body of the brief; mere repetition of the headings under which the argument is arranged is not sufficient.*

   (i) *The argument, exhibiting clearly the points of fact and of law presented and citing the authorities and statutes relied on.*

   (j) *A conclusion specifying with particularity the relief the party seeks.*

2. *A brief on the merits for a respondent or an appellee shall conform to the foregoing requirements, except that items required by subparagraphs 1(a), (b), (d), (e), (f), and (g) of this Rule need not be included unless the respondent or appellee is dissatisfied with their presentation by the opposing party.*

3. *A brief on the merits may not exceed the word limitations specified in Rule 33.1(g). An appendix to a brief may include only relevant material, and counsel is cautioned not to include in an appendix arguments or citations that properly belong in the body of the brief.*

4. *A reply brief shall conform to those portions of this Rule applicable to the brief for a respondent or an appellee but, if appropriately divided by topical headings, need not contain a summary of the argument.*

5. *A reference to the joint appendix or to the record set out in any brief shall indicate the appropriate page number. If the reference is to an exhibit, the page numbers at which the exhibit appears, at which it was offered in evidence, and at which it was ruled on by the judge shall be indicated, e. g., Pl. Exh. 14, Record 199, 2134.*

6. *A brief shall be concise, logically arranged with proper headings, and free of irrelevant, immaterial, or scandalous matter. The Court may disregard or strike a brief that does not comply with this paragraph.*

Rule 25. Briefs on the Merits: Number of Copies and Time to file

1. The petitioner or appellant shall file 40 copies of the brief on the merits within 45 days of the order granting the writ of certiorari, noting probable jurisdiction, or postponing consideration of jurisdiction. Any respondent or appellee who supports the petitioner or appellant shall meet the petitioner's or appellant's time schedule for filing documents.

2. The respondent or appellee shall file 40 copies of the brief on the merits within 30 days after the brief for the petitioner or appellant is filed.

3. The petitioner or appellant shall file 40 copies of the reply brief, if any, within 30 days after the brief for the respondent or appellee is filed, but any reply brief must actually be received by the Clerk not later than 2 p.m. one week before the date or oral argument. Any respondent or appellee supporting the petitioner or appellant may file a reply brief.

4. If cross-petitions or cross-appeals have been consolidated for argument, the Clerk, upon request of the parties, may designate one of the parties to file an initial brief and reply brief as provided in paragraphs 1 and 3 of this Rule (as if the party were petitioner or appellant), and may designate the other party to file an initial brief as provided in paragraph of this Rule and, to the extent appropriate, a supplemental brief following the submission of the reply brief. In such a case, the Clerk may establish the time for the submission of the briefs and alter the otherwise applicable word limits. Except as approved by the Court or a Justice, the total number of words permitted for the briefs of the parties cumulative shall not exceed the maximum that would have been allowed in the absence of an order under this paragraph.

5. The time periods stated in paragraphs 1, 2, and 3 of this rule may be extended as provided in rule 30. An application to extend the time to file a brief on the merits is not favored. If a case is advanced for hearing, the time to file briefs on the merits may be abridged as circumstances require pursuant to an order of the Court on its own motion or that of a party.

6. A party wishing to present late authorities, newly enacted legislation, or other intervening matter that was not available in time to be included in a brief may file 40 copies of a supplemental brief, restricted to such new matter and otherwise presented in conformity with these Rules, up to the time the case is called for oral argument or by leave of the Court thereafter.

7. After a case has been argued or submitted, the Clerk will not file any brief, except that of a party filed by leave of the Court.

8. *The Clerk will not file any brief that is not accompanied by proof of service as required by Rule 29.*

Rule 26. Joint Appendix

1. Unless the Clerk has allowed the parties to use the deferred method described in paragraph 4 of this Rule, the petitioner or appellant, within 45 days after entry of the order granting the writ of certiorari, noting probable jurisdiction, or postponing consideration of jurisdiction, shall file 40 copies of a joint appendix, prepared as required by Rule 33.1. the joint appendix shall contain: (l) the relevant docket entries in all the courts below; (2) any relevant pleadings, jury instructions, findings, conclusions, or opinions; (3) the judgment, order, or decision under review; and (4) any other parts of the record that the parties particularly wish to bring to the Court's attention. Any of the foregoing items already reproduced in a petition for a writ of certiorari, jurisdictional statement, brief in opposition to a petition for a writ of certiorari, motion to dismiss or affirm, or any appendix to the foregoing, that was prepared as required by Rule 33.1, need not be reproduced again in the joint appendix. The petitioner or appellant shall serve three copies of the joint appendix on each of the other parties to the proceeding as required by Rule 29.

2. The parties are encouraged to agree on the contents of the joint appendix. In the absence of agreement, the petitioner or appellant, within 10 days after entry of the order granting the writ of certiorari, noting probable jurisdiction, or postponing consideration of jurisdiction, shall serve on the respondent or appellee a designation of parts of the record so designated insufficient shall serve on the petitioner or appellant a designation of additional parts to be included in the joint appendix, and the petitioner or appellants shall include the parts so designated. If the Court has permitted the respondent or appellee to proceed *in forma pauperis*, the petition or appellant may seek by motion to be excused from printing portions of the record the petitioner or appellant considers unnecessary. In making these designations, counsel should include only those materials the Court should examine; unnecessary designations should be avoided. The record is on file with the Clerk and available to the Justices, and counsel may refer in briefs and in oral argument to relevant portions of the record not included in the joint appendix.

3. When the joint appendix is filed, the petitioner or appellant immediately shall file with the Clerk a statement of the cost of printing 50 copies and shall serve a copy of the statement on each of the other parties as required by Rule 29. Unless the parties agree otherwise, the cost of producing the joint appendix shall be paid initially by the petitioner or appellant, but a petitioner or appellant who considers that parts of the record designated by the respondent or appellee are unnecessary for the determination of the issues presented may so advise the respondent or appellee, who then shall advance the cost of printing the additional parts, unless the court of a Justice otherwise fixes the initial allocation of the costs. The cost of printing the joint appendix is taxed as a cost in the case, but if a party unnecessarily causes matter to be included in the joint appendix or prints excessive copies, the Court may impose these costs on that party.

4. (a) On the parties' request, the Clerk may allow the preparation of the joint appendix to be deferred until after the briefs have been filed. In that event, the petitioner or appellant shall file the joint appendix no more than 14 days after receiving the brief for the respondent or appellee. The provisions of paragraphs 1, 2, and 3 of this Rule shall be followed, except that the designations referred to therein shall be made by each party when that party's brief is served Deferral of the joint appendix is not favored.

   (b) If the deferred method is used, the briefs on the merits may refer to the pages of the record.

In that event, the joint appendix shall include in brackets on each page thereof the page number of the record where that material may be found. A party wishing to refer directly to the pages of the joint appendix may serve and file copies of its brief prepared as required by Rule 33.2 within the time provided by Rule 25, with appropriate references to the pages of the record. In that event, within 10 days after the joint appendix is filed, copies of the brief prepared as required by Rule 33.1 containing references to the pages of the joint appendix in place of, or in addition to, the initial references to the pages of the record, shall be served and filed. No other change may be made in the brief as initially served and filed except that typographical errors may be corrected.

5. The joint appendix shall be prefaced by a table of contents showing the parts of the record that it contains, in the order in which the parts are set out, with references to the pages of the joint appendix at which each part begins. The relevant docket entries shall be set out after the table of contents, followed by the other parts of the record in chronological order. When testimony contained in the reporter's transcript of proceedings is set out in the joint appendix, the page of the transcript at which the testimony appears shall be indicated in brackets immediately before the statement that is set out. Omissions in the transcript or in any other document printed in the joint appendix shall be indicated by asterisks. Immaterial formal matters (e.g., captions, subscriptions, acknowledgments) shall be omitted. A question and its answer may be contained in a single paragraph.

6. Two lines must appear at the bottom of the cover of the joint appendix: (1) The first line must indicate the date the petition for the writ of certiorari was filed or the date the appeal was docketed; (2) the second line must indicate the date certiorari was granted or the date jurisdiction of the appeal was noted or postponed.

7. Exhibits designated for inclusion in the joint appendix may be contained in a separate volume or volumes suitably indexed. The transcript of a proceeding before an administrative agency, board, commission, or officer used in an action in a district court or court of appeals is regarded as an exhibit for the purposes of this paragraph.

8. The Court, on its own motion or that of a party, may dispense with the requirement of a joint appendix and may permit a case to be heard on the original record (with such copies of the record or relevant parts thereof, as the Court may require) or on the appendix used in the court below if it conforms to the requirement of this Rule.

9. For good cause, the time limits specified in this Rule may be shortened or extended by the Court or a Justice or by the clerk under Rule 30.4.

Rule 27. Calendar

1. From time to time, the Clerk will prepare a calendar of cases ready for argument. A case ordinarily will not be called for argument less than two weeks after the brief on the merits for the respondent or appellee is due.

2. The clerk will advise counsel when they are required to appear for oral argument and will publish a hearing list in advance of each argument session for the convenience of counsel and the information of the public.

3. The Court, on its own motion or that of a party, may order that two or more cases involving the same or related questions be argued together as one case or on such other terms as the Court may prescribe.

Rule 28. Oral Argument

1. Oral argument should emphasize and clarify the written arguments in the briefs on the merits. Counsel should assume that all Justices have read the briefs before oral argument. Oral argument read from a prepared text is not favored.

2. The petitioner or appellant shall open and may conclude the argument. A cross-writ of certiorari or cross-appeal will be argued with the initial writ of certiorari or appeal as one case in the time allowed for that one case, and the Court will advise the parties who shall open and close.

3. Unless the Court directs otherwise, each side is allowed one-half hour for argument. Counsel is not required to use all the allotted time. Any request for additional time to argue shall be presented by motion under Rule 21 in time to be considered at a scheduled Conference prior to the date of oral argument and no later than 7 days after the respondent's or appellee's brief on the merits is filed, and shall set out specifically and concisely why the case cannot be presented within the half-hour limitation. Additional time is rarely accorded.

4. Only one attorney will be heard for each side, except by leave of the Court on the motion filed in time to be considered at a scheduled Conference prior to the date of oral argument and no later than 7 days after the respondent's or appellee's brief on the merits is filed. Any request for a divided argument shall be presented by motion under Rule 21 and shall set out specifically and concisely why more than one attorney should be allowed to argue. A divided argument is not favored.

5. Regardless of the number of counsel participating in oral argument, counsel making the opening argument shall present the case fairly and completely and not reserve points of substance for rebuttal.

6. Oral argument will not be allowed on behalf of any party for whom a brief has not been filed.

7. By leave of the Court, and subject to paragraph 4 of this Rule, counsel for an *amicus curiae* whose brief has been filed as provided in Rule 37 may argue orally on the side of a party, with the consent of that party. In the absence of consent, counsel for an *amicus curiae* may seek leave of the Court to argue orally by a motion setting out specifically and concisely why oral argument would provide assistance to the Court not otherwise available. Such a motion will be granted only in the most extraordinary circumstances.

8. Oral arguments may be presented only by members of the Bar of this Court. Attorneys who are not members of the Bar of this Court may make a motion to argue *pro hac vice* under the provisions of rule 6.

PART VII. PRACTICE AND PROCEDURE

Rule 29. Filing and Service of Documents; Special Notifications; Corporate Listing

1. *Any document required or permitted to be presented to the Court or to a Justice shall be filed with the Clerk in paper form.*

2. A document is timely filed if it is received by the Clerk within the time specified for filing; or if it is sent to the Clerk through the United States Postal Service by first-class mail (including express or priority mail), postage prepaid, and bears a postmark, other than a commercial postage meter label, showing that the document was mailed on or before the last day for filing; or if it is delivered on or before the last day for filing to a third-party commercial carrier for delivery to the Clerk within 3 calendar days. *If submitted by an inmate confined in an institution,*

a document is timely filed if it is deposited in the institution's internal mail system on or before the last day for filing and is accompanied by a notarized statement or declaration in compliance with 28 U. S. C. § 1746 setting out the date of deposit and stating that first-class postage has been prepaid. If the postmark is missing or not legible, or if the third-party commercial carrier does not provide the date the document was received by the carrier, the Clerk will require the person who sent the document to submit a notarized statement or declaration in compliance with 28 U.S.C. §1746 setting out the details of the filing and stating that the filing took place on a particular date within the permitted time.

3. Any document required by these Rules to be served may be served personally, by mail, or by a third-party commercial carrier for delivery within 3 calendar days on each party to the proceeding at or before the time of filing. If the document has been prepared as required by Rule 33.1, three copies shall be served on each other party separately represented in the proceeding. If the document has been prepared as required by rule 33.2, the service of a single copy on each other separately represented party suffices. If personal service is made, it shall consist of delivery at the office of the counsel of record, either to counsel or to an employee therein. If service is by mail or third-party commercial carrier, it shall consist of depositing the document with the United States Postal Service, with no less than first-class postage prepaid, or delivery to the carrier for delivery within 3 calendar days, addressed to the counsel of record at the proper address. When a party is not represented by counsel, service shall be made on the party, personally, by mail, or by commercial carrier. Ordinarily, service on a party must be by a manner at least as expeditious as the manner used to file the document with the court. *An electronic version of the document shall also be transmitted to all other parties at the time of filing or reasonably contemporaneous therewith unless the party filing the document is proceeding pro se and in forma pauperis or the electronic service address of the party being served is unknown and not identifiable through reasonable efforts.*

4. (a) *If the United States or any federal department, office, agency, officer, or employee is a party to be served, service shall be made on the Solicitor General of the United States, Room 5616, Department of Justice, 950 Pennsylvania Ave., N. W., Washington, DC 20530-0001. When an agency of the United States that is a party is authorized by law to appear before this Court on its own behalf, or when an officer or employee of the United States is a party, the agency, officer, or employee shall be served in addition to the Solicitor General.*

(b) *In any proceeding in this Court in which the constitutionality of an Act of Congress is drawn into question, and neither the United States nor any federal department, office, agency, officer, or employee is a party, the initial document filed in this Court shall recite that 28 U. S. C. § 2403(a) may apply and shall be served on the Solicitor General of the United States, Room 5616, Department of Justice, 950 Pennsylvania Ave., N. W., Washington, DC 20530-0001. In such a proceeding from any court of the United States, as defined by 28 U. S. C. § 451, the initial document also shall state whether that court, pursuant to 28 U. S. C. § 2403(a), certified to the Attorney General the fact that the constitutionality of an Act of Congress was drawn into question, see Rule 14.1(e)(v).*

(c) *In any proceeding in this Court in which the constitutionality of any statute of a State is drawn into question, and neither the State nor any agency, officer, or employee thereof is a party, the initial document filed in this Court shall recite that 28 U. S. C. § 2403(b) may apply and shall be served on the Attorney General of that State. In such a proceeding from any court of the United States, as defined by 28 U. S. C. § 451, the initial document also shall state whether that court, pursuant to 28 U. S. C. § 2403(b), certified to the State Attorney General the fact that the constitutionality of a statute of that State was drawn into question, see Rule 14.1(e)(v).*

5. *Proof of service, when required by these Rules, shall accompany the document when it is presented to the Clerk for filing and shall be separate from it. Proof of service shall contain, or be accompanied by, a statement that all parties required to be served have been served, together with a list of the names, addresses, and telephone numbers of counsel indicating the name of the party or parties each counsel represents. It is not necessary that service on each party required to be served be made in the same manner or evidenced by the same proof. Proof of service may consist of any one of the following:*

   (a) an acknowledgment of service, signed by counsel of record for the party served, and bearing the address and telephone number of such counsel;

   (b) a certificate of service, reciting the facts and circumstances of service in compliance with the appropriate paragraph or paragraphs of this Rule, and signed by a member of the Bar of this Court representing the party on whose behalf service is made or by an attorney appointed to represent that party under the Criminal Justice Act of 1964, see 18 U.S.C. §3006A(d)(6), or under any other applicable federal statute; or

   (c) a notarized affidavit or declaration in compliance with 28 U.S.C. §1746, reciting the facts and circumstances of service in accordance with the appropriate paragraph or paragraphs of this Rule, whenever service is made by a person not a member of the Bar of this Court and not an attorney appointed to represent a party under the Criminal Justice Act of 1964, see 18 U.S.C. §3006A(d)(6), or under any other applicable federal statute.

6. *Every document, except a joint appendix or amicus curiae brief, filed by or on behalf of a nongovernmental corporation shall contain a corporate disclosure statement identifying the parent corporations and listing any publicly held company that owns 10% or more of the corporation's stock. If there is no parent or publicly held company owning 10% or more of the corporation's stock, a notation to this effect shall be included in the document. If a statement has been included in a document filed earlier in the case, reference may be made to the earlier document (except when the earlier statement appeared in a document prepared under Rule 33.2), and only amendments to the statement to make it current need be included in the document being filed. In addition, whenever there is a material change in the identity of the parent corporation or publicly held companies that own 10% or more of the corporation's stock, counsel shall promptly inform the Clerk by letter and include, within that letter, any amendment needed to make the statement current.*

7. In addition to the filing requirement set forth in this Rule, all filers who are represented by counsel must submit documents to the Court's electronic filing system in conformity with the "Guidelines for the Submission of Documents to the Supreme Court's Electronic Filing System" issued by the Clerk.

Rule 30. Computation and Extension of Time

1. In the computation of any period of time prescribed or allowed by these Rules, by order of the Court, or by an applicable statute, the day of the act, event, or default from which the designated period begins to run is not included. The last day of the period shall be included unless it is a Saturday, Sunday, federal legal holiday listed in 5 U.S.C. §6103 or the day on which the Court building is closed by order of the Court or the Chief Justice, in which event the period shall

extend until the end of the next day that is not a Saturday, Sunday, federal legal holiday, or day on which the Court building is closed.

2. Whenever a Justice or the Clerk is empowered by law or these Rules to extend the time to file any document, an application or motion seeking an extension shall be filed within the period sought to be extended. An application to extend the time to file a petition for a writ of certiorari or to file a jurisdictional statement must be filed at least 10 days before the specified final filing date as computed under these Rules; if filed less than 10 days before the final filing date, such application will not be granted except in the most extraordinary circumstances.

3. An application to extend the time to file a petition for a writ of certiorari, to file a jurisdictional statement, to file a reply brief on the merits, or to file a petition for rehearing of any judgment or decision of the Court: on the merits shall be made to an individual Justice and presented and served on all other parties as provided by Rule 22. Once denied, such an application may not be renewed.

4. A motion to extend the time to file any document or paper other than those specified in paragraph 3 of this Rule may be presented in the form of a letter to the Clerk setting out specific reasons why an extension of time is justified. The letter shall be served on all other parties as required by Rule 29. The motion may be acted on by the Clerk in the first instance, and any party aggrieved by the Clerk's action may request that the motion be submitted to a Justice or to the Court. The Clerk will report action under this paragraph to the Court as instructed.

Rule 31. Translations

Whenever any record to be transmitted to this Court contains material written in a foreign language without a translation made under the authority of the lower court or admitted to be correct, the clerk of the court transmitting the record shall advise the Clerk of this Court immediately so that this Court may order that a translation be supplied and, if necessary, printed as part of the joint appendix.

Rule 32. Models, Diagrams, Exhibits, and Lodgings

1. Models, diagrams, and exhibits of material forming part of the evidence taken in a case and brought to this Court for its inspection shall be placed in the custody of the Clerk at least two weeks before the case is to be heard or submitted.

2. All models, diagrams, exhibits, and other items placed in the custody of the Clerk shall be removed by the parties no more than 40 days after the case is decided. If this is not done, the Clerk will notify counsel to remove the articles forthwith. If they are not removed within a reasonable time thereafter, the Clerk will destroy them or dispose of them in any other appropriate way.

3. Any party or *amicus curiae* desiring to lodge non-record material with the Clerk must set out in a letter, served on all parties, a description of the material proposed for lodging and the reasons why the non-record material may properly be considered by the Court. The material proposed for lodging may not be submitted until and unless requested by the Clerk.

Rule 33. Document Preparation: Booklet Format; 8 ½ by 11-Inch Paper Format

1. *Booklet Format:* (a) Except for a document expressly permitted by these Rules to be submitted on 8½ - by 11-inch paper, see, e.g., Rules 21, 22, and 39, every document filed with the Court shall be prepared in a 6 1/8- by 9 1/4-inch booklet format using a standard typesetting process (e.g., hot metal, photocomposition, or computer typesetting) to produce text printed in typographic (as opposed to typewriter) characters. The process used must produce a clear, black

image on white paper. The text must be reproduced with a clarity that equals or exceeds the output of a laser printer.

(b) The text of every booklet-format document, including any appendix thereto, shall be typeset in a Century family (e.g., Century Expanded, New Century Schoolbook, or Century Schoolbook) 12-point type with 2-point or more leading between lines. Quotations in excess of 50 words shall be indented. The typeface of footnotes shall be 10-point type with 2-point or more leading between lines. The text of the document must appear on both sides of the page.

(c) Every booklet-format document shall be produced on paper that is opaque, unglazed, and not less than 60 pounds in weight and shall have margins of at least three-fourths of an inch on all sides. The text field, including footnotes, may not exceed 4 1/8 by 7 1/8 inches. The document shall be bound firmly in at least two places along the left margin (saddle stitch or perfect binding preferred) so as to permit easy opening, and no part of the text should be obscured by the binding. Spiral, plastic, metal, or string bindings may not be used. Copies of patent documents, except opinions, may be duplicated in such size as is necessary in a separate appendix.

(d) Every booklet-format document shall comply with the word limits shown on the chart in subparagraph 1(g) of this Rule. The word limits do not include the questions presented, the list of parties and the corporate disclosure statement, the tables of contents, the table of cited authorities, the listing of counsel at the end of the document, or any appendix. The word limits include footnotes. Verbatim quotations required under Rule 14.1(f), if set out in the text of a brief rather than in the appendix, are also excluded For good cause, the Court or a Justice may grant leave to file a document in excess of the word limits, but application for such leave is not favored. An application to exceed word limits shall comply with Rule 22 and must be received by the Clerk at least 15 days before the filing date of the document in question, except in the most extraordinary circumstances.

(e) Every booklet-format document shall have a suitable cover consisting of 65-pound weight paper in the color indicated on the chart in subparagraph 1(g) of this Rule. If a separate appendix to any document is filed, the color if its cover shall be the same as that of the cover of the document it supports. The Clerk will furnish a color chart upon request. Counsel shall ensure that there is adequate contrast between the printing and the color of the cover. A document filed by the United States, or by any other federal party represented by the Solicitor General, shall have a gray cover. A joint appendix, answer to a bill of complaint, motion for leave to intervene, and any other document not listed in subparagraph 1(g) of this Rule shall have a tan cover.

(f) Forty copies of a booklet-format document shall be filed, and one unbound copy of the document on 8½ - by 11-inch paper shall also be submitted.

(g) Word limits and cover colors for booklet-format documents are as follows:

	Type of Document	Word Limits	Color of Cover
(i)	Petition for a writ of Certiorari (Rule 14): Motion for Leave to File a Bill of Complaint and Brief in Support (Rule 17.3); Jurisdictional Statement (Rule 18.3); Petition for an Extraordinary Writ (Rule 20.2)	9,000	white

KELLY PATRICK RIGGS

(ii)	Brief in Opposition (Rule 15.3) ; Brief in Opposition to Motion for Leave to file an Original Action (Rule 17.5); Motion to Dismiss or Affirm (Rule 18.6); Brief in Opposition to Mandamus or Prohibition (Rule 20.3(b)); Response to a Petition for Habeas Corpus (Rule 20.4); Respondent's Brief in Support of Certiorari (Rule 12.6)	9,000	orange
(iii)	Reply to Brief in Opposition (Rules 15.6) and 17.5); Brief Opposing a Motion to Dismiss or Affirm (Rule 18.8)	3,000	tan
(iv)	Supplemental Brief (Rules 15.8, 17, 18.10, and 25.6)	3,000	tan
(v)	Brief on the Merits for Petitioner or Appellant (Rule 24); Exceptions by Plaintiff to Report of Special Master (Rule 17)	13,000	light blue
(vi)	Brief on the Merits for Respondent or Appellee Rule 24.2); Brief on the Merits for Respondent or Appeal Supporting Petitioner or Appellant Rule 12.6); Exceptions by Party Other Than Plaintiff to Report of Special Mater (Rule 17)	13,000	light red
(vii)	Reply Brief on the Merits (Rule 24.4)	6,000	yellow
(viii)	Reply to Plaintiff's Exceptions to Report of Special Master (Rule 17)	13,000	orange
(ix)	Reply to Exceptions by Party Other Than Plaintiff to Report of Special Master (Rule 17)	13,000	yellow
(x)	Brief for an *Amicus Curiae* at the Petition State or pertaining to a Motion for Leave to file a Bill of Complaint (Rule 37.2)	6,000	cream
(xi)	Brief for an *Amicus Curiae* in Support of the Plaintiff, Petitioner, or Appellant, or in Support of Neither Party, on the Merits or in an Original Action at the Exceptions Stage (Rule 37.3)	9,000	light green
(xii)	Brief for any Other *Amicus Curiae* in Support of the Plaintiff, Petitioner, or Appellant, or in Support of Neither Party, on the Merits or in an Original Action at the Exceptions Stage (Rule 37.3)	8,000	light green
(xiii)	Brief for an *Amicus Curiae* Identified in Rule 37.4 in Support of the Defendant,	9,000	dark green

66

	Respondent, or Appellee, on the Merits or in an Original Action at the Exceptions Stage (Rule 37.3)		
(xiv)	Brief for any Other *Americus Curiae* in Support of the Defendant, Respondent, or Appellee, on the Merits or in an Original Action at the Exceptions Stage (Rule 37.3)	8,000	dark green
(xv)	Petition for Rehearing (Rule 44)	3,000	tan

(h) A document prepared under Rule 33.1 must be accompanied by a certificate signed by the attorney, the unrepresented party, or the preparer of the document stating that the brief complies with the word limitations. The person preparing the certificate may rely on the word count of the word-processing system used to prepare the document. The word-processing system must be set to include footnotes in the word count. The certificate must state the number of the words in the document. The certificate shall accompany the document when it is presented to the Clerk for filing and shall be separate from it. If the certificate is signed by a person other than a member of the Bar of this Court, the counsel of record, or the unrepresented party, it must contain a notarized affidavit or declaration in compliance with 28 U.S.C. §1746.

2. *8½-by 11-inch Paper Format: (a) The text of every document, including any appendix thereto, expressly permitted by these Rules to be presented to the Court on 8½-by 11-inch paper shall appear double-spaced, except for indented quotations, which shall be single spaced, on opaque, un glazed, white paper. The document shall be stapled or bound at the upper left-hand corner. Copies, if required, shall be produced on the same type of paper and shall be legible. The original of any such document (except a motion to dismiss or affirm under Rule 18.6) shall be signed by the party proceeding pro se or by counsel of record who must be a member of the Bar of this Court or an attorney appointed under the Criminal Justice Act of 1964, see 18 U. S. C. § 3006A(d)(7), or under any other applicable federal statute. Subparagraph 1(g) of this Rule does not apply to documents prepared under this paragraph.*

(b) Page limits for documents presented on 8½-by 11-inch paper are 40 pages for a petition for a writ of certiorari, jurisdictional statement, petition for an extraordinary writ, brief in opposition, or motion to dismiss or affirm and 15 pages for a reply to a brief in opposition, brief opposing a motion to dismiss or affirm, supplemental brief, or petition for rehearing. The exclusions specified in subparagraph 1(d) of this Rule apply.

Rule 34. Document Preparation: General Requirements

Every document, whether prepared under Rule 33.1 or Rule 33.2, shall comply with the following provisions:

1. *Each document shall bear on its cover, in the order indicated, from the top of the page:*

   (a) *the docket number of the case or, if there is none, a space for one;*

   (b) *the name of this Court;*

   (c) *the caption of the case as appropriate in this Court;*

   (d) *the nature of the proceeding and the name of the court from which the action is brought (e. g., "On Petition for Writ of Certiorari to the United States Court of Appeals for the Fifth*

Circuit"; or, for a merits brief, "On Writ of Certiorari to the United States Court of Appeals for the Fifth Circuit");

(e) *the title of the document (e.g., "Petition for Writ of Certiorari," "Brief for Respondent," "Joint Appendix");*

(f) *the name of the attorney who is counsel of record for the party concerned (who must be a member of the Bar of this Court except as provided in Rule 9.1) and on whom service is to be made, with a notation directly thereunder identifying the attorney as counsel of record and setting out counsel's office address, e-mail address, and telephone number. Only one counsel of record may be noted on a single document, except that counsel of record for each party must be listed on the cover of a joint appendix. The names of other members of the Bar of this Court or of the Bar of the highest court of State acting as counsel, and, if desired, their addresses may be added, but the counsel of record shall be clearly identified. Names of persons other than attorneys admitted to a state bar may not be listed unless the party is appearing pro se, in which case the party's name, address, and telephone number shall appear.*

(g) *The foregoing shall be displayed in an appropriate typographical manner and, except for identification of counsel, may not be set in type smaller than standard 11-point if the document is prepared as required by Rule 33.1.*

2. *Every document (other than a joint appendix) that exceeds 1,500 words when prepared under Rule 33.1 or that exceeds five pages when prepared under Rule 33.2, shall contain a table of contents and a table of cited authorities (i.e., cases alphabetically arranged, constitutional provisions, statutes, treatises, and other materials) with references to the pages in the document where such authorities are cited.*

3. *The body of every document shall bear at its close the name of counsel of record and such other counsel, identified on the cover of the document in conformity with subparagraph 1(f) of this Rule, as may be desired.*

4. *Every appendix to a document must be preceded by a table of contents that provides a description of each document in the appendix.*

5. *All references to a provision of federal statutory law should ordinarily be cited to the United States Code if the provision has been codified therein. In the event the provision has not been classified to the United States Code, citation should be to the Statutes at Large. Additional or alternative citations should be provided only if there is a particular reason why those citations are relevant or necessary to the argument.*

6. *A case in which privacy protection was governed by Federal Rule of Appellate Procedure 25(a)(5), Federal Rule of Bankruptcy Procedure 9037, Federal Rule of Civil Procedure 5.2, or Federal Rule of Criminal Procedure 49.1 is governed by the same Rule in this Court. In any other case, privacy protection is governed by Federal Rule of Civil Procedure 5.2, except that Federal Rule of Criminal Procedure 49.1 governs when an extraordinary writ is sought in a criminal case. If the Court schedules briefing and oral argument in a case that was governed by Federal Rule of Civil Procedure 5.2(c) or Federal Rule of Criminal Procedure 49.1(c), the parties shall submit electronic versions of all prior and subsequent filings with this Court in the case, subject to the redaction Rules set forth above.*

Rule 35. Death, Substitution, and Revivor; Public Officers

1. If a party dies after the filing of a petition for a writ of certiorari to this Court or after the filing of a notice of appeal, the authorized representative does not voluntarily become a party, any other party may suggest the death on the record and, on motion, seek an order requiring the representative to become a party within a designated time. If the representative then fails to become a party, the party so moving, if a respondent or appellee, is entitled to have the petition for a writ of certiorari or the appeal dismissed, and if a petitioner or appellant, is entitled to proceed as in any other case of nonappearance by a respondent or appellee. If the substitution of a representative of the deceased is not made within six months after the death of the party, the case shall abate.

2. Whenever a case cannot be revived in the court whose judgment is sought to be reviewed because the deceased party's authorized representative is not subject to that court's jurisdiction, proceedings will be conducted as this Court may direct.

3. When a public officer who is a party to a proceeding in this Court in an official capacity dies, resigns or otherwise ceases to hold office, the action does not abate, and any successor in office is automatically substituted as a party. The parties shall notify the Clerk in writing of any such successions. Proceedings following the substitution shall be in the name of the substituted party, but any misnomer not affecting the substantial rights of the parties will be disregarded.

4. A public officer who is a party to a proceeding in this Court in an official capacity may be described as a party by the officer's official title rather than by name, but the Court may require the name to be added.

Rule 36. Custody of Prisoners in Habeas Corpus Proceedings

1. *Pending review in this Court of a decision in a habeas corpus proceeding commenced before a court, Justice, or judge of the United States, the person having custody of the prisoner may not transfer custody to another person unless the transfer is authorized under this Rule.*

2. *Upon application by a custodian, the court, Justice, or judge who entered the decision under review may authorize transfer and the substitution of a successor custodian as a party.*

3. *(a) Pending review of a decision failing or refusing to release a prisoner, the prisoner may be detained in the custody from which release is sought or in other appropriate custody or may be enlarged on personal recognizance or bail, as may appear appropriate to the court, Justice, or judge who entered the decision, or to the court of appeals, this Court, or a judge or Justice of either court.*

   (b) Pending review of a decision ordering release, the prisoner shall be enlarged on personal recognizance or bail unless the court, Justice, or judge who entered the decision, or the court of appeals, this Court, or a judge or Justice of either court, orders otherwise.

4. *An initial order respecting the custody or enlargement of the prisoner, and any recognizance or surety taken, shall continue in effect pending review in the court of appeals and in this Court unless, for reasons shown to the court of appeals, this Court, or a judge or Justice of either court, the order is modified or an independent order respecting custody, enlargement, or surety is entered.*

Rule 37. Brief for an *Amicus Curiae*

1. an *amicus curiae* brief that brings to the attention of the Court a relevant matter not already brought to its attention by the parties may be of considerable help to the Court. An *amicus curiae* brief that does not serve this purpose burdens the Court, and its filing is not favored. An *amicus curiae* brief may be filed only by an attorney abutted to practice before this Court as provided in Rule 5.

2. (a) An *amicus curiae* brief submitted before the Court's consideration of a petition for a writ of certiorari, motion for leave to file a bill of complaint, jurisdictional statement, or petition for an extraordinary writ may be filed if it reflects that written consent of all parties has been provided, or if the Court grants leave to file under subparagraph 2(b) of this Rule. An *amicus curiae* brief in support of a petitioner or appellant shall be filed within 30 days after the case is placed on the docket or response is called for by the Court, whichever is later, and that time will not be extended. An *amicus curiae* brief in support of a motion of a plaintiff for leave to file a bill of complaint in. An original action shall be filed within 60 days after the case is placed on the docket, and that time will not be extended. An *amicus curiae* brief in support of a respondent, an appellee, or a defendant shall be submitted within the time allowed for filing a brief in opposition or a motion to dismiss or affirm. An *amicus curiae* filing a brief under this subparagraph shall ensure that the counsel of record for all parties receive notice of its intention to file an *amicus curiae* brief at least 10 days prior to the due date for the *amicus curiae* brief unless the *amicus curiae* brief is filed earlier than 10 days before the due date. Only one signatory to any *amicus curiae* brief filed jointly by more than one *amicus curiae* must timely notify the parties of its intent to file that brief. The *amicus curiae* brief shall indicate that counsel of record received timely notice of the intent to file the brief under this Rule and shall specify whether consent was granted, and its cover shall identify the party supported. Only one signatory to an *amicus curiae* brief filed jointly by more than one *amicus curiae* must obtain the consent of the parties to file that brief. A petitioner or respondent may submit to the Clerk a letter granting blanket consent to *amicus curiae* briefs, stating that the party consents to the filing of amicus curiae briefs in support of either party. The Clerk will note all notices of blanket consent on the docket.

   (b) When a party to the case has withheld consent, a motion for leave to file an *amicus curiae* brief before the (hurt's consideration of a petition for a writ of certiorari, motion for leave to file a bill of complaint, jurisdictional statement, or petition for an extraordinary writ may be presented to the Court. The motion, prepared as required by Rule 33.1 and as one document with the brief sought to be filed, shall be submitted within the time allowed for filing an *amicus curiae* brief and shall indicate the party or parties who have withheld consent and state the nature of the movant's interest. Such a motion is not favored.

3. (a) An *amicus curiae* brief in a case before the Court for oral argument may be filed if it reflects that written consent of all parties has been provided or if the Court grants leave to file under subparagraph 3(b) of this Rule. The brief must be submitted within 7 days after the brief for the party supported is filed, or if in support of neither party, within 7 days after the time allowed for filing the petitioner's or appellant's brief. Motions to extend the time for filing an *amicus curiae* brief will not be entertained. The 10-day notice requirement of subparagraph 2(a) of this Rule does not apply to an *amicus curiae* brief in a case before the Court for oral argument. The *amicus curiae* brief shall specify whether consent was granted, and its cover shall identify the party supported or indicate whether it suggests affirmance or reversal. The Clerk will not file a reply brief for an *amicus curiae* or a brief for an *amicus curiae* in support of, or in opposition to,

a petition for rehearing. Only one signatory to an *amicus curiae* brief filed jointly by more than one *amicus curiae* must obtain consent of the parties to file that brief. A petitioner or respondent may submit to the Clerk a letter granting blanket consent to *amicus curiae* briefs, stating that the party consents to the filing of *amicus curiae* briefs in support of either or of neither party. The Clerk will note all notices of blanket consent on the docket.

(b) When a party to a case before the Court for oral argument has withheld consent, a motion for leave to file an *amicus curiae* brief may be presented to the Court. The motion, prepared as required by rule 33.1 and as one document with the brief sought to be filed, shall be submitted within the time allowed for filing an *amicus curiae* brief and shall indicate the party or parties who have withheld consent and state the nature of the movant's interest.

4. No motion for Leave to file an *amicus curiae* brief is necessary If the brief is presented on behalf of the United States by the Solicitor General; on behalf of any agency of the United States allowed by law to appear before this Court when submitted by the agency's authorized legal representative; on behalf of a State, Commonwealth, Territory, or Possession when submitted by its Attorney General; or on behalf of a city, county, town, or similar entity when submitted by its authorized law officer.

5. A brief or motion filed under this Rule shall be accompanied by proof of service as required by Rule 29, and shall comply with the applicable provisions of Rules 21, 24, and 33.1 (except that it suffices to set out in the brief the interest of the *amicus curiae*, the summary of the argument, the argument, and the conclusion). A motion for leave to file may not exceed 1,500 words. A party served with the motion may file an objection thereto, stating concisely the reasons for withholding consent; the objection shall be prepared as required by Rule 33.2.

6. Except for briefs presented on behalf of *amicus curiae* listed in Rule 37.4, a brief filed under this Rule shall indicate whether counsel for a party authored the brief in whole or in part and whether such counsel or a party made a monetary contribution intended to fund the preparation or submission of the brief, and shall identify every person other than the *amicus curiae*, its members, or its counsel, who made such a monetary contribution. The disclosure shall be made in the first footnote on the first page of text.

Rule 38. Fees

Under 28 U. S. C. § 1911, the fees charged by the Clerk are:

(a) *for docketing a case on a petition for a writ of certiorari or on appeal or for docketing any other proceeding, except a certified question or a motion to docket and dismiss an appeal under Rule 18.5, $300;*

(b) *for filing a petition for rehearing or a motion for leave to file a petition for rehearing, $200;*

(c) *for reproducing and certifying any record or paper, $1 per page; and for comparing with the original thereof any photographic reproduction of any record or paper, when furnished by the person requesting its certification, $.50 per page;*

(d) *for a certificate bearing the seal of the Court, $10; and*

(e) *for a check paid to the Court, Clerk, or Marshal that is returned for lack of funds, $35.*

Rule 39. Proceedings *In Forma Pauperis*

1. *A party seeking to proceed in forma pauperis shall file a motion for leave to do so, together with the party's notarized affidavit or declaration (in compliance with 28 U. S. C. § 1746) in the form*

prescribed by the Federal Rules of Appellate Procedure, Form 4. The motion shall state whether leave to proceed in forma pauperis was sought in any other court and, if so, whether leave was granted. If the court below appointed counsel for an indigent party, no affidavit or declaration is required, but the motion shall cite the provision of law under which counsel was appointed, or a copy of the order of appointment shall be appended to the motion.

2. *If leave to proceed in forma pauperis is sought for the purpose of filing a document, the motion, and an affidavit or declaration if required, shall be filed together with that document and shall comply in every respect with Rule 21. As provided in that Rule, it suffices to file an original and 10 copies, unless the party is an inmate confined in an institution and is not represented by counsel, in which case the original, alone, suffices. A copy of the motion, and affidavit or declaration if required, shall precede and be attached to each copy of the accompanying document.*

3. *Except when these Rules expressly provide that a document shall be prepared as required by Rule 33.1, every document presented by a party proceeding under this Rule shall be prepared as required by Rule 33.2 (unless such preparation is impossible). Every document shall be legible. While making due allowance for any case presented under this Rule by a person appearing pro se, the Clerk will not file any document if it does not comply with the substance of these Rules or is jurisdictionally out of time.*

4. *When the documents required by paragraphs 1 and 2 of this Rule are presented to the Clerk, accompanied by proof of service as required by Rule 29, they will be placed on the docket without the payment of a docket fee or any other fee.*

5. *The respondent or appellee in a case filed in forma pauperis shall respond in the same manner and within the same time as in any other case of the same nature, except that the filing of an original and 10 copies of a response prepared as required by Rule 33.2, with proof of service as required by Rule 29, suffices. The respondent or appellee may challenge the grounds for the motion for leave to proceed in forma pauperis in a separate document or in the response itself.*

6. *Whenever the Court appoints counsel for an indigent party in a case set for oral argument, the briefs on the merits submitted by that counsel, unless otherwise requested, shall be prepared under the Clerk's supervision. The Clerk also will reimburse appointed counsel for any necessary travel expenses to Washington, D. C., and return in connection with the argument.*

7. *In a case in which certiorari has been granted, probable jurisdiction noted, or consideration of jurisdiction postponed, this Court may appoint counsel to represent a party financially unable to afford an attorney to the extent authorized by the Criminal Justice Act of 1964, 18 U. S. C. § 3006A, or by any other applicable federal statute.*

8. *If satisfied that a petition for a writ of certiorari, jurisdictional statement, or petition for an extraordinary writ is frivolous or malicious, the Court may deny leave to proceed in forma pauperis.*

Rule 40. Veterans, Seamen, and Military Cases

1. A veteran suing under any provision of law exempting veterans from the payment of fees or court costs, may proceed without prepayment of fees or costs or furnishing security therefor and may file a motion for leave to proceed on papers prepared as required by Rule 33.2. The motion shall ask leave to proceed as a veteran and be accompanied by an affidavit or declaration setting out the moving party's veteran status. A copy of the motion shall proceed and be attached to

each copy of the petition for a writ of certiorari or other substantive document filed by the veteran.

2. A seaman suing under 28 U.S.C. §1916 may proceed without prepayment of fees or costs or furnishing security therefor and may file a motion for leave to proceed on papers prepared as required by rule 33.2. The motion shall ask leave to proceed as a seaman and be accompanied by an affidavit or declaration setting out the moving party's seaman status. A copy of the motion shall precede and be attached to each copy of the petition for a writ of certiorari or other substantive document filed by the seaman.

3. An accused person petitioning for a writ of certiorari to review a decision of the United States Court of Appeals for the Armed Forces under 28 U.S.C. §1259 may proceed without prepayment of fees or costs or furnishing security therefor and without filing an affidavit of indigency but is not entitled to proceed on papers prepared as required by rule 33.2, except as authorized by the Court on a separate motion under Rule 39.

PART VIII. DISPOSITION OF CASES

Rule 41. Opinions of the Court

Opinions of the Court will be released by the Clerk immediately upon their announcement from the bench or as the Court otherwise directs. Thereafter, the Clerk will cause the opinions to be issued in slip form, and the Reporter of Decisions will prepare them for publication in the preliminary prints and bound volumes of the United States Reports.

Rule 42. Interest and Damages

1. If a judgment for money in a civil case is affirmed, any interest allowed by law is payable from the date the judgment under review was entered. If a judgment is modified or reversed with a direction that a judgment for money be entered below, the courts below may award interest to the extent permitted by law. Interest in cases arising in a state court is allowed at the same rate that similar judgments bear interest in the courts of the State in which judgment is directed to be entered. Interest in cases arising in a court of the United States is allowed at the interest rate authorized by law.

2. When a petition for a writ of certiorari, an appeal, or an application for other relief is frivolous, the Court may award the respondent or appellee just damages and single or double costs under Rule 43. Damages or costs may be awarded against the petitioner, appellant, or applicant, against the party's counsel, or against both party and counsel.

Rule 43. Costs

1. If the Court affirms a judgment, the petitioner or appellant shall pay costs unless the Court otherwise orders.

2. If the Court reverses or vacates a judgment, the respondent or appellee shall pay costs unless the Court otherwise orders.

3. The Clerk's fees and the cost of printing the joint appendix are the only taxable items in this Court. The cost of the transcript of the record from the court below is also a taxable item, but shall be taxable in that court as costs in the case. The expenses of printing briefs, motions, petitions, or jurisdictional statements are not taxable.

4. In a case involving a certified question, costs are equally divided unless the Court otherwise orders, except that if the Court decides the whole matter in controversy, as permitted by Rule 19.2, costs are allowed as provided in paragraphs 1 and 2 of this Rule.

5. To the extent permitted by 28 U.S.C. §2412, costs under this rule are allowed for or against the United States or an officer or agent thereof, unless expressly waived or unless the Court otherwise orders.

6. When costs are allowed in this Court, the Clerk will insert an itemization of the costs in the body of the mandate or judgment sent to the court below. The prevailing side may not submit a bill of costs.

7. In extraordinary circumstances, the Court may adjudge double costs.

Rule 44. Rehearing

1. *Any petition for the rehearing of any judgment or decision of the Court on the merits shall be filed within 25 days after entry of the judgment or decision unless the Court or a Justice shortens or extends the time. The petitioner shall file 40 copies of the rehearing petition and shall pay the filing fee prescribed by Rule 38(b), except that a petitioner proceeding in forma pauperis under Rule 39, including an inmate of an institution, shall file the number of copies required for a petition by such a person under Rule 12.2. The petition shall state its grounds briefly and distinctly and shall be served as required by Rule 29. The petition shall be presented together with certification of counsel (or of a party unrepresented by counsel) that it is presented in good faith and not for delay; one copy of the certificate shall bear the signature of counsel (or of a party unrepresented by counsel). A copy of the certificate shall follow and be attached to each copy of the petition. A petition for rehearing is not subject to oral argument and will not be granted except by a majority of the Court at the instance of a Justice who concurred with the judgment or decision.*

2. *Any petition for the rehearing of an order denying a petition for a writ of certiorari or extraordinary writ shall be filed within 25 days after the date of the order of denial and shall comply with all the form and filing requirements of paragraph 1 of this Rule, including the payment of the filing fee if required, but its grounds shall be limited to intervening circumstances of a substantial or controlling effect or to other substantial grounds not previously presented. The time for filing a petition for the rehearing of an order denying a petition for a writ of certiorari or extraordinary writ will not be extended. The petition shall be presented together with certification of counsel (or of a party unrepresented by counsel) that it is restricted to the grounds specified in this paragraph and that it is presented in good faith and not for delay; one copy of the certificate shall bear the signature of counsel (or of a party unrepresented by counsel). The certificate shall be bound with each copy of the petition. The Clerk will not file a petition without a certificate. The petition is not subject to oral argument.*

3. *The Clerk will not file any response to a petition for rehearing unless the Court requests a response. In the absence of extraordinary circumstances, the Court will not grant a petition for rehearing without first requesting a response.*

4. *The Clerk will not file consecutive petitions and petitions that are out of time under this Rule.*

5. *The Clerk will not file any brief for an amicus curiae in support of, or in opposition to, a petition for rehearing.*

6. *If the Clerk determines that a petition for rehearing submitted timely and in good faith is in a form that does not comply with this Rule or with Rule 33 or Rule 34, the Clerk will return it with a letter indicating the deficiency. A corrected petition for rehearing submitted in accordance with Rule 29.2 no more than 15 days after the date of the Clerk's letter will be deemed timely.*

Rule 45. Process; Mandates

1. All process of this court issues in the name of the President of the United States.

2. In a case on review from a state court, the mandate issues 25 days after entry of the judgment, unless the Court or a Justice shortens or extends the time, or unless the parties stipulate that it issue sooner. The filing of a petition for rehearing stays the mandate until disposition of the petition, unless the Court orders otherwise. If the petition is denied, the mandate issues forthwith.

3. In a case on review from any court of the United States as defined by 28 U.S.C. §451, a formal mandate does not issue unless specially directed; instead, the Clerk of this Court will send the clerk of the lower court a copy of the opinion or order of this Court and a certified copy of the judgment. The certified copy of the judgment, prepared and signed by this Court's Clerk, will provide for costs if any are awarded. In all other respects, the provisions of paragraph 2 of this Rule apply.

Rule 46. Dismissing Cases

1. At any stage of the proceedings, whenever all parties file with the Clerk an agreement in writing that a case be dismissed, specifying the terms for payment of costs, and pay to the Clerk any fees then due, the Clerk, without further reference to the Court, will enter an order of dismissal.

2. (a) A petitioner or appellant may file a motion to dismiss the case, with proof of service as required by Rule 29, tendering to the Clerk any fees due and costs payable. No more than 15 days after service thereof, an adverse party may file an objection, limited to the amount of damages and costs in this Court alleged to be payable or to showing that the moving party does not represent all petitioners or appellants. The Clerk will not file any objection not so limited.

   (b) When the objection asserts that the moving party does not represent all the petitioners or appellants, the party moving for dismissal may file a reply within 10 days, after which time the matter will be submitted to the Court for its determination.

   (c) If no objection is filed – or if upon objection going only to the amount of damages and costs in this Court, the party moving for dismissal tenders the additional damages and costs in full within 10 days of the demand therefor-the Clerk, without further reference to the Court, will enter an order of dismissal. If, after objection as to the amount of damages and costs in this court, the moving party does not respond by a tender within 10 days, the Clerk will report the matter to the Court for its determination.

3. No mandate or other process will be issued on a dismissal under this Rule without an order of the Court.

PART IX. DEFINITIONS AND EFFECTIVE DATE

Rule 47. Reference to "State Court" and "State Law"

The term "state court," when used in these Rules, includes the District of Columbia Court of Appeals, the Supreme Court of the Commonwealth of Puerto Rico, the courts of the Northern Mariana Islands, the local courts of Guam, and the Supreme Court of the Virgin Islands. References in these Rules to the statutes of a

State include the statutes of the District of Columbia, the Commonwealth of Puerto Rico, the Commonwealth of the Northern Mariana Islands, the Territory of Guam, and the Territory of the Virgin Islands.

Rule 48. Effective Date of Rules

1. These Rules, adopted April 18, 2019, will be effective July 1, 2019.

2. The Rules govern all proceedings after their effective date except that the amendments to Rules 25.3 and 33.1(g) will apply only to cases in which certiorari was granted or a direct appeal or original action was set for argument after the effective date.

CHAPTER THREE

STATUTES AND LAWS

First, let me clarify that 'statute' is a fancy word for "a law enacted by a legislative body." After reading the rules of the Supreme Court, you likely discovered that the rules referred to a number of statutes or laws that are equally important to be aware of. Keep in mind that the Supreme Court is the ultimate example of a bureaucracy. The clerk's office of the Supreme Court has a primary purpose of discarding any petition it possibly can for failure to comply with the rules, see Rule 1.1. Notice also in Rule 1.3, the reference to 5 U.S.C. §6103

Although you have no need to memorize the rules and the statutes, it is very important to become familiar with the applicable laws before you file your petition. Again, you have about thirty days to get prepared, so please apply yourself by giving this list of statutes a cursory read, at a minimum. Once you have completed that task, we will continue to prepare your own personal claim before you get the forms packet from the Supreme Court.

28 U.S.C.

§1 Number of justices; quorum

The Supreme Court of the United States shall consist of a Chief Justice of the United States and eight associate justices, any six of whom shall constitute a quorum.

§2 Terms of court

The Supreme Court shall hold at the seat of government a term of court commencing on the first Monday in October of each year and may hold such adjourned or special terms as may be necessary.

§3 Vacancy in office of Chief Justice; disability

Whenever the Chief Justice is unable to perform the duties of his office or the office is vacant, his powers and duties shall devolve upon the associate justice next in precedence who is able to act, until such disability is removed or another Chief Justice is appointed and duly qualified.

§4 Precedence of associate justices

Associate justices shall have precedence according to the seniority of their commissions. Justices whose commissions bear the same date shall have precedence according to seniority in age.

§6 Records of former court of appeals

The records and proceedings of the court of appeals, appointed previously by the adoption of the Constitution, shall be kept until deposited with the National Archives of the United States in the office of the clerk of the Supreme Court, who shall furnish copies thereof to any person requiring and paying for them, in the manner provided by law for giving copies of the records and proceedings of the Supreme Court. Such copies shall have the same faith and credit as proceedings of the Supreme Court.

§1251 Original jurisdiction

> a) The Supreme Court shall have original and exclusive jurisdiction of all controversies between two or more states.

The Supreme Court shall have original but not exclusive jurisdiction of:

All actions or proceedings to which ambassadors, other public ministers, consuls, or vice consuls of foreign states are parties;

All controversies between the United States and a State;

All actions or proceedings by a State against the citizens of another State or against aliens.

§1253   Direct appeals from decisions of three-judge courts

Except as otherwise provided by law, any party may appeal to the Supreme Court from an order granting or denying, after notice and hearing, an interlocutory or permanent injunction in any civil action, suit or proceeding required by any Act of Congress to be heard and determined by a district court of three judges.

§1254   Courts of appeals; certiorari; certified questions

Cases in the courts of appeals may be reviewed by the Supreme Court by the following methods:

1. By writ of certiorari granted upon the petition of any party to any civil or criminal case, before or after rendition of judgment or decree;

2. By certification at any time by a court of appeals of any question of law in any civil or criminal case as to which instructions are desired, and upon such certification, the Supreme Court may give binding instructions or require the entire record to be sent up for decision of the entire matter in controversy.

§1257   STATE COURTS; CERTIORARI

a) Final judgments or decrees rendered by the highest court of a State in which a decision could be had may be reviewed by the Supreme Court by writ of certiorari where the validity of a treaty or statute of the United States is drawn in question or where the validity of a statute of any State is drawn in question on the ground of its being repugnant to the Constitution, treaties, or laws of the United States, or where any title, right, privilege, or immunity is specially set up or claimed under the Constitution or the treaties or statues of, or any commission held or authority exercised under, the United States.

§1258   Supreme Court of Puerto Rico; certiorari

Final judgments or decrees rendered by the Supreme Court of the Commonwealth of Puerto Rico may be reviewed by the Supreme Court by writ of certiorari where the validity of a treaty or statute of the United States is drawn in question or where the validity of a statute of the Commonwealth of Puerto Ricco is drawn in question on the ground of its being repugnant to the Constitution, treaties, or laws of the United States, or where any title, right, privilege, or immunity is specially set up or claimed under the Constitution or the treaties or statues of, or any commission held or authority exercised under, the United States.

§1259   Court of Appeals for the Armed Forces; certiorari

Decisions of the United States Court of Appeals for the Armed Forces may be reviewed by the Supreme Court by writ of certiorari in the following cases:

1. Cases reviewed by the Court of Appeals for the Armed Forces under section 867(a)(1) of title 10.

2. Cases certified to the Court of Appeals for the Armed Forces by the Judge Advocate General under section 867(a)(2) of title 10.

3. Cases in which the Court of Appeals for the Armed Forces granted a petition for review under sections 867(a)(3) of title 10.

4. Cases other than those described in paragraphs (1), (2), and (3) of this subsection in which the Court of Appeals for the Armed Forces granted relief.

§1260 Supreme Court of the Virgin Islands; certiorari

Final judgments or decrees rendered by the Supreme Court of the Virgin Islands may be reviewed by the Supreme Court by writ of certiorari where the validity of a treaty or statute of the United States is drawn in question or where the validity of a treaty or statute of the Virgin Islands is drawn in question on the ground of its being repugnant to the Constitution, treaties, or laws of the United States, or where any title, right, privilege, or immunity is specially set up or claimed under the Constitution or the treaties of, or any commission held or authority exercised under, the United States.

§1651 Writs

The Supreme Court and all courts established by Act of Congress may issue all writs necessary or appropriate in aid of their respective jurisdictions and agreeable to the usages and principles of law.

An alternative writ or rule nisi may be issued by a justice or judge of a court which has jurisdiction.

§1872 Issues of fact in Supreme Court

In all original actions at law in the Supreme Court against citizens of the United States, issues of fact shall be tried by jury.

§1911 Supreme Court

The Supreme Court may fix fees to be charged by its clerk.

The fees of the clerk, cost of serving process and other necessary disbursements incidental to any case before the court, may be taxed against the litigants as the court directs.

§1912 Damages and costs on affirmance

Where a judgment is affirmed by the Supreme Court or a court of appeals, the court in its discretion may adjudge to the prevailing party damages for his delay, and single or double costs.

§1925 Admiralty and maritime cases

Except as otherwise provided by Act of Congress, the allowance and taxation of costs in admiralty and maritime cases shall be prescribed by rules promulgated by the Supreme Court.

§2071 Rule-making power generally

a) The Supreme Court and all courts established by Act of Congress may from time to time prescribe rules for the conduct of their business. Such rules shall be consistent with Acts of Congress and rules of practice and procedure prescribed under section 2072 of this title [28 USCS §2072].

b) Any rule prescribed by a court, other than the Supreme Court, under subsection (a) shall be prescribed only after giving appropriate public notice and an opportunity for comment. Such rule shall take effect upon the date specified by the prescribing court and shall have such effect on pending proceedings as the prescribing court may order.

c) (1) A rule of a district court prescribed under subsection (a) shall remain in effect unless modified or abrogated by the judicial council of the relevant circuit.

(2) Any other rule prescribed by a court other than the Supreme Court under subsection (a) shall remain in effect unless modified or abrogated by the Judicial Conference.

d) Copies of rules prescribed under subsection (a) by a district court shall be furnished to the judicial council, and copies of all rules prescribed by a court other than the Supreme Court under subsection

(a) shall be furnished to the Director if the Administrative Office of the United States Courts and be made available to the public.

e) If the prescribing court determines that there is an immediate need for a rule, such court may proceed under this section without public notice and opportunity for comment, but such court shall promptly thereafter afford such notice and opportunity for comment.

f) No rule may be prescribed by a district court other than this section.

§2072   Rules of procedure and evidence; power to prescribe

a) The Supreme Court shall have the power to prescribe general rules of practice and procedure and rules of evidence for cases in the United States district courts (including proceedings before magistrates [magistrate judges] thereof) and courts of appeals.

b) Such rules shall not abridge, enlarge, or modify any substantive right. All laws in conflict with such rules shall be of no further force or effect after such rules have taken effect.

c) Such rules may define when a ruling of a district court is final for purposes of appeal under section 1291 of this title [28 USCS §1291].

§2074   Rules of procedure and evidence; submission to Congress; effective date

a) The Supreme Court shall transmit to Congress not later than May 1 of the year in which a rule prescribed under section 2072 [28 USCS §2072] is to become effective a copy of the proposed rule. Such rule shall take effect no earlier than December 1 of the year in which such rule is transmitted unless otherwise permitted by law. The Supreme Court may fix the extent such rule shall apply to proceedings then pending, except that the Supreme Court shall not require the application of such rule to further proceedings then pending to the extent that. in the opinion of the court in which such proceedings are pending, the application of such rule in such proceedings would not be feasible or would work injustice, in which event the former rule applies.

b) Any such rule creating, abolishing, or modifying an evidentiary privilege shall have no force or effect unless approved by an Act of Congress.

§2075   Bankruptcy Rules

The Supreme Court shall have the power to prescribe by general rules, the forms of process, writs, pleadings, and motions, and the practice and procedure in cases under title 11 [11 USCS § § 1 et seq.].

Such rules shall not abridge, enlarge, or modify any substantive right.

The Supreme Court shall transmit to Congress not later than May 1 of the year in which a rule prescribed under this section is to become effective a copy of the proposed rule. The rule shall take effect no earlier than December 1 of the year in which it is transmitted to Congress unless otherwise provided by law.

The bankruptcy rules promulgated under this section shall prescribe a form for the statement required under section 707(b)(2)(C) of title 11 [11 USCS §707(b)(2)(C)] and may provide general rules on the content of such statement.

§2101   Supreme Court; time for appeal or certiorari; docketing; stay

a) A direct appeal to the Supreme Court from any decision under section 1253 of this title [28 USCS §1253], holding unconstitutional in whole or in part, any Act of Congress, shall be taken within thirty days after the entry of the interlocutory or final order, judgment or decree. The record shall be made up, and the case docketed within sixty days from the time such appeal is taken under rules prescribed by the Supreme Court.

b) Any other direct appeal to the Supreme Court which is authorized by law from a decision of a district court in any civil action, suit, or proceeding, shall be taken within thirty days from the judgment, order, or decree, appealed from, if interlocutory, and within sixty days if final.

c) Any other appeal or any writ of certiorari intended to bring any judgment or decree in a civil action, suit, or proceeding before the Supreme Court for review shall be taken or applied for within ninety days after the entry of such judgment or decree. A justice of the Supreme Court, for good cause shown, may extend the time for applying for a writ of certiorari for a period not exceeding sixty days.

d) The time for appeal or application for a writ of certiorari to review the judgment of a State court in a criminal case shall be as prescribed by the rules of the Supreme Court.

e) An application to the Supreme Court for a writ of certiorari to review a case before judgment has been rendered in the court of appeals may be made at any time before judgment.

f) In any case in which the final judgment or decree of any court is subject to review by the Supreme Court on writ of certiorari, the execution and enforcement of such judgment or decree may be stayed for a reasonable time to enable the party aggrieved to obtain a writ of certiorari from the Supreme Court. The stay may be granted by a judge of the court rendering the judgment or decree or by a justice of the Supreme Court and may be conditioned on the giving of security, approved by such judge or justice, that if the aggrieved party fails to make application for such writ within the period allotted therefore, or fails to obtain an order granting his application, or fails to make his plea good in the Supreme Court, he shall answer for all damages and costs which the other party may sustain by reason of the stay.

g) The time for application for a writ of certiorari to review a decision of the United States Court of Appeals for the Armed Forces shall be as prescribed by the rules of the Supreme Court.

§2102   Priority of criminal case on appeal from State court

Criminal cases on review from State courts shall have priority on the docket of the Supreme Court over all cases except cases to which the United States is a party and such other cases as the court may decide to be of public importance.

§2104   Reviews of States court decisions

A review by the Supreme Court of a judgment or decree of a State court shall be conducted in the same manner and under the same regulations, and shall have the same effect, as if the judgment or decree reviewed had been rendered in a court of the United States.

§2105   Scope of review; abatement

There shall be no reversal in the Supreme Court or a court of appeals for error in ruling upon matters in abatement which do not involve jurisdiction.

§2106   Determination

The Supreme Court or any other court of appellate jurisdiction may affirm, modify, vacate, set aside, or reverse any judgment, decree, or order of a court lawfully brought before it for review and may remand the cause and direct the entry of such appropriate judgment, decree, or order, or require such further proceedings to be had as may be just under the circumstances.

§2109 Quorum of Supreme Court justices absent

If a case brought to the Supreme Court by direct appeal from a district court cannot be heard and determined because of the absence of a quorum of qualified justices, the Chief Justice of the United States may order it remitted to the Court of Appeals for the circuit including the district in which the case arose, to be heard and determined by that court either sitting *en banc* or specially constituted and composed of the three circuit judges senior in commission who are able to sit, as such order may direct. The decision of such court shall be final and conclusive. In the event of the disqualification or disability of one or more of such circuit judges, such court shall be filled as provided in Chapter 15 [28 USCS §§331 et seq.].

In any other case brought to the Supreme Court for review, which cannot be heard and determined because of the absence of a quorum of qualified justices, if a majority of the qualified justices shall be of the opinion that the case cannot be heard and determined at the next ensuing term, the court shall enter its order affirming the judgment of the court from which the case was brought for review with the same effect as upon affirmance by an equally divided court.

§2241 Power to grant writ

a) Writs of habeas corpus may be granted by the Supreme Court, any justice thereof, the district courts, and any circuit judge within their respective jurisdictions. The order of a circuit judge shall be entered in the records of the district court wherein the restraint complained of it had.

b) The Supreme Court, any justice thereof, and any circuit judge may decline to entertain an application for a writ of habeas corpus and may transfer the application for hearing and determination to the district court having jurisdiction to entertain it.

c) The writ of habeas corpus shall not extend to a prisoner unless-

   1. He is in custody under or by color of the authority of the United States or is committed for trial before some court thereof; or

   2. He is in custody for an act done or omitted in pursuance of an Act of Congress or an order, process, judgment, or decree of a court or judge of the United States; or

   3. He is in custody in violation of the Constitution or laws or treaties of the United States; or

   4. He, being a citizen of a foreign state and domiciled therein is in custody for an act done or omitted under any alleged right, title, authority, privilege, protection, or exemption claimed under the commission, order, or sanction of any foreign state, or under color thereof, the validity and effect of which depend upon the law of nations; or

   5. It is necessary to bring him into court to testify or for trial.

d) Where an application for a writ of habeas corpus is made by a person in custody under the judgment and sentence of a State court of a State which contains two or more Federal judicial districts, the application may be filed in the district court for the district wherein such person is in custody or in the district court for the district within which the State court was held which convicted and sentenced him and each of such district courts shall have concurrent jurisdiction to entertain the application. The district court for the district wherein such an application is filed in the exercise of its discretion and in furtherance of justice may transfer the application to the other district court for hearing and determination.

e) (1) No court, justice, or judge shall have jurisdiction to hear or consider an application for a writ of habeas corpus filed by or on behalf of an alien detained by the United States who has been determined by the United States to have been properly detained as an enemy combatant or is awaiting such determination. Except as provided in paragraphs (2) and (3) of section 1005(e) of the Detainee Treatment Act of 2005 (10 USCS 801 note), no court, justice, or judge shall have jurisdiction to hear or consider any other action against the United States or its agents relating to any aspect of the detention, transfer, treatment, trial, or conditions of confinement of an alien who is or was detained by the United States and has been determined by the United States to have been properly detained as an enemy combatant or is awaiting such determination.

§2263 Filing of habeas corpus application; time requirements; tolling rules

a) Any application under this chapter [28 USCS §2261 et seq.] for habeas corpus relief under section 2254 [18 USCS §2254] must be filed in the appropriate district court not later than 180 days after final State court affirmance of the conviction and sentence on direct review or the expiration of the time for seeking such review.

b) The time requirements established by subsection (a) shall be tolled—

　　1. From the date that a petition for certiorari is filled in the Supreme Court until the date of final disposition of the petition if a State prisoner files the petition to secure review by the Supreme Court of the affirmance of a capital sentence on direct review by the court of last resort of the State or other final State court decision on direct review;

　　2. From the date on which the first petition for post-conviction review or other collateral relief is filed until the final State court disposition of such petition; and

　　3. During an additional period not to exceed 30 days, if—

　　　　a) A motion for an extension of time is filed in the Federal district court that would have jurisdiction over the case upon the filing of a habeas corpus application under section 2254 [28 USCS §2254]; and

　　　　b) A showing of good cause is made for the failure to file the habeas corpus application within the time period established by this section.

§2265 Certification and judicial review

A Certification.

　　1. In general. If requested by an appropriate State official, the Attorney General of the United States shall determine—

　　　　a) Whether the State has established a mechanism for the appointment, compensation, and payment of reasonable litigation expenses of competent counsel in State postconviction proceedings brought by indigent prisoners who have been sentenced to death;

　　　　b) The date on which the mechanism described in subparagraph (1) (A) was established; and

　　　　c) Whether the State provides standards of competency for the appointment of counsel in proceedings described in subparagraph (A)

　　2. Effective date. The date the mechanism described in paragraph (1)(A) was established shall be the effective date of the certification under this subsection.

　　3. Only express requirements. There are no requirements for certification or for application of this chapter other than those expressly stated in this chapter [28 USCS §§2261 et seq.].

2. Regulations. The Attorney General shall promulgate regulations to implement the certification procedure under subsection (a).

3. Review of certification.

    1. In general. The determination by the Attorney General regarding whether to certify a State under this section is subject to review exclusively as provided under chapter 158 of this title [28 USCS §§2341 et seq.].

    2. Venue. The Court of Appeals for the District of Columbia Circuit shall have exclusive jurisdiction over matters under paragraph (1), subject to review by the Supreme Court under section 2350 of this title [28 USCS §2350].

    3. Standard of review. The determination by the Attorney General regarding whether to certify a State under this section shall be subject to de novo review.

§2266 Limitation periods for determining applications and motions

a) The adjudication of any application under section 2254 [28 USCS §2254] that is subject to this chapter [28 USCS §2255] by a person under sentence of death shall be given priority by the district court and by the court of appeals overall noncapital matters.

b) (1)(A) A district court shall render a final determination and enter a final judgment on any application for a writ of habeas corpus brought under this chapter [28 USCS §§2261 et seq.] in a capital case not more than 450 days after the date on which the application is filed, or 60 days after the date on which the case is submitted for decision, whichever is earlier.

(B) A district court shall afford the parties at least 120 days in which to complete all actions, including the preparation of all pleadings and briefs, and if necessary, a hearing, prior to the submission of the case for decision.

(C) (i) A district court may delay for not more than one additional 30-day period beyond the period specified in subparagraph (A), the rendering of a determination of an application for a writ of habeas corpus if the court issues a written order making a finding, and stating the reasons for the finding, that the ends of justice would be served by allowing the delay outweigh the best interests of the public and the applicant in a speedy disposition of the application.

    ii. The factors, among others, that a court shall consider in determining whether a delay in the disposition of an application is warranted are as follows:

        I. Whether the failure to allow the delay would be likely to result in a miscarriage of justice.

        II. Whether the case is so unusual or so complex, due to the number of defendants, the nature of the prosecution, or the existence of novel questions of fact or law, that it is unreasonable to expect adequate briefing within the time limitations established by subparagraph (A).

        III. Whether the failure to allow a delay in a case that, taken as a whole, is not so unusual or so complex as described in subclause (II), but would otherwise deny the applicant reasonable time to obtain counsel, would unreasonably deny the applicant or the government continuity of counsel, or would deny counsel for the applicant or the government the reasonable time necessary for effective preparation, taking into account the exercise of due diligence.

      iii.   No delay in disposition shall be permissible because of general congestion of the court's calendar.

      iv.   The court shall transmit a copy of any order issued under clause (i) to the Director of the Administrative Office of the United States Courts for inclusion in the report under paragraph (5).

(2) The time limitations under paragraph (1) shall apply to—

    (A) an initial application for a writ of habeas corpus;

    (B) any second or successive application for a writ of habeas corpus; and

    (C) any redetermination of an application for a writ of habeas corpus following a remand by the court of appeals or the Supreme Court for further proceedings, in which case the limitation period shall run from the date the remand is ordered.

(3) (A) the time limitations under this section shall not be construed to entitle an applicant to a stay of execution, to which the applicant would otherwise not be entitled, for the purpose of litigating any application or appeal.

(B) No amendment to an application for a writ of habeas corpus under this chapter [28 USCS §§2261 et seq.] shall be permitted after the filing of the answer to the application, except on the grounds specified in section 2244(b) [28 USCS §2244(b)].

(4) (A) The failure of a court to meet or comply with a time limitation under this section shall not be a ground for granting relief from a judgment of conviction or sentence.

(B) The State may enforce a time limitation under this section by petitioning for a writ of mandamus to the court of appeals. The court of appeals shall act on the petition for a writ of mandamus not later than 30 days after the filing of the petition.

(5) (A)The Administrative Office of the United States Courts shall submit to Congress an annual report on the compliance by the district courts with the time limitations under this section.

(B) The report described in subparagraph (A) shall include copies of the orders submitted by the district courts under paragraph (l)(B)(iv).

(C)(1)(A) A court of appeals shall hear and render a final determination of any appeal of an order granting or denying, in whole or in part, an application brought under this chapter]28 USCS §§2261 et seq.] in a capital case not later than 120 days after the date on which the reply brief is filed, or if no reply brief is filed, not later than 120 days after the date on which the answering brief is filed.

(B)(i) A court of appeals shall decide whether to grant a petition for rehearing or other request for rehearing *en banc* not later than 30 days after the date on which the petition for rehearing is filed unless a responsive pleading is required, in which case the court shall decide whether to grant the petition not later than 30 days after the date on which the responsive pleading is filed.

(ii) If a petition for rehearing or rehearing *en banc* is granted, the court of appeals shall hear and render a final determination of the appeal not later than 120 days after the date on which the order granting rehearing or rehearing *en banc* is entered.

(2)   The time limitations under paragraph (1) shall apply to—

    (A) an initial application for a writ of habeas corpus;

    (B) any second or successive application for a writ of habeas corpus; and

(C) any redetermination of an application for a writ of habeas corpus or related appeal following a remand by the court of appeals *en banc* or the Supreme Court for further proceedings, in which case the limitation period shall run from the date the remand is ordered.

(3) The time limitations under this section shall not be construed to entitle an applicant to a stay of execution, to which the applicant would otherwise not be entitled, for the purpose of litigating any application or appeal.

(4) (A) The failure of a court to meet or comply with a time limitation under this section shall not be a ground for granting relief from a judgment of conviction or sentence.

(B) The States may enforce a time limitation under this section by applying for a writ of mandamus to the Supreme Court.

(5) The Administrative Office of the United States Courts shall submit to Congress an annual report on the compliance by the courts of appeals with the time limitations under this section.

§2350 Review in Supreme Court on certiorari or certification

(a) An order granting or denying an interlocutory injunction under section 2349(b) of this title [28 USCS §2349(b)] and a final judgment of the court of appeals in a proceeding to review under this chapter [28 USCS §2341 et seq.] are subject to review by the Supreme Court on a writ of certiorari as provided by section 1254(1) of this title [28 USCS §1254(1)]. Application for the writ shall be made within 45 days after entry of the order and within 90 days after entry of the judgment, as the case may be. The United States, the agency, or an aggrieved party may file a petition for a writ of certiorari.

(b) The provisions of section 1254(2) of this title [28 USCS §1254(2)], regarding certification, and of section 2101(f) of this title [28 USCS §2101(f)], regarding stays, also apply to proceedings under this chapter [28 USCS §§2341 et seq.].

§2516 Interest on claims and judgments

(a) Interest on a claim against the United States shall be allowed in a judgment of the United States Court of Federal Claims only under a contract or Act of Congress expressly providing for payment thereof.

(b) Interest on a judgment against the United States affirmed by the Supreme Court after review on petition of the United States is paid at a rate equal to the weekly average 1-year constant maturity Treasury yield, as published by the Board of Governors of the Federal Reserve System, for the calendar week preceding the date of the judgment.

§3904 Expedited review of certain appeals

(a) In general. An appeal may be taken directly to the Supreme Court of the United States from any interlocutory or final judgment, decree, or order of a court upon the constitutionality of any provision of chapter 5 of title 3 [3 USCS §§401 et seq.] .

(b) Jurisdiction. The Supreme Court shall, if it has not previously ruled on the question, accept jurisdiction over the appeal referred to in subsection (a), advance the appeal on the docket, and expedite the appeal to the greatest extent possible.

18 U.S.C.

§202   Definitions

(1) For the purpose of sections 203, 205, 207, 208, and 209 of this title [18 USCS §§203, 205, 207, 208, and 209] the term "special Government employee" shall mean an officer or employee of the executive or legislative branch of the United States Government, of any independent agency of the United States or of the District of Columbia, who is retained, designated, appointed, or employed to perform, with or without compensation, for not to exceed one hundred and thirty days during any period of three hundred and sixty-five consecutive days, temporary duties either on a full-time or intermittent basis, or a part-time United States commissioner, a part-time United States magistrate [United States magistrate judge], or, regardless of the number of days of appointment, an independent counsel appointed under chapter 40 of title 28 and any person appointed by that independent counsel under section 594(c) of title 28. Notwithstanding the next preceding sentence, every person serving as a part-time local representative of a Member of Congress in the Member's home district or State shall be classified as a special Government employee. Notwithstanding section 29(c) and (d) of the Act of August 10, 1956 (70A Stat. 632; 5 U.S.C. 30r(c) and (d)), a Reserve officer of the Armed Forces, or an officer of the National Guard of the United States, unless otherwise an officer or employee of the United States, shall be classified as a special Government employee while on active duty solely for training. A reserve officer of the Armed Forces or an officer of the National Guard of the United States who is voluntarily serving a period of extended active duty in excess of one hundred and thirty days shall be classified as an officer of the United States within the meaning of section 203]18 USCS §203] and sections 205 through 209 and 218 [18 USCS §§205-209 and 218]. A Reserve officer of the Armed Forces or an officer of the National Guard of the United States who is serving involuntarily shall be classified as a special Government employee. The terms "officer or employee" and "special Government employee" as used in sections 203, 205, 207 through 209, and 218 [18 USCS §§ 203, 205, 207-209, and 218], shall not include enlisted members of the Armed Forces/

(2) For the purposes of sections 205 and 207 of this title [18 USCS §§ 205 and 207], the term "official responsibility" means the direct administrative or operating authority, whether immediate or final, and either exercisable alone or with others, and either personally or through subordinates, to approve, disapprove, or otherwise direct Government action.

(3) Except as otherwise provided in such sections, the terms "officer" and "employee" in sections 203, 205, 207 through 209, and 218 of this title [18 USCS §§ 203, 205, 207-209, and 218] shall not include the President, the Vice President, a Member of Congress, or a Federal judge.

(4) The term "Member of Congress" in sections 204 and 207 [18 USCS §§204 and 207] means—

    (1) a United States senator; and

    (2) a Representative in, or Delegate or Resident Commissioner to, the House of Representatives.

(5) As used in this chapter [18 USCS §§201 et seq.], the term—

    (1) "executive branch" includes each executive agency as defined in title 5, and any other entity or administrative unit in the executive branch;

    (2) "judicial branch" means the Supreme Court of the United States; the United States courts of appeals; the United States district courts; the Court of International Trade; the United States bankruptcy courts; any court created pursuant to article I of the United States Constitution, including the Court of Appeals for the Armed Forces, the United States Claims Court [United States Court of Federal Claims], and the United States Tax Court, but not including

a court of a territory or possession of the United States; the Federal Judicial Center; and any other agency, office, or entity in the judicial branch; and

(3) "legislative branch" means—

    (A) the Congress; and

    (B) the Office of the Architect of the Capitol, the United States Botanic Garden, the General Accounting Office (Government Accountability Office), the Government Printing Office [Government Publishing Office], the Library of Congress, the Office of Technology Assessment, the Congressional Budget Office, the United States Capitol Police, and any other agency, entity, office, or commission established in the legislative branch.

§3041 Power of courts and magistrates [United States magistrate judges]

For any offense against the United States, the offender may, by any justice or judge of the United States, or by any United States magistrate [United States magistrate judge] , or by any chancellor, judge of a supreme or superior court, chief or first judge of common pleas, mayor of a city, justice of the peace, or other magistrate, of any state where the offender may be found, and at the expense of the United States, be arrested and imprisoned, or released as provided in chapter 207 of this title [18 USCS § 3141 et seq.], as the case may be, for trial before such court of the United States as by law has cognizance of the offense. Copies of the process shall be returned as speedily as may be into the office of the clerk of such court, together with the recognizances of the witnesses for their appearances to testify in the case.

A United States judge or magistrate [United States magistrate judge] shall proceed under this section to rules promulgated by the Supreme Court of the United States. Any state judge or magistrate acting hereunder may proceed according to the usual mode of procedure of his state but his acts and orders shall have no effect beyond determining, pursuant to the provisions of section 3142 of this title [18 USCS § 3142], whether to detain or conditionally release the prisoner prior to trial or to discharge him from arrest.

CHAPTER FOUR

ABOUT THE SUPREME COURT

First, understand that there is more than one Supreme Court. Every state in the union has its own independent Judicial System, and every one of them has its own Supreme or Superior Court. This book, however, is strictly concerning The Supreme Court of the United States. The high court is the only court empowered by The Constitution of The United States, see Article III, Section I, which states in pertinent part that:

> "The judicial power of the United States shall be vested in one Supreme Court"

As you read, in the statutes of the previous chapter, The Supreme Court is vested with a wide variety of powers. The most important to a prisoner who seeks a certificate of appealability, however, is the power which is codified under 28 U.S.C. §1254(1).

AUTHOR'S NOTE

> You must remember that the request for post-conviction relief under both §2255 and §2254 is a federal court action. Thus, if you are seeking a writ of certiorari, it will be to The United States Court of Appeals. If you misquote the jurisdictional basis in your petition, you will be denied without question.

A fact that is largely unknown to the American people is that The Supreme Court of the United States is not a forum for an additional appeal. The court does, in fact, exercise an appellate jurisdiction, but it is also a court of discretion. If you don't remember Rule 10, please go back and read it again before you go on. Rule 10 states, in part, that:

> "Review on a writ of certiorari is not a matter of right, but of judicial discretion. A petition for a writ of certiorari will be granted only for compelling reasons. The following, although neither controlling nor fully measuring the Court's discretion, indicate the character of the reasons the Court considers: …
>
> A petition for a writ of certiorari is rarely granted when the asserted error consists of erroneous factual findings or the misapplication of a properly stated rule of Law."

In other words, the Court hears only the cases it wants to, and I can assure you that the Court is only interested in big issues. There is no doubt that the Supreme Court follows one of the oldest philosophical maximums of all time. "The needs of the many outweigh the needs of the few, or the one." This has been a constant since the time of Aristotle, all the way to Mr. Spock in the Star Trek movies, and certainly followed by the Supreme Court.

THE ODDS OF REVIEW

The odds of being granted a writ of certiorari are stacked against you because of the number of people who seek the court's attention. On average, the clerk of The Supreme Court will receive six to seven hundred petitions every month. The Court, however, only has time to hear less than one hundred cases every year. What's most important to remember is that The Supreme Court Justices have a lot more to consider than just the impact that the case will have on the individual petitioner. Regardless of how simple we think our issue may be, we can easily be passed over for a petition containing a bigger issue that may have a national impact.

THE SELECTION PROCESS

Know that even if you send your petition to the court on toilet paper and handwritten in pencil, it will be read by someone. The Supreme Court is not like the District Court or the Circuit; the clerks will not just throw your petitions away like the lower courts; they don't want to miss the big issues. And, yes, I know of three petitions that were filed on toilet paper, one was granted certiorari, see *Boag v. MacDougall*, 454 U.S. 364.

The selection process starts with the clerk's initial review. As soon as he or she opens the cover of your petition, they will be looking for compelling federal and Constitutional questions, see Rule 14,

"1. A petition for a writ of certiorari shall contain, IN THE ORDER INDICATED:

(a) The questions presented for review …"

Needless to say, if the clerk does not find questions directly under your cover sheet, your petition will be summarily denied.

AUTHOR'S NOTE

The Supreme Court is likely the only Court that seeks to do justice in a post-conviction proceeding. Although the lower courts grudgingly grant a few cases here and there, The Supreme Court, on the other hand, is tasked with maintaining a uniform national standard.

Once the clerk who is handling your petition finds a compelling question, he or she moves on to ensure that the petition is in order before passing it on. The next step is review by a law clerk. Each justice has a few law clerks who have most likely graduated from law school recently and have an impressive resume that includes being a clerk before, with a raving letter of recommendation from another judge or two. The law clerk will scrutinize the petition a bit more carefully. This review is often referred to as the initial review even though the clerk of courts office reviewed it before filing.

When the law clerk is finished, he or she will prepare a memorandum for the justice he or she works for. The memo will summarize the facts and law of the case, and then suggest whether the case should be heard by the Court. With their clerks memos in hand, the nine justices gather together to discuss which petitions should be granted and which should be denied.

In the event a petition is granted, the parties are asked to file a more extensive briefing to support their case. The brief will always go into more detail than the petition does. It is important to provide the Court with a clear view of your position. For those of you who must file in Pro Se because of financial limitations; don't worry, if you get this far you will be appointed counsel.

ORAL ARGUMENT

Once counsel for each side has refined their case with additional briefing, the case is scheduled for an oral argument. By this time each of the nine justices has a firm idea as to their position on the issues raised. At the hearing itself each side has a specific amount of time in which they are expected to emphasize and/or clarify the merits of their case. The allotted time for each side is thirty (30) minutes. During the presentation of each side of the case the justices will ask questions of the representatives (lawyers) to clarify any questionable issue.

It is an unwritten rule that, the side that is questioned the most is often the one that loses, see *Yates v. United States*, 574 U.S. _____,135 S. Ct._____ (2015).

You can review the case of John L. Yates in any law library. What you won't see is how harshly the justices questioned the government about their theory of the case, or that Justice Kennedy suggested that not anyone should ever refer to prosecutorial discretion again. In that case the government received the harshest questioning of any case I have ever read from the Supreme Court. The case resulted in the holdings that follow:

(1) The U.S. Court of Appeals for the Eleventh Circuit erred when it found that the captain of a fishing boat was properly convicted of violating 18 U.S.C. §1519 because he told a member of his crew to throw undersized fish his crew caught overboard, instead of complying with an order issued by a Florida Fish and Wildlife Conservation Commission officer who was deputized as a federal agent which required him to segregate the undersized fish from other fish and return with them to port;

(2) The term "tangible object" that appeared in §1519 covered only objects that were used to record or preserve information, not all objects in the physical world, and did not include fish.

CONFERENCE

Usually, days and sometimes months after the oral argument, the case will be conferenced. Also, on any given day, several cases will be heard in an oral argument. Another common occurrence is when cases that are heard the same day will likewise be conferenced together on a later day. A good example of this phenomenon is *United States v. Cronic*, 466 U.S. 648; and *Strickland v. Washington*, 466 U.S. 668. Notice both cases were heard at oral argument on January 10, 1984 and both were decided on May 14, 1984.

"The case is conferenced" simply means that the justices gather together in a Supreme Court conference room in obscurity. At the mysterious "Conference," there are no clerks, no staff, and no stenographer. This means that there is no minutes recording. The justices discuss the cases previously argued to gain additional insight as to how each justice feels about how they will vote.

AUTHOR'S NOTE

It is my personal belief that the discussions, in the conference, are highly sophisticated conversations of complex law. This arena may very well be more likened unto a legal debate among friends, one attempting to persuade the other, about the law on any given subject.

I can only imagine that the level of legal reasoning in any of those conferences is that of intellectual giants. Perhaps, the equivalent of debating physics with Albert Einstein.

Following the conference, a decision has to be made about who will write the Court's opinion. If the Chief Justice is in the majority, he or she will appoint a justice from the majority to write the opinion, or elect to write it himself. When the Chief Justice is not in the majority, then the most senior justice in the majority will assign a justice form that majority to write it.

All in all, The Supreme Court is still just a court. It is made up of people attempting to reach the ends of justice, within their limited authority to do so.

CHAPTER FIVE

PROMPT HEARING

Another issue that must be addressed is that of a prompt hearing. In the thousands of post-convictions relief cases that have been filed since the enactment of 28 U.S.C. §2255, one constant remains: the district and appellate court will delay all meaningful claims. A meaningful claim requires a "prompt hearing," under the mandates of §2255(b). Unfortunately, §2255(b) does not specify what the word "prompt" means in the terms of time.

In my own personal case, and that of many others, I was forced to seek a writ of mandamus in the court of appeals. The writ of mandamus was filed because the presiding district judge, Karon Owen Bowdre, refused to provide her honest service. This, as many of you know, is a common occurrence. After filing the writ, Judge Bowdre began to execute her duties hastily in the pending §2255 action. Ordinarily, this would be a good thing. But, in my case, Judge Bowdre employed a new method of delay. She decided on three of my four claims and denied me relief in my post-conviction case (§2255).

The failure to reach the merits of all my claims in the §2255 proceeding was a direct and purposeful disregard for the mandates set forth by the Eleventh Circuit in *Clisby v. Jones*, 960 F.2d. 925. She had effectively evaded a meaningful claim by withholding her honest service consideration of the claim. Her intention was to use the appeals process to further delay her Constitutional and Statutory obligation to grant relief. This is what I call "kicking the can down the road to appeal."

Once in the appeals court, the panel joined the bandwagon by employing their own delay to stack upon the delay employed by the district court. The federal rules of appellate procedure define absolutely no time limitation that requires a panel to rule within a specific period. District judges know that the rules allow the Court of Appeals to wait, literally years, before handing down an opinion. Thus, in an extraordinary case where a judge is obstructing justice, in an unsolved murder, for example, they will send it to the Court of Appeals unresolved. The collective hope, in such a sensitive case, is that they can delay the relief until the specifically requested relief would be moot.

In this context, you will discover that the courts are using the respective rules to circumvent the Congressional mandates enacted in 28 U.S.C. §2255(b).

This method of delaying /justice is made possible because of the vague nature of the text in the statute that would otherwise require a prompt hearing.

When reading the federal statute, 28 U.S.C. §2255 in any law library, you find that the statute is followed by the notes of Congress. Those notes define the intent of Congress at the time of the statute's enactment. At the end of 28 U.S.C. §2255 you find the following:

> "This section restates, clarifies, and simplifies the procedure in the nature of the ancient writ of error Coram Nobis. It provides an expeditious remedy for correcting erroneous sentences without resorting to habeas corpus. It has the approval of the Judicial Conference of the United States. Its principal provisions are incorporated in H.R. 4233, Seventy-Ninth Congress."

This statement in itself seems clear enough, the intent is for district courts to correct their own errors quickly. Unfortunately, the courts follow the text of the statute; that ordinarily are written to instruct courts how Congress' intent is to be carried out. Although the Congressional notes and the text of 28 U.S.C. §2255 sound similar, you will find one particularly misleading element. The text of the statute provides no bright line limitation that defines what an expeditious remedy is. Thus, district courts are impermissibly required to determine for themselves what Congress meant. The particularly troubling part of 28 U.S.C. §2255(b) states the following:

> "Unless the motion and the files and records of the case conclusively show that the prisoner is entitled to no relief, the Court shall cause notice thereof to be served upon the United States attorney, grant a PROMPT HEARING thereon, determine the issues and make findings of fact and conclusions of law with respect thereto. If the Court finds that the judgment was rendered without jurisdiction, or that the sentence imposed was not authorized by law or otherwise open to collateral attack, or that there has been such a denial or infringement of the Constitutional rights of the prisoner as to render the judgment vulnerable to collateral attack, the Court shall vacate and set the judgment aside and shall discharge the prisoner or resentence him or grant a new trial or correct the sentence as may appear appropriate." 28 U.S.C. §2255(b).

As you can see here, the statute is full of mandatory language that requires the Court to perform its duties under some very specific circumstances. Unfortunately, you will also find that Congress did not specifically set out when the Court is required to do so. Thus, most Courts will wait until the prisoner can no longer possibly present a case or until he or she has completed their sentence.

This chapter is added for those of you who are suffering from the inordinate delay employed by the Court of Appeals. When this happens, you may file a mandamus to the Supreme Court of the United States. Don't misunderstand, it is very unlikely that your petition will be heard, but it will light a particularly hot fire under the butt of the Court of Appeals. It is also the prelude to another claim you will see in *Post-Conviction Relief: Second Last Chance*. The remainder of this chapter is the petition I filed in the Supreme Court regarding this very specific issue.

NO.:_____

_____

_____

_____

IN THE
SUPREME COURT OF THE UNITED STATES

_____

IN RE: KELLY PATRICK RIGGS

_____

PROOF OF SERVICE

I, Kelly Patrick Riggs, do declare on February 21, 2019, as required by Supreme Court Rule 29, I have served the enclosed PETITION FOR LEAVE TO PROCEED *IN FORMA PAUPERIS* and PETITION FOR A WRIT OF MANDAMUS on the clerk of this Honorable Court, by depositing an envelope containing the above documents in the United States mail, properly addressed, and with first-class postage pre-paid. The Solicitor General of The United States and The Eleventh Circuit Court of Appeals were served in like manner at the following addresses:

U.S. Solicitor General
Room 5614
U.S. Dept. of Justice
950 Pennsylvania Ave., N.W.
Washington, D.C. 20530

Eleventh Circuit
Court of Appeals
56 Forsyth St. N.W.
Atlanta, GA 30303

I declare under the penalty of perjury that the foregoing is true and correct. Executed on February 21, 2019.

X_____
Kelly Patrick Riggs, Pro Se
Reg. Number

Address

CERTIFICATE OF COMPLYING WITH TYPE-VOLUME LIMITATION, TYPEFACE REQUIREMENTS, AND TYPE-STYLE REQUIREMENTS

The Petition along with this certificate of compliance complies with the type-volume limitation of Supreme Court Rule 33 because this petition contains 4177 words.

The petition was typed in Prestige Pica 10.

X_____
Kelly Patrick Riggs, Pro Se
Reg. Number

Address

Docket No.:_____

_____
_____
_____

IN THE
SUPREME COURT OF THE UNITED STATES

IN RE: KELLY PATRICK RIGGS
[INCARCERATED}

Petition for Writ of
MANDAMUS

Motion for Leave to Proceed *in forma pauperis*

The Petitioner, Kelly Patrick Riggs, requests leave to file the attached petition for a writ of Mandamus without prepayment of costs and to proceed *in forma pauperis*. As for grounds, Mr. Riggs asserts that counsel has previously be appointed pursuant to The Criminal Justice Act.

Submitted by and for:

X_____
Kelly Patrick Riggs, Pro Se
Reg. Number

Address

KELLY PATRICK RIGGS

Docket No.:_____

_____
_____
_____

IN THE
SUPREME COURT OF THE UNITED STATES

IN RE: KELLY PATRICK RIGGS

On Petition for a Writ of Mandamus to The United States
Court of Appeals for The Eleventh Circuit
18-12111

PETITION FOR WRIT OF MANDAMUS

Submitted by and for:

X_____
Kelly Patrick Riggs, Pro Se
Reg. Number

Address

QUESTIONS PRESENTED

This case presents an important nationwide issue concerning what constitutes an expeditious remedy and/or a prompt hearing under 28 U.S.C. §2255. The question of what constitutes a "prompt hearing" and/or an "expeditious remedy" has gone unanswered since the enactment of §2255 in 1948. This petition represents an opportunity for the Supreme Court to provide a bright line limitation that defines the meaning of a "prompt hearing" under the law. Mr. Riggs presents the questions that follow:

(1) Did Congress, with the enactment of 28 U.S.C. §2255 intend to restate, clarify, and simplify the procedure in the nature of the ancient writ of error Coram Nobis. Does it provide an expeditious remedy for correcting erroneous sentences without resorting to habeas corpus, as suggested by the Seventy-Ninth Congress in H.R. 4233?

(2) Does 28 U.S.C. §2255(b) provide a bright line limitation to define the meaning of "… a prompt hearing …" in the statute.

(3) Did Congress intend to allow district courts around the country to employ inordinate delay by failing to define "… an expeditious remedy …" in H.R. 4233?

(4) Did Congress impermissibly delegate its law making authority, to the U.S. district courts, to determine for themselves what prompt means under the law?

(5) Does the text of 28 U.S.C. §2255(b) require adherence to Congress' intent for the statute to "provide an expeditious remedy for correcting erroneous sentences?"

(6) Is 28 U.S.C. §2255(b) unconstitutionally void-for-vagueness where it fails to define a bright line limitation as to the meaning of "prompt," allowing many district and appellate courts to leave a claim to lay stagnant.

KELLY PATRICK RIGGS

LISTS OF PARTIES

All parties appear on the caption to the case on the cover page. Mr. Riggs is the Appellant below. The United States is the Appellee below.

DISCLOSURE OF CORPORATE AFFILIATIONS
AND FINANCIAL INTEREST

Pursuant to Supreme Court Rule 29.6, Kelly Patrick Riggs, makes the following disclosure:

1) Mr. Riggs is not a subsidiary or affiliate of a publicly owned corporation.

2) There is no publicly owned corporation, not a party to the appeal, that has a financial interest in the outcome of this case.

By: _____
    Kelly Patrick Riggs, Pro Se
    Reg. Number

    Address

TABLE OF CONTENTS

TABLE OF AUTHORITIES

STATUETS:

OTHER AUTHORITIES:

SUPREME COURT RULES:

KELLY PATRICK RIGGS

PETITION FOR A WRIT OF MANDAMUS

Mr. Riggs respectfully petitions the Supreme Court to issue a writ of mandamus to the Eleventh Circuit of the United States Court of Appeals. He asks this court to order the Eleventh Circuit to provide its honest service, to fulfill its duty, and to follow its very own mandates in *Clisby v. Jones*, 960 F.2d 925.

JURISDICTIONAL STATEMENT

The Supreme Court of the United States has the original and exclusive jurisdiction in any case where the Constitutional validity of an act of Congress is questioned. In Mr. Riggs's case, he questions if 28 U.S.C. §2255(b) is void for vagueness.

Moreover, the Supreme Court has exclusive jurisdiction because Mr. Riggs seeks a writ of mandamus to the Eleventh Circuit, Court of Appeals, asking that the Court of Appeals be ordered to execute its duty. Under 28 U.S.C. §165l(a), the remedy of mandamus against a lower federal court is a drastic and extraordinary remedy reserved for really extraordinary causes. It is given that the writ's traditional use in aid of appellate jurisdiction, both at common law and in the federal courts, has been to confine the lower court against which mandamus is sought to a lawful exercise of the lower court's prescribed jurisdiction. Because of the Eleventh Circuit's failure to exercise its jurisdiction in Mr. Riggs's case, the effectiveness and validity of an act of Congress is left in question.

The Supreme Court has exclusive jurisdiction to issue a writ of mandamus to a circuit of the United States Court of Appeals. That authority is vested in the Supreme Court by 28 U.S.C. §1651 and the Rules of the Supreme Court, Rule 20.

The Supreme Court has recognized that "where a district court persistently and without reason refuses to adjudicate a case properly before it, the Court of Appeals may issue the writ 'in order that it may exercise the jurisdiction of review given by law." *Will v. Calvert Fire Ins. Co.*, 437 U.S. 655, 662-63, 98 S.Ct. 2552, 57 L.Ed. 2d 504 (1978) (quoting *Ins. Co. v. Comstock*, 83 U.S. 258, 16 Wall. 258, 270, 21 L.Ed. 2d 493 (1873)). Indeed, this court is not alone in recognizing that a writ may be appropriate to address a district court's undue delay in adjudicating a case properly before it, see In re: Hood, 135 F. appx 709, 711 (5th Cir. 2005) (holding writ of mandamus was appropriate to address district court's seven-month delay in entering judgment); *Madden v. Myers*, 102 F. 3d 74, 79, (3rd Cir. 1996) ("an appellate court may issue a writ of mandamus on the ground that undue delay is tantamount to failure to exercise jurisdiction."); *Johnson v. Rogers*, 917 F. 2d 1283, 1285 (10th Cir. 1990) (granting writ of mandamus where district court failed to rule on a petition for writ of habeas which had been pending for fourteen months); *McClellan v. Young*, 421 F. 2d 690, 691 (6th Cir. 1970)(granting writ of mandamus to address delay in ruling on pending petition for writ of habeas). In Mr. Riggs's case, the Eleventh Circuit has had ample time to issue an order of remand in the past eight months, where the Circuit Court precedent in *Clisby v. Jones* leaves the panel no other option. As the Tenth Circuit aptly put it, "justice delayed is justice denied." Johnson, 917 F. 2d at 1285.

Additionally, the Supreme Court of the United States is the only court in the country that has the authority to decide the question of whether 28 U.S.C. §2255 is void for vagueness.

CONSTITUTIONAL AND STATUTORY PROVISIONS INVOLVED

28 U.S.C. §1651 which states:

> "(a) The Supreme Court and all courts established by an act of Congress may issue all writs necessary or appropriate in aid of these respective jurisdictions and agreeable to the usage and principles of law.
> (b) An alternative writ or rule nisi may be issued by a justice or judge of a court which has jurisdiction."

28 U.S.C. §2255(b) which states:

> "(b) Unless the motion and the files and records of the case conclusively show that the prisoner is entitled to no relief, the court shall cause notice thereof to be served upon the United States attorney, grant a prompt hearing thereon, determine the issues and make findings of fact and conclusion of law with respect thereto. If the court finds that the judgment was rendered without jurisdiction, that the sentence imposed was not authorized by law or otherwise open to collateral attack, or that there has been such a denial or infringement of the Constitutional rights of the prisoner as to render the judgment vulnerable to collateral attack, the court shall discharge the prisoner or resentence him or grant a new trial or correct sentence as may appear appropriate."

STATEMENT OF THE CASE

On or about November 11, 2015, Mr. Riggs submitted an instant motion seeking post-conviction relief pursuant to 28 U.S.C. §2255. His primary claims – although poorly particularized because of his ignorance of law – where based on four basic events: 1) he and his defense counsel, Glennon F. Threatt, Jr., suffered from two distinct and separate conflicts of interest; 2) that he had been outright denied counsel at critical, pre-guilt, stages of the criminal proceeding; 3) he suffered from a constructive denial of counsel at a critical stage; and 4) he had been abandoned by counsel on direct appeal.

Mr. Riggs raised four very specific grounds for relief which are particularized in his §2255 and made a part of the corresponding appendix. App-1.

After thirty-one (31) months of delay and several requests for judgement, and an amendment, the district court denied Mr. Riggs's request for relief, under §2255, based on only three of Mr. Riggs's four grounds for relief, see the courts memorandum opinion issued by the district court on May 2, 2018, and made a part of the corresponding appendix. App - 28.

In addition to the courts May 2, 2018, memorandum, it issued an order that denied Mr. Riggs a certificate of appealability on the same day. Which is also made a part of the corresponding appendix. App - 46.

On or about May 14, 2018, Mr. Riggs filed a notice of appeal from the district court's denial of a certificate of appealability, made a part of the corresponding appendix. App - 47. On or about June 6, 2018, Mr. Riggs filed his "Motion for Issuance of a Certificate of Appealability" in the Eleventh Circuit of the United States Court of Appeals. Within his motion to the court of appeals Mr. Riggs notified the court that the Eleventh Circuit's long-standing mandate, in *Clisby v. Jones*, 960 F.2d 925 (11th Cir. 1992) (enbanc), requires the court of appeals to vacate and remand for consideration on all grounds for habeas relief, made a part of the corresponding appendix. App - 52.

On or about June 25, 2018, the government provided its certificate of interested persons. Made a part of the corresponding appendix. App - 61.

On or about October 10, 2018, Mr. Riggs filed a motion in the Court of Appeals to expedite the proceeding from the Special Housing Unit (S.H.U.) at Coleman F.C.C. low security prison. The motion was written in pencil and Mr. Riggs was not allowed access to produce a copy. Thus, there is not a copy in the corresponding appendix.

Now thirty-nine months after raising ground three in his §2255, Mr. Riggs questions if 28 U.S.C. §2255(b) is unconstitutionally void-for-vagueness where it's text fails to provide a bright line time limitation, allowing the lower courts to disregard Congress' intent to provide an "expeditious remedy" and employing years of unnecessary delay in the average case.

REASONS TO GRANT THE WRIT

The federal statute, 28 U.S.C. §2255, was enacted with an ambiguity that allows lower courts to disregard the intentions of Congress, leaving to the courts to decide what the law really means. The ambiguity between Congress' intent in enacting 28 U.S.C. §2255 and the text of 28 U.S.C. §2255(b) leaves the courts rather than Congress to decide what Congress really intended when they enacted §2255 into law. The lack of particularity in §2255(b) has cost the taxpayers billions of dollars, years of false incarceration that were later overturned, and thousands of hours of wasted judicial resources over the last seventy-one years. This ambiguity is one of the many causes that has resulted in prisons being overcrowded and has never before been addressed by the Supreme Court. This case represents an issue of national importance and very likely a huge step in Criminal Justice Reform. This court, in giving a definition of two words, could have the largest impact on mass incarceration in history. The one question that has been before all lower courts, producing a different answer in each, is, "What does 'prompt hearing' really mean?"

A definition of this term for all courts to follow would almost immediately end all frivolous litigation in the lower courts. The largest number of frivolous filings is from Pro Se litigants trying to obtain a "prompt hearing." If this court were to provide a definition similar to:

> "The term 'prompt hearing,' for the purpose of 28 U.S.C.§2255(b), is defined as a period of time not to exceed seventy (70) days following the final substantive pleading or order filed in the case."

With such a definition in force, Pro Se litigants would end their filings to allow the seventy (70) days to elapse in hopes of a prompt hearing; the court of appeals would no longer receive petitions for writs of mandamus; and district courts would never again be burdened with deciding what constitutes unnecessary delay in a pest conviction proceeding.

Providing a definition for these two words, "prompt hearing," would save the Supreme Court hours of work, a ruling on this issue will determine once and for all what a "prompt hearing" is. Most importantly, the public won't be able to assume that the denial of this opportunity is the invalidation of Congress' intent to provide an "expeditious remedy." Simply put, an expeditious remedy is impossible to achieve without first providing a bright-line definition of what a "prompt hearing" really is.

In comparing one hundred cases of exonerations, this court would discover that the average time spent in prison waiting for a "prompt hearing" is an estimated sixty (60) months. That is five years that an American

Citizen must wait in prison before overturning a manifest miscarriage of justice. Mr. Riggs has waited eighty (80) months so far and still has unresolved grounds for relief.

On or about November 11, 2015, Mr. Riggs filed his second motion for relief raising four grounds. Mr. Riggs's ground three very specifically states:

GROUND THREE:

Mr. Riggs was deprived of counsel at multiple critical stages in his criminal case. Thus, he was deprived of a speedy public trial with a compulsory process for compelling his ten alibi witnesses.

(a) Supporting facts:

Mr. Riggs adopts by reference the facts contained in ground one and two, here in ground three. Mr. Riggs is further explicating that he was deprived of counsel at three critical stages in his criminal case. Because of these errors Mr. Riggs was deprived of the trial he so desperately desired.

The record reflects two constants throughout Mr. Riggs's criminal case; One) he demanded a fair trial; and Two) he repeatedly requested the appointment of the effective assistance of counsel. One such record entry was memorialized on or about December 13, 2012. In that hearing Mr. Riggs made verbal requests of the court for the effective assistance of counsel, that would present his alibi defense, in a fair trial. The court concluded that Mr. Riggs needed "a more extensive mental evaluation."

Mr. Riggs shows:

1. On or about September 5, 2013, Mr. Riggs was brought to court to determine if a conflict of interest existed between Mr. Riggs, the Federal Public Defender's office, and Mr. Alvin Ray Johnson, Jr.

2. At the hearing Mr. Riggs and Glennon Threatt, assistant public defender, were present expressing opposite sides of the controversy. The court did not appoint unconflicted counsel for the hearing. Mr. Riggs was forced to decide between proceeding without counsel or proceeding with conflicted counsel. Mr. Riggs did not waive his right to counsel and/or unconflicted counsel. The court did not advise Mr. Riggs concerning the dangers of proceeding through the hearing with conflicted counsel. Thus, Mr. Riggs fell prey to the effect of counsel who represented interest that were in conflict to Mr. Riggs.

3. A conflict of interest hearing is a critical stage in the trial process because it holds significant consequences for the accused. A conflict of interest hearing is a qualitatively distinct, discrete, and separate phase or step of a criminal proceeding where the defendant has a right to counsel.

4. In Mr. Riggs's case counsel desperately endeavored to avoid a trial because, in the event of a trial, counsel's conflict would have become known. If Mr. Riggs had been allowed to proceed to trial, the proceeding would have implicated others known to Mr. Riggs and Mr. Threatt in criminal conduct that was, or is still not yet, indicted in state proceedings. People such a Brad Taylor, LaKendrick Dunn, Eric Marriono, Brandon Moody, and others.

5. Had the court-appointed unconflicted counsel, Mr. Threatt and the Federal Public Defender's office would have been dismissed from Mr. Riggs's case. He would have proceeded to trial, where proof of official misconduct at the state level, Mr. Riggs' alibi defense, and his efforts as a C.I. would have been proven. Mr. Riggs would have proven his innocence rather than just legal insufficiency; his life and social status would have been restored years ago. Mr. Riggs would have also proven that Mr. Threatt and Allison's case employed the services of Alvin Ray

Johnson, Jr. - who was known to intimidate witnesses - to coerce guilty pleas from other witnesses, such as Ray Allan, Gregory Robinson, and others.

6. On or about September 27, 2013, Mr. Threatt engaged in a conversation with another assistant federal public defender, Sabra M. Barnett, concerning Mr. Riggs's activities as a C.I. against a Mexican cartel operating in the Northern District of Alabama. Ms. Barnett advised her client, Lois Rodriguez, that Mr. Riggs was a danger to the criminal cases of cartel members. Mr. Riggs was incarcerated amongst. Ms. Barnett represented to the Alabama State Bar that Mr. Rodriguez was 'naive about prison life,' notwithstanding his extensive criminal history that extended from Birmingham, Alabama, to Barstow, California. Mr. Rodriguez was formerly a subject of information Mr. Riggs supplied to a multi-agency task force.

7. On or about October 5, 2013, Mr. Rodriguez advised Mr. Riggs about Ms. Barnett's notification and advised Mr. Riggs that he could not remain in the same cell block with the cartel. Upon making this discovery, Mr. Riggs moved to withdraw his plea agreement, realizing he was only endangered by the Federal Public Defender's office.

8. On or about October 18, 2013, Mr. Riggs was present in another hearing to determine if a conflict existed. Mr. Riggs had filed for the appointment of unconflicted counsel once again and again present in the courtroom without the benefit of counsel. The motion for counsel was granted.

9. On or about October 30, 2013, Mr. Brett Bloomston filed his notice of appearance. (DE-60) Mr. Bloomston filed no substantive motion from the time of his appointment. However, Mr. Riggs's filing of motions in Pro Se and the government's motions in response constitute a lengthy dialogue. Mr. Bloomston failed to even amend or clarify Mr. Riggs's motion to withdraw his guilty plea. Thus, Mr. Riggs was constructively denied counsel at a critical, post-plea, but pre-sentence stage in his criminal proceeding.

10. On or about April 30, 2014, Mr. Riggs filed his notice of appeal, and Mr. Bloomston was appointed as appellate counsel. Notwithstanding the obvious errors, Mr. Bloomston withdrew as appellate counsel. Mr. Riggs was once again abandoned by counsel at a critical stage of his criminal proceeding. Mr. Riggs was forced to proceed in appeal without the benefit of counsel."

Mr. Riggs filed his grounds for relief pursuant to 28 U.S.C. §2255. In doing so he invoked the intentions of Congress that were particularized by the Seventy-ninth Congress in H.R. 4233.

"This section restates , clarifies, and simplifies the procedure in the nature of the ancient writ of error Coram Nobis. It provides an expeditious remedy for correcting erroneous sentences without resort to habeas corpus. It has the approval of the Judicial Conference of the United States."

The text of the corresponding statute however provides for anything but an "expeditious remedy." Although the text of the statute uses the mandatory language, "the court shall … grant a prompt hearing," the courts are not bound to schedule such a hearing because there is no definition of the term "prompt hearing."

The district court, in Mr. Riggs's case, disregarded the intent of Congress and, on May 2, 2018, outright defied the Eleventh Circuit's mandate in *Clisby v. Jones*, 960 F.2d 925. The district court, in its memorandum, openly denied Mr. Riggs's §2255/reviewing and/or addressing only three of his four grounds.

App - 28. The ground that goes unaddressed is ground three, thus the district court uses the appeals process to further delay a "prompt hearing" on ground three. The district court, in following its own interpretation of 28 U.S.C. §2255(b), believes it is following the instructions of Congress by denying Mr. Riggs's §2255 on three grounds and preserving the last ground for a "prompt hearing" after the court of appeals remands for the Clisby error.

Mr. Riggs filed a motion for a certificate of appealability and/or summary judgment to vacate and remand. The Eleventh Circuit's long-standing mandate of *Clisby v. Jones*, *960 F.2d 925 (11th Cir. 1992) (*en banc*) holds that:

> "until [federal habeas] proceedings have been concluded, they cast doubt on a prisoner's conviction and interfere with the state's administration of its correction program. Our procedures for handling habeas petitions are designed, in part to minimize such disruption … and we emphasize the importance of litigating all of a petitioner's claims in one habeas proceeding, both at the trial and appellate levels.

> We are disturbed by the growing number of cases in which we are forced to remand for consideration of issues the district court chose not to resolve, see e.g., *Alderman v. Zant*, no. 90-8981 (11th Cir. 1991); *Mathis v. Zant*, 903 F.2d 1368 (11th Cir. 1990); *Smith v. Zant*, 887 F.2d 1407 (11th Cir. 1989)(*en banc*); *Lindsey v. Smith*, 820 F.2d 1137 (11th Cir. 1987), cert, denied, 489 U.S. 1059, 109 S.Ct. 1327, 103 L.Ed. 2d 595 (1989); *Wilson v. Kemp*, 777 F.2d 621 (11th Cir. 1985), cert, denied, 4/6 U.S. 1153, 106 S.Ct. 2258, 90 L.Ed 2d 703 (1986), etc."

In a recent appeal in the Eleventh Circuit, the court held:

> "'under well settled principles in this circuit, Pro Se applications for post-conviction relief are to be liberally construed.' *United States v. Brown*, 117 F.3d 471, 475 (11th Cir. 1997). And under Clisby, district courts are to resolve all claims for relief raised in a petition for writ of habeas corpus, 'regardless [of] whether habeas relief is granted or denied.' 960 F.2d at 936; see *Rhode v. United States*, 583 F.3d 1289, 1291 (11th Cir. 2009)(Per Curiam)(holding that Clisby applies to motions to vacate under 28 U.S.C. §2255). When a district court has overlooked a claim, our practice is to vacate the judgment without prejudice and remand the case for consideration of that claim Clisby, 960 F.2d at 938." See *Heffield v. United States*, case no. 17-14480 (11th Cir. 2019).

The law and controlling precedent indicates that Mr. Riggs is due his requested relief that is currently before the Eleventh Circuit of the court of appeals. The question before The Supreme Court of the United States is when exactly is this relief due. It's unfortunate for Mr. Riggs, and thousands of prisoners around the country as well as tax payers, that the courts have the latitude to hold them for years before they decide to grant what is due under the law and the Constitution. In most cases relief is withheld until the end of the prisoner's sentence, when the delay of justice constitutes the denial of justice.

One of the most concerning civil rights issues, of our modern time, is the Mass-incarceration of American citizens. According to a recent report – issued by the National Association of Criminal Defense Lawyers, titled The Trial Penalty – the most aggravating elements of the Mass-incarceration issue is that a number of innocent people, like Mr. Riggs, are coerced to plead guilty every day. The conviction of the innocent, is propagated by the government's broad charging discretion, see *Yates v. United States*, 574 U.S. (2015); *United States v. Theodor Stevens*, U.S. Dist., Washington D.C., 593 F. Supp. 2d 177 (2009); United *States v. Arthur Anderson LLP.*, 544 U.S. 696 (2005); and *United States v FedEx*, U.S. Dist., Northern District of California, Lexis 36383 (2016). Mass incarceration is further aggravated by inadequate defense lawyers who virtually eliminate the option of taking a case to trial. On a more human level, for some defense lawyers, there cannot be a more heart-wrenching task than to have to explain to a client, who very likely may be innocent, that they must seriously consider pleading guilty or risk the absolute devastation of the remainder of his or her life, that includes the unimaginable impact to their families. To further perpetuate Mass-incarceration, and pertinent to this petition, the lower courts around the country –

including the thirteen Circuits of the court of appeals – delay, deny, and/or ignore nearly all meaningful Constitutional claims that warrant post-conviction relief.

In the case of *United States v. Kelly Patrick Riggs*, 2:12-cr-297- KOB-JEO, in the Northern District of Alabama, Mr. Riggs and his counsel, Glennon F. Threatt, Jr., suffered from a conflict of interest prior to the guilt phase of the criminal proceeding. Mr. Riggs raised the issue before the district court and was granted a hearing. Mr. Riggs also requested unconflicted counsel to advise him of his rights concerning the conflict of interest, but the district court declined to appoint unconflicted counsel. Mr. Riggs proceeded through the hearing without counsel, represented only by conflicted counsel, which gives rise to a distinctly separate claim. Mr. Riggs was coerced to plead guilty and was later steamrolled through sentencing. Mr. Riggs raised his issues on appeal which was summarily dismissed after being abandoned by counsel, Brett M. Bloomston.

Mr. Riggs filed for post-conviction relief pursuant to 28 U.S.C. §2255, in which he raised claims that are undeniably due relief. His claims have been volleyed back and forth between the District Court and the Eleventh Circuit of The Court of Appeals for the last thirty-nine months, which are left unresolved still today. Mr. Riggs's claims have laid docile before the Eleventh Circuit panel for the last eight months, see Case No.: 18-12111. Mr. Riggs now petitions The Supreme Court of The United States to intervene by issuing a writ of mandamus; not only for resolution of his own Constitutional claims, but also to set a standard for all courts to follow in subsequent cases.

CONCLUSION

Mr. Riggs moves this Supreme Court of The United States to grant the writ of mandamus, thereby providing a "Bright Line" definition for the term "prompt hearing."

X_____

Kelly Patrick Riggs, Pro Se
Reg. Number

Address

DOCKET NO.: _____

_____
_____
_____

IN THE
SUPREME OOURT OF THE UNITED STATES

IN RE: KELLY PATRICK RIGGS

On Petition for a Writ of Mandamus to the United States
Court of Appeals for The Eleventh Circuit
18-12111

APPENDIX

Submitted by and for:

X_____

Kelly Patrick Riggs, Pro Se
Reg. Number

Address

KELLY PATRICK RIGGS

TABLE OF CONENTS

POST-CONVICTION RELIEF: C.O.A. IN THE SUPREME COURT

AMENDED

MOTION UNDER 28 U.S.C. § 2255 TO VACATE, SET ASIDE, OR CORRECT

SENTENCE BY A PERSON IN FEDERAL CUSTODY.

United States District Court	District Northern District of Alabama	
Name *(under which you were convicted):* Kelly Patrick Riggs		Docket or Case No.: 2:15-CV-8043-KOB
Place of Confinement:	Prisoner No.:	
UNITED STATES OF AMERICA V.	Movant *(include name under which convicted)* Kelly Patrick Riggs	

MOTION

1.   (a) Name and location of court which entered the judgment of conviction you are challenging:

   U.S.D.C. Northern District of Alabama
   Southern Division
   Birmingham, AL

   (b) Criminal docket or case number (if you know): 2:12-CR-297-KOB-JEO

2.   (a) Date of the judgment of conviction (if you know): September 6, 2013

   (b) Date of sentencing: April 22, 2014

3.   Length of sentence: 120 Months   Text

4.   Nature of crime (all counts):
   Count One: Enticing a Minor 18 U.S.C. §2422(b)

   Count Two: Transferring Obscene Material to a Minor 18 U.S.C. §1470

5.   (a) What was your plea? (Check one)
   (1) Not guilty ☐   (2) Guilty ☒   (3) Nolo contendere (no contest) ☐

   (b) If you entered a guilty plea to one count or indictment, and a not guilty plea to another count or
   what did you plead guilty to and what did you plead not guilty to?   N/A

6.   If you went to trial, what kind of trial did you have? (Check one) N/A   Jury ☐   Judge only ☐

7.   Did you testify at a pretrial hearing, trial, or post-trial hearing?   Yes ☐   No ☒

8.   Did you appeal from the judgment of conviction?   Yes ☒   No ☐

App - 1

113

9. If you did appeal, answer the following:
    (a) Name of court: Eleventh Circuit
    (b) Docket or case number (if you know): 14-11917-CC
    (c) Result: Affirmed
    (d) Date of result (if you know): March 2, 2015
    (e) Citation to the case (if you know): Unknown
    (f) Grounds raised:

    Ineffective assistance of counsel, deprived of counsel, conflict of
    interest, lack of jurisdiction, and rush to judgment.

    (g) Did you file a petition for certiorari in the United States Supreme Court?   Yes [X]   No [ ]
        If "Yes," answer the following:
        (1) Docket or case number (if you know): 14-9985
        (2) Result: Certiorari denied

        (3) Date of result (if you know): June 29, 2015
        (4) Citation to the case (if you know): WL 245 7924(U.S.), 83 USLW 3929
        (5) Grounds raised:

        Fraud on the court, ineffective assistance of counsel, plain error,
        manufactured jurisdiction, falsified indictment, prosecution without
        jurisdiction, rush to judgment, entered plea under threat and duress.

10. Other than the direct appeals listed above, have you previously filed any other motions, petitions, or applications, concerning this judgment of conviction in any court?
    Yes [X]   No [ ]

11. If your answer to Question 10 was "Yes," give the following information:
    (a) (1) Name of court: U.S.D.C Northern District of Alabama
        (2) Docket or case number (if you know): 2:15-CV-8005-KOB
        (3) Date of filing (if you know): March 9, 2015

        (4) Nature of the proceeding: Recharacterized as motion under §2255
        (5) Grounds raised: Fraud on the court, outrageous government conduct,
        ineffective assistance of counsel, deprived of civil rights, prosecution

App - 2

114

without jurisdiction, and manufactured jurisdiction, .

(6) Did you receive a hearing where evidence was given on your motion, petition, or application?

Yes [ ]   No [X]

(7) Result: Dismissed without prejudice

(8) Date of result (if you know): March 19, 2015

(b) If you filed any second motion, petition, or application, give the same information:

(1) Name of court: U.S.D.C. Northern District of Alabama

(2) Docket of case number (if you know): 2:12-CR-297-KOB-JEO

(3) Date of filing (if you know): April 11, 2015

(4) Nature of the proceeding: Writ of error coram nobis

(5) Grounds raised:

Fraud on the court, outrageous government conduct, depravation of civil rights, prosecution without jurisdiction, and prosecutorial misconduct.

(6) Did you receive a hearing where evidence was given on your motion, petition, or application?

Yes [ ]   No [X]

(7) Result: Denied

(8) Date of result (if you know): May 6, 2015

(c) Did you appeal to a federal appellate court having jurisdiction over the action taken on your motion, petition, or application?

(1) First petition: Yes [X]   No [ ]

(2) Second petition: Yes [X]   No [ ]

(d) If you did not appeal from the action on any motion, petition, or application, explain briefly why you did not:

N/A

12. For this motion, state every ground on which you claim that you are being held in violation of the Constitution, laws, or treaties of the United States. Attach additional pages if you have more than four grounds. State the facts supporting each ground.

App - 3

GROUND ONE:

Mr. Riggs' Criminal Judgement violates due process because it was not intelligent, knowing, or voluntary.

Mr. Riggs is actually innocent and his conviction was cultivated by conflicted counsel who provided false information. Thus, Mr. Riggs' trial process was fundamentally unfair. These two claims identify that a fundamental miscarriage of justice occured. Succinctly, an actually innocent person was found guilty because conflicted counsel facilitated an involuntary plea agreement.

(a) Supporting facts (Do not argue or cite law. Just state the specific facts that support your claim.):

Mr. Riggs believed that if he did not sign the plea agreement then his wife and children would be at risk of being killed by Mr. Alvin Ray Johnson, Jr., whom Mr. Riggs gave a statement against hours earlier. At the time of the plea agreement, Mr. Riggs informed counsel about a threat against Mr. Riggs' wife and children. Counsel stated that the Marshals Service would provide protection for Mr. Riggs' family and move Mr. Riggs away from Mr. Johnson, but only if Mr. Riggs would plea guilty. Counsel did not apprise Mr. Riggs of his right to protection from other inmates or his right to proceed to trial. Mr. Riggs did not understand the options available to him at the time of the guilty plea, nor did he know the consequences of the choices he was presented. Therefore, Mr. Riggs' guilty plea was invalied, which in turn invalidates his conviction. This court should set aside the Judgement and return Mr. Riggs to the pre-plea agreement stage of the proceedings.

Mr. Riggs' prosecution stems from his efforts as a C.I. who provided information to law enforcement entities in the State of Alabama. As the records obtained from the Freedom of Information Act show, Mr. Riggs has provided critical information to task force officers in Cherokee, Blount, Shelby, and Jefferson counties. Over a ten year period he has discovered public officials who were involved in the drug trade. By 2010, Mr. Riggs had inadverently identified the involvement of a state prosecutor, in Shelby County, and his relation to Mexican Cartel members. By 2011, Mr. Riggs suffered two attempts on his life and then notified of a contract, to

App - 4

GROUND ONE:

(a) Supporting facts (Continued):

kill him, with the Cartel. Mr. Riggs made reports to Cornelius Harris in the FBI's Birmingham field office and, shortly after, police officers and confidential informants, from Shelby County, Alabama, i.e, Hoover City Police Department, staged a crime and then kidnapped Mr. Riggs three days later. He was held without official charge until May 28, 2012, when he was charged by Homeland Security.

1) In or around December of 2011, and while still recovering from surgery after donating a kidney, Mr. Riggs committed to rent space in his home in an effort to supplement his income.

2) In or around February of 2012, Mr. Riggs, with the assistance of an acquaintance, listed said space for rent in an ad on craigslist.com.

3) Mr. Riggs' ad was answered by a Hoover City Police Detective in or around March, 2012. After much consideration, Mr. Riggs rented the space to police informant Joy Brown, who was operating under the alias Laney Jones. Police informant Joy Brown moved into the home of Mr. Riggs on May 14, 2012.

4) On or about May 16, 2012, Ms. Brown purchased an internet-ready cellular phone at Wal-Mart in Trussville, Alabama. Upon purchasing the phone, Ms. Brown asked for Mr. Riggs' permission to use one of the SIM cards from his broken cellular phone for the new phone she had purchased.

5) On or about May 23, 2012, Ms. Brown engaged in a detailed conversation with a Hoover City Police detective on her new cellular phone while Mr. Riggs was elsewhere with many alibi witnesses. The text messages were a very explicitly detailed sexual dialogue between Ms. Brown, pretending to be Mr. Riggs, and the police detective, pretending to be a 14-year-old girl.

6) On or about May 26, 2012, Mr. Riggs arrived at an insurance company, riding a newly obtained motorcycle, to purchase insurance. While waiting for the insurance agent he was brutally attacked by 6-8 heavily armed men. He was then transported to Hoover City Police Department where he met and was interviewed by Special Agent Daniel McKenzie. Agent McKenzie discovered that Mr. Riggs was confused about why the police personnel would kidnap him while he was shopping for insurance.

App - 5

117

GROUND ONE: (a) Supporting facts (continued) :

7) On or about May 30, 2012, Mr. Riggs was appointed counsel, Jeffrey Bramer, and appeared in court for a preliminary hearing. During trial preparations, many alibi witnesses called and attempted to visit Jeffrey Bramer to offer their testimony. Jeffrey Bramer refused to take any of the many witness statements and/or memorialize their testimony.

8) From on or about May 30, 2012, through on or about October 9, 2012, Jeffrey Bramer refused to assert Mr. Riggs' alibi defense, take witness statements, and/or prepare for trial.

9) On or about June 1, 2012, Joy Brown, while attempting to extract evidence against Mr. Riggs, inadvertently confessed to staging the crime for which he is incarcerated for, to include but not limited to, sending obscene pictures to detectives and having dialogue with detectives on May 23, 2012, on her phone. This confession was memorialized on jail telephone recordings at Shelby County Jail.

10) On or about October 10, 2012, David Luker was appointed by the court to defend Mr. Rigg' interests. David Luker refused to assert Mr. Riggs' alibi defense, interview a single witness, and/or do any other meaningful thing to benefit Mr. Riggs.

11) On or about May 29, 2012, Mr. Riggs, being refused assistance of counsel, filed a Pro Se motion to appeal to the District Judge. Mr. Riggs was attempting, by his filing, to inform the Judge that he had an air-tight alibi defense that a second lawyer refused to assert or otherwise defend his interests.

12) On or about June 4, 2013, the court appointed the Federal Public Defender's Office to represent Mr. Riggs' interests.

13) During his pre-trial detention Mr. Riggs was exposed to an individual who confessed to the drug-related murder-for-hire of DeAndre Washington, a federal defendant. Within the confession of the "hit-man", Mr. Riggs was provided with the names of two residents of Birmingham, Alabama who hired him.

14) Mr. Riggs notified the U.S. District Court, the U.S. Marshal's Service, and the U.S. Federal Defender's Office. Mr. Riggs was shocked to learn that the "hit-man" was appointed the same Assistant Federal Public Defender as Mr. Riggs, Glennon F. Threatt, Jr.

App - 6

Ground One: (a) Supporting facts (continued) :

15) In or around August, 2013, Mr. Johnson had contact with his court-appointed counsel, Glennon Threatt, who informed Mr. Johnson that there would be no downward departure because Mr. Johnson informed others that he had murdered Mr. Washington. Mr. Johnson began making arrangements to kill his counsel, Glennon Threatt.

16) Mr. Riggs, and fellow detainee Greg Robinson, reported this threat to the U.S. District Court in an effort to prevent harm to Glennon Threat. Additionally, Mr. Riggs personally alerted Glennon Threatt by phone.

17) On or about August 31, 2013, Mr. Riggs filed a Pro Se motion asking for a hearing to determine if it was a conflict of interest for the Federal Public Defender's Office to represent both Mr. Riggs and someone who he reported for murder at the same time, while even more specifically, they were both being represented by the very same lawyer. It was later discovered that Mr. Glennon F. Threatt, Jr. was aware of the unsolved murder.

18) On September 4, 2013, Mr. Riggs' Pro Se motion was received and filed under seal by the United States District Court Clerk. The court issued an order setting a hearing to determine if a conflict of interest was indeed an issue.

19) On or about September 5, 2013, Mr. Riggs was taken from Cullman County Jail and transported to the United States Courthouse (Hugo L. Black Bldg.) in Birmingham, Alabama. While in holding downstairs, Mr. Riggs was counseled by Glennon F. Threatt, Jr., who advised Mr. Riggs that he would soon be getting time served for his assistance. That afternoon Mr. Riggs was taken into a hearing. The hearing was to determine if a conflict of interest existed between Mr. Riggs and counsel Glennon F. Threatt, Jr. At that hearing, Mr. Riggs' position was that Mr. Threatt's representation was in conflict for serving two masters. Mr. Threatt was forced to decide which client he was going to be loyal to: Mr. Riggs, who is a witness to the murder confession, or the murderer.

20) At the hearing, Mr. Threatt's interests were in conflict with Mr. Riggs' own because Mr. Threatt had to remain Mr. Riggs' representative so he could manipulate Mr. Riggs' testimony concerning his other client, Alvin Ray Johnson, Jr. Silencing Mr. Riggs' testimony was the only way for Mr. Threatt to protect his other client from a prosecution of an unsolved, drug-related murder, which

GROUND ONE: (a) Supporting facts (continued) :
   is subject of an FBI investigation.

21) On September 5, 2013, Mr. Threatt was directed by the court to represent Mr. Riggs' position in the hearing where Mr. Riggs challenged Mr. Threatt's loyalties. At that hearing, Mr. Riggs was denied counsel at a critical stage. Mr. Threatt's interests were to represent his very own position that was in conflict with Mr. Riggs' interests. Magistrate Judge John E. Ott inquired of Mr. Threatt, who stated he had advised Mr. Riggs that no conflict existed. Mr. Riggs also agreed due to a misunderstanding concerning the complexities of the conflict of interest that occured where Mr. Threatt represented Mr. Riggs in a controversy to which Mr. Threatt was the adversarial party.

22) Magistrate Judge John E. Ott determined that there was no conflict based upon Mr. Threatt's statement without further inquiry. Later that afternoon Mr. Threatt and Allison Case advised Mr. Riggs concerning the events and requirements of a downward departure pursuant to U.S.S.G. §5k.1.

23) On or about September 5, 2013, shortly after following a hearing, court-appointed counsel, Glennon Threatt, compelled Mr. Riggs to provide statements to Deputy Marshal Keith Blakenship concerning Alvin Ray Johnson, Jr.'s confession to murdering DeAndre Washington and Mr. Johnson's threat to murder Glennon Threatt and his family.

24) Upon Mr. Riggs' return to Cullman County Jail, Mr. Riggs was confronted by Mr. Johnson because of Mr. Riggs' statement to the Marshals. Mr. Johnson then made threats against Mr. Riggs' family and, additionally, Mr. Johnson ordered Mr. Riggs to withdraw his statement.

25) Mr. Riggs immediately called Glennon Threatt about the confrontation. Having been advised earlier, Mr. Riggs decided to take the offered plea, expecting the downward departure, and more importantly, protection for his family.

26) At around 8:00 P.M. on September 5, 2013, Mr. Threatt arrived at the Cullman County Jail, once again alone, and advised Mr. Riggs about how a plea agreement would protect Mr. Riggs' family and get Mr. Riggs moved for his protection. Mr. Riggs was earlier advised that he would get time served for his assistance persuant to a §5k.1 departure. Mr. Riggs was, later that night,

GROUND ONE: (a) Supporting facts (continued) :

coerced into signing a plea agreement. Mr. Threatt led Mr. Riggs to believe that the plea agreement would protect his family and himself, and then Mr. Threatt would appeal for Mr. Riggs.

27) On September 6, 2013, Mr. Riggs was rushed into a change of plea hearing only 18 hours later. The court was in such a hurry that it allowed the reading of the factual basis to be waived.

28) Mr. Riggs continued to provide information to Mr. Threatt by mail which Mr. Threatt shared with a colleague in the Federal Defender's Office by name of Sabra Barnett.

29) On or about October 5, 2013, Mr. Riggs learned through a fellow inmate, who was incarcerated for illegal re-entry and distribution of methamphetamine, that Ms. Barnett advised Cartel associates that Mr. Riggs was providing information that was dangerous to their case. On or about October 5, 2013, Mr. Riggs filed a motion to withdraw his plea agreement.

30) On or about October 18, 2013, Mr. Riggs was once again denied counsel at another conflict of interest hearing.

31) On or about October 21, 2013, the court granted Mr. Riggs' motion for appointment of new counsel.

32) On or about December 20, 2013, the court heard Mr. Riggs' motion to withdraw his guilty plea. Mr. Riggs and court-appointed counsel Brett Bloomston were present in court before United States Chief District Judge Karen Owen Bowdre. During the course of the hearing the court attempted to determine the claims in Mr. Riggs' Pro Se motion. Mr. Riggs' motion was not refined or clarified by court-appointed counsel Brett Bloomston. The court received testimony from former counsel Glennon Threatt. Mr. Threatt testified in particular part, and relevent to this action, that he, Mr. Threatt, did give the court and the government Notice of Alibi in Mr. Riggs' case. Furthermore, Mr. Threatt testified that he had issued subpoenas to ten (10) witnesses in Mr. Rigg's case.

App - 9

121

GROUND ONE: (a) Supporting facts (continued) :

Court-appointed counsel Brett Bloomston was present in the court when Mr. Threatt testified in support of Mr. Riggs' alibi defense to support his actual innocence. Mr. Bloomston was also present when the court took judicial notice of the accuracy of Glennon Threatt's testimony. Mr. Riggs was denied leave to withdraw his plea of guilty, notwithstanding two structural errors.

33) On or about April 22, 2014, at a sentencing hearing before Judge Karen O. Bowdre, Mr. Riggs was sentenced notwithstanding his protest and unequivocal assertation of innocence. While in court, and subsequent to the court's rendering an unlawful sentence, Mr. Riggs stood and made his Declaration of Verbal Notice of Appeal based on his alibi defense, alibi witnesses, and his actual innocence, all in the presence of counsel Brett Bloomston.

34) On appeal, counsel promptly filed an <u>Anders</u> brief, identifying there were no possible issues for appeal. Once notified by the Court of Appeals of his right to object, Mr. Riggs filed his own brief- particularizing to the best of his ability- raising the claim of actual innocence and the outright denial of counsel at a critical stage. On January 8, 2015, the Court of Appeals issued an order granting counsel's motion to withdraw and affirming the sentence and conviction. (App-1)

35) On or about November 10, 2015, Mr. Riggs blindly filed for post-conviction relief pursuant to 28 U.S.C. §2255 without his case file or any other discovery materials.

(b) **Direct Appeal of Ground One:**

    (1) If you appealed from the judgment of conviction, did you raise this issue?

        Yes [X]   No [ ]

    (2) If you did not raise this issue in your direct appeal, explain why:

        N/A

(c) **Post-Conviction Proceedings:**

    (1) Did you raise this issue in any post-conviction motion, petition, or application?

        Yes [X]   No [ ]

    (2) If you answer to Question (c)(1) is "Yes," state:

    Type of motion or petition: §2255

    Name and location of the court where the motion or petition was filed:

      U.S.D.C. Northern District of Alabama

    Docket or case number (if you know): 2:15-CV-8043-KOB

    Date of the court's decision: January 12, 2018

    Result (attach a copy of the court's opinion or order, if available):

    Mr. Riggs granted leave to amend his §2255

    (3) Did you receive a hearing on your motion, petition, or application?

        Yes [ ]   No [X]

    (4) Did you appeal from the denial of your motion, petition, or application? N/A

        Yes [ ]   No [ ]

    (5) If your answer to Question (c)(4) is "Yes," did you raise the issue in the appeal? N/A

        Yes [ ]   No [ ]

    (6) If your answer to Question (c)(4) is "Yes," state:

    Name and location of the court where the appeal was filed:

      N/A

    Docket or case number (if you know):

    Date of the court's decision:

    Result (attach a copy of the court's opinion or order, if available):

    (7) If your answer to Question (c)(4) or Question (c)(5) is "No," explain why you did not appeal or raise this issue:

    This is a step in an ongoing litigation that is not yet final.

App - 11

GROUND TWO:

Mr. Riggs was deprived of the effective assistance of counsel at all stages of his criminal proceedings. Thus, he was denied a speedy and public trial.

(a) Supporting facts (Do not argue or cite law. Just state the specific facts that support your claim.):

Mr. Riggs adopts by reference the facts contained in ground One. Mr. Riggs is further explicating that trial counsel either misapprehanded the settled law concerning guilty pleas or misrepresented the law to Mr. Riggs. Under either scenario, counsel breached his duty to ensure Mr. Riggs' decision to plead guilty was informed. Counsel's breach of duty not only caused Mr. Riggs to plead guilty unintelligently, but also deprived Mr. Riggs of the effective assistance of counsel at a fair trial.

Mr. Riggs is actually innocent of the crimes of conviction, a claim supported by ten alibi witnesses, Mr. Glennon F. Threatt, Jr.'s testimony, and this courts judicial notice issued on March 17, 2016. Mr. Riggs has raised issue concerning defense counsel's actual conflict of interest that denied Mr. Riggs the effective assistance of counsel.

These two claims identify that a fundamental miscarriage of justice occured. Succincly, an actually innocent person was found guilty because conflicted counsel facilitated an involuntary guilty plea.

In September of 2013, Mr. Riggs alerted the court concerning an actual conflict of interest that affected Mr. Riggs, his attorney Glennon Threatt, the Federal Public Defender's Office, and Alvin Ray Johnson, Jr. As a result of this notice, and because of the seriousness of the claim, the court ordered Mr. Threatt to address

App - 12

124

GROUND TWO: (a) Supporting facts (continued):

Mr. Riggs' claim about the conflict, without the benefit of unconflicted counsel to protect Mr. Riggs' interests.

Unsurprisingly, Mr. Threatt denied a conflict existed or that the dual representation conflict impaired his ability to represent Mr. Riggs. Mr. Threatt's representation was inaccurate. The conflict required counsel to avoid a trial because the evidence and facts of Mr. Riggs trial- ' had he had the opportunity to procede to trial - would have made Mr. Threatt's conflict apparent. Correspondingly, the attorneys, Mr. Threatt and Allison Case, convinced Mr. Riggs to enter into a plea agreement, in essence advising Mr. Riggs to forgo his alibi defense, cooperate with authorities, and that both he and his family would receive assistance and protection. This representation likely was untrue rather than merely inaccurate.

Due to the seriousness of the conflict, the court should have appointed unconflicted counsel to advise Mr. Riggs about the conflict. Because unconflicted counsel was not appointed, Mr. Riggs' trial was fundamentally unfair. This court should set aside the judgement and return Mr. Riggs to the pre-plea agreement stage of the proceedings.

1) During Mr. Riggs' pre-trial detention he was exposed to Alvin Ray Johnson, Jr., who confessed to the drug-related murder-for-hire of DeAndre Washington. Within the confession, Mr. Johnson provided the names of others involved in the scheme. Mr. Riggs reported Mr. Johnson's confession to the district court, the U.S. Marshals Service and to Glennon Threatt. Mr. Threatt in turn advised Mr. Johnson that he would not be receiving the expected downward departure because he had told other inmates about the murder. Mr. Johnson then made additional threats against the lives of both   Mr. Threatt and his family.

2) These events were again reported by inmate Gregory Robinson and Mr. Riggs. Following the second event, Mr. Riggs' trial preperations were reduced to discussing Mr. Johnson's case and Mr. Riggs' reports. After two weeks of failed trial preperation- and discovering that Mr. Threatt's representation of Mr. Johnson was a distraction- Mr. Riggs filed a motion raising a conflict of interest in pro se.

3) Mr. Riggs' motion, filed on September 3, 2012, requested a hearing to determine if it was a conflict of interest for the Federal Public Defender's Office to

App - 13

125

GROUND TWO: (a) Supporting facts (continued):

represent Mr. Riggs, a witness to a confession of murder, and Mr. Johnson, who confessed the murder. More specifically, Mr. Riggs and Mr. Johnson were both represented by the same lawyer, Mr. Threatt.

4) On or about September 5, 2013, Mr. Riggs was transported to the federal court house in Birmingham, Alabama. While in holding in the court's basement Mr. Riggs was counseled by Mr. Threatt, who advised that Mr. Riggs would soon be getting time served for his assistance if he would plead guilty.

5) Later that afternoon, Mr. Riggs was taken into a hearing to determine if a conflict of interest existed. The court failing to appoint unconflicted counsel, conducted the hearing with Mr. Threatt as Mr. Riggs' counsel. On the day of the hearing Mr. Riggs' interests were to prove a conflict of interest existed. Mr. Threatt's interest was to prove that a conflict did not exist. The interests of Mr. Riggs and Mr. Threatt were in conflict on September 5, 2013. On that day Mr. Riggs was either represented by conflicted counsel or he had no counsel at all.

6) Based upon Mr. Threatt's representation, Magistrate Judge John E. Ott determined that no conflict existed. Upon returning to the basement, Mr. Threatt and Ms. Case visited with Mr. Riggs, giving counsel concerning the events and requirements of a downward departure under U.S.S.G. §5k.1. Mr. Riggs gave protest because he was going to trial and a downward departure would be meaningless. Just the same, Mr. Riggs provided his statement to U.S. Deputy Marshal Keith Blakenship without the benefit of counsel.

7) Upon returning to his place of detention Mr. Riggs was confronted by Mr. Johnson, who declared that Mr. Riggs gave a statement against him. Mr. Johnson made threats against the lives of Mr. Riggs' wife and children. Mr. Riggs, distraught about the the events and possibility of yet more killings by Mr. Johnson, this time of Mr. Riggs' own family, called Mr. Threatt after hours. Mr. Riggs, having been earlier advised, decided to take the offered plea, expecting the downward departure and, more importantly, protection for his family.

8) At or around 8:00 P.M on September 5, 2013, Mr. Threatt arrived at Cullman County Jail and advised Mr. Riggs about how the plea agreement would protect his family. Mr. Riggs was earlier advised that he would get time served for his

App - 14

126

GROUND TWO: (a) Supporting facts (continued):

assistance under a §5k.1 departure. Mr. Threatt represented that the plea agreement would provide protection for his family. It was unknown to Mr. Riggs that he was being directed by conflicted counsel to plea guilty under false pretences. Mr. Riggs was deprived of a speedy and public trial by conflicted counsel.

App - 15

(b) Direct Appeal of Ground Two:

    (1) If you appealed from the judgment of conviction, did you raise this issue?

        Yes ☒   No ☐

    (2) If you did not raise this issue in your direct appeal, explain why:

        N/A

(c) Post-Conviction Proceedings:

    (1) Did you raise this issue in any post-conviction motion, petition, or application?

        Yes ☒   No ☐

    (2) If you answer to Question (c)(1) is "Yes," state:

Type of motion or petition: §2255

Name and location of the court where the motion or petition was filed:

  U.S.D.C. Northern District of Alabama

Docket or case number (if you know):   2:15-CV-8043-KOB

Date of the court's decision: January 12, 2018

Result (attach a copy of the court's opinion or order, if available):
Mr. Riggs granted leave to amend his §2255

    (3) Did you receive a hearing on your motion, petition, or application?

        Yes ☐   No ☒

    (4) Did you appeal from the denial of your motion, petition, or application? N/A

        Yes ☐   No ☐

    (5) If your answer to Question (c)(4) is "Yes," did you raise the issue in the appeal? N/A

        Yes ☐   No ☐

    (6) If your answer to Question (c)(4) is "Yes," state:

Name and location of the court where the appeal was filed: N/A

N/A

Docket or case number (if you know):

Date of the court's decision:

Result (attach a copy of the court's opinion or order, if available):

(7) If your answer to Question (c)(4) or Question (c)(5) is "No," explain why you did not appeal or raise this issue:

This a step in an ongoing litigation that is not yet final.

GROUND THREE:

Mr. Riggs was deprived of counsel of multiple critical stages in his criminal case. Thus, he was deprived of a speedy public trial with a compulsory process for compelling his ten alibi witness.

(a) Supporting facts (Do not argue or cite law. Just state the specific facts that support your claim.):

Mr. Riggs adopts by reference the facts contained in grounds One and Two, here in ground Three. Mr. Riggs is further explicating that he was deprived of counsel at three critical stages in his criminal case. Because of these errors Mr. Riggs was deprived of the trial he so desperately desired.

The record reflects two constants throughout Mr. Riggs' criminal case: One) He demanded a fair trial; and Two) He repeatedly requested the appointment of the effective assistance of counsel. One such record entry was memoralized on or about December 13, 2012. In that hearing Mr. Riggs made verbal requests of the court for the effective assistance of counsel, that would present his alibi defense, in a fair trial. The court concluded that Mr. Riggs needed "a more extensive mental evaluation." Mr. Riggs shows:

1) On or about September 5, 2013, Mr. Riggs was brought to court to determine if a conflict of interest existed between Mr. Riggs, the Federal Public Defender's Office, and Mr. Alvin Ray Johnson, Jr.

2) At the hearing Mr. Riggs and Glennon Threatt, assistant public defender, were present expressing opposite sides of the controversy. The court did not appoint unconflicted counsel for the hearing. Mr. Riggs was forced to decide between proceeding without counsel or proceeding with conflicted counsel. Mr. Riggs did not waive his right to counsel and/or unconflicted counsel. The court did not advise Mr. Riggs concerning the dangers of proceeding through the hearing with

App - 17

129

KELLY PATRICK RIGGS

GROUND THREE: (a) Supporting facts (continued):

conflicted counsel. Thus, Mr. Riggs fell prey to the effects of counsel who represented interests that were in conflict to Mr. Riggs'.

3) A conflict of interest hearing is a critical stage in the trial process because it holds significant consequences for the accused. A conflict of interest hearing is a qualitatively distinct, discrete, and seperate phase or step of a criminal proceeding where the defendant has a right to counsel.

4) In Mr. Riggs' case counsel desperately endeavored to avoid a trial because, in the event of trial, counsel's conflict would have become known. If Mr. Riggs had been allowed to proceed to trial, the proceeding would have implicated others known to Mr. Riggs and Mr. Threatt in criminal conduct that was, or is still not yet, indicted in state proceedings. People such as Brad taylor, Lakendrick Dunn, Eric Mariono, Brandon Moody, and others.

5) Had the court appointed unconflicted counsel, Mr Threatt and the Federal Public Defender's Office would have been dismissed from Mr. Riggs' case. He would have proceeded to trial, where proof of official misconduct at the state level, Mr. Riggs' alibi defense, and his efforts as a CI would have been proven. Mr. Riggs would have proven his innocence rather than just legal insufficiancy; his life and social status would have been restored years ago. Mr. Riggs would have also proven that Mr. Threatt and Allison Case employed the services of Alvin Ray Johnson, Jr.- who was known to intimidate witnesses- to coerce guilty pleas from other witnesses. Such as Ray Allen, Gregory Robinson, and others.

7) On or about September 27, 2013, Mr. Threatt engaged in a conversation with another assistant federal public defender, Sabra M. Barnett, concerning Mr. Riggs' activities as a C.I. against a Mexican cartel operating in the Northern District of Alabama. Ms. Barnett advised her client, Lois Rodriguez, that Mr. Riggs was a danger to the criminal cases of cartel members Mr. Riggs was incarcerated with. Ms. Barnett represented to the Alabama State Bar that Mr. Rodriguez was "naive about prison life", not withstanding his extensive criminal history that extended from Birmingham, Alabama to Barstow, California. MR. Rodriguez was formerly a subject of information Mr. Riggs supplied to a multi agency task force.

App - 18

130

GROUND THREE: (a) Supporting facts (continued):

8) On or about October 5, 2013, Mr. Rodriguez advised Mr. Riggs about Ms. Barnett's notification and advised Mr. Riggs that he could not remain in the same cell block with the Cartel. Upon making this discovery Mr. Riggs moved to withdraw his plea agreement, realizing he was only endangered by the Federal Public Defender's Office.

9) On or about October 18, 2013, Mr. Riggs was present in another hearing to determine if a conflict existed. Mr. Riggs had filed for the appointment of unconflicted counsel once again and again present in the court room without the benefit of counsel. The motion for counsel was granted.

10) On or about October 30, 2013, Mr. Brett Bloomston filed his notice of appearance. (DE-60) Mr. Bloomston filed no substantive motion from the time of his appointment. Although Mr. Riggs' filing of motions in pro se and the governments motions in reponse constituted a lengthy dialog, Mr. Bloomston failed to even amend or clarrify Mr. Riggs' motion to withdraw his guilty plea. Thus, Mr. Riggs was constructively denied counsel at a critical, post plea but pre-sentence, stage in his criminal proceeding.

11) On or about April 30, 2014, Mr. Riggs filed his notice of appeal and Mr. Bloomston was appointed as appellate counsel. Notwithstanding the obvious errors, Mr. Bloomston withdrew as appellate counsel. Mr. Riggs was once again abandoned by counsel at a critical stage of his criminal proceeding. Mr. Riggs was forced to proceed in appeal without the benefit of counsel.

(b) **Direct Appeal of Ground Three:**

    (1) If you appealed from the judgment of conviction, did you raise this issue?

        Yes [X]   No [ ]

    (2) If you did not raise this issue in your direct appeal, explain why:

        N/A

(c) **Post-Conviction Proceedings:**

    (1) Did you raise this issue in any post-conviction motion, petition, or application?

        Yes [X]   No [ ]

    (2) If you answer to Question (c)(1) is "Yes," state:

    Type of motion or petition: §2255

    Name and location of the court where the motion or petition was filed:

    U.S.D.C. Northern District of Alabama

    Docket or case number (if you know): 2:15-CV-8043-KOB

    Date of the court's decision: January 12, 2018

    Result (attach a copy of the court's opinion or order, if available):

    Mr. Riggs granted leave to amend his §2255

    (3) Did you receive a hearing on your motion, petition, or application?

        Yes [ ]   No [X]

    (4) Did you appeal from the denial of your motion, petition, or application? N/A

        Yes [ ]   No [ ]

    (5) If your answer to Question (c)(4) is "Yes," did you raise the issue in the appeal? N/A

        Yes [ ]   No [ ]

    (6) If your answer to Question (c)(4) is "Yes," state: N/A

    Name and location of the court where the appeal was filed:

    N/A

    Docket or case number (if you know): _____

    Date of the court's decision: _____

    Result (attach a copy of the court's opinion or order, if available):

    (7) If your answer to Question (c)(4) or Question (c)(5) is "No," explain why you did not appeal or raise this issue:

    This is a step in an ongoing litigation that is not yet filed.

GROUND FOUR:

Mr. Riggs' incarceration is unconstitutional because his conviction is a manifest miscarriage of justice:

Mr. Riggs is actually innocent and has been incarcerated without the benefit of a fair trial.

(a) Supporting facts (Do not argue or cite law. Just state the specific facts that support your claim.):

Mr. Riggs adopts by reference the facts contained in grounds One, Two, and Three here in ground Four. Mr. Riggs is further explicating that his actual innocence serves to overcome all procedural bars. Thus, his claims require resolution on their merits. The claims and facts herein must be presumed as true unless definitively rebutted by the record.

Had Mr. Riggs been appointed adequate representation he would have been able to present the evidence in his criminal case, above and beyond his alibi defense that would have proven his innocence at a fair trial. At trial Mr. Riggs would have proven:

1) In or about October of 2008, Mr. Riggs and his family moved to St. Clair County Alabama. By the next spring Mr. Riggs began work in Jefferson County Alabama, the Northern district of Alabama. A short time into employment Mr. Riggs found himself, once again, assisting law enforcement. He was helping to identify opioid and amphatamine dealers who catered to those employed in the construction fields.

2) Within 18 months of service, to random task force officers, Mr. Riggs' efforts began to take its toll on Mr. Riggs' marriage. After giving birth to her fourth child Mrs. Riggs had little toleration for the long nights and sporatic absences of Mr. Riggs. By the fall of 2011 a seperation was imminent.

3) In November of 2011, Mr. Riggs donated a kidney to a fellow veteran at the University of Alabama at Birmingham Hospital. Upon his discharge Mr. Riggs was required to find another home. The voluntary surgery was an additional stress Mrs. Riggs could not bear. Mr. Riggs then rented an additional home at 801 Argo Margarette Road; Trussville, Alabama.

App - 21

133

GROUND FOUR: (a) Supporting facts (continued):

4) Within a couple of months Mr. and Mrs. Riggs began to see each other romantically on a regular basis. Mrs. Riggs would often stay overnight with Mr. Riggs at his home. During their courtship Mr. and Mrs. Riggs had taken amature nude pictures of one another which they maintained in their cellular phones.

5) In March or possibly in early April of 2012, Mrs Riggs fell ill. Mr. Riggs, unable to reach Mrs. Riggs, went to Mrs. Riggs' home and found her unresponsive on her livingroom floor. Once hospitalized, Mr. Riggs stayed by Mrs. Riggs' side for approximately three days.

6) Upon Mrs. Riggs being discharged from the hospital, Mr. Riggs took her to her home. Upon arrival Mr. Riggs found her home had been broken into. Mr. and Mrs. Riggs left and went to Mr. Riggs' home and found it had been broken into as well. After evaluating the damages to both properties Mr. and Mrs. Riggs discovered that their only losses were two door locks, a SIM card belonging to Mrs. Riggs, and a phone from Mr. Riggs' home.

7) In or around March, 2012, Mr. Riggs' roommate ad was answered. Unknown to Mr. Riggs, however, it was answered by police informant Joy Brown, who was operating under the alias "Laney Jones". Ms. Brown and Mr. Riggs had become acquainted over the next couple of months. Mr. Riggs also introduced her to others acquainted to Mr. Riggs. Ms. Brown took a specific interest in Tim Simmons and his cousin Breanna.

8) On or about May 14, 2012, Ms. Brown rented the space in Mr. Riggs' home. The next day, May 15, 2012, Ms. Brown asked that Mr. Riggs allow an internet connection in his home. Mr. Riggs refused.

9) On or about May 16, 2012, Ms. Brown purchased an internet-ready cellular phone at Wal-Mart in Trussville, Alabama. After purchasing her new phone Ms. Brown asked to use the SIM card of one of Mr. Riggs' broken cellular phones.

10) After Mr. Riggs' arrest, and within the first week, Ms. Brown, speaking with Mr. Riggs over jail house phone, admitted to sending nude pictures of Mr. Riggs from her cellular phone.

App - 22

134

GROUND FOUR: (a) Supporting facts (continued):

11) In a meeting with his first appointed lawyer, Jeffrey Bramer, Mr. Riggs expressed what he had talked to Ms. Brown about during their phone conversation. Mr. Riggs also gave Mr. Bramer a list of many alibi witnesses and discussed everything he knew about "Breanna". Mr. Riggs informed Mr. Bramer that he had only known Breanna for a couple of months. Mr. Riggs explained that he had worked on her car, that she was a waitress at Olive Garden in Gardendale, Alabama, and that he had only talked to her a couple of times over the phone.

12) Mr. Bramer had shown Mr. Riggs pictures of Mr. Riggs and Mrs. Riggs- the nude pictures they had made of each other and kept in their respective phones- and Mr. Riggs immediately identified the pictures as the ones contained only in the phones that had been stolen during the break-ins. Mr. Bramer had also disclosed that the alleged girl in the charged offense used the name "Breanna".

13) Mr. Bramer was adamant that Mr. Riggs was set up for some unknown reason and that he would have the case in a trial very quickly. After only a few days Mr. Bramer had confirmed all that Mr. Riggs had told him. Mr. Bramer informed Mr. Riggs that Joy Brown was working-off charges.

14) A couple of weeks later Mr. Bramer visited Mr. Riggs at Shelby County Jail and asked only one additional question. Mr. Bramer asked Mr. Riggs if he had been assisting law enforcement officers in drug related investigations. After Mr. Riggs answered in the affirmative, Mr. Bramer advised that Mr. Riggs should plead guilty if he knew what was good for him.

Had Mr. Riggs been granted the opportunity to present the facts of his criminal case in a fair trial with the effective assistance of counsel Mr. Riggs could have proven that he is innocent. Additionally, and as a matter of fact, Mr. Riggs could have proven he wasn't even present when the alleged conduct occured.

App - 23

(b) Direct Appeal of Ground Four:

   (1) If you appealed from the judgment of conviction, did you raise this issue?

      Yes [X]   No [ ]

   (2) If you did not raise this issue in your direct appeal, explain why:

     N/A

(c) Post-Conviction Proceedings:

   (1) Did you raise this issue in any post-conviction motion, petition, or application?

      Yes [X]   No [ ]

   (2) If you answer to Question (c)(1) is "Yes," state:

   Type of motion or petition: §2255

   Name and location of the court where the motion or petition was filed:

   U.S.D.C. Northern District of Alabama

   Docket or case number (if you know): 2:15-CV-8043-KOB

   Date of the court's decision: January 12, 2018

   Result (attach a copy of the court's opinion or order, if available):

   Mr. Riggs granted leave to amend his §2255

   (3) Did you receive a hearing on your motion, petition, or application?

      Yes [ ]   No [X]

   (4) Did you appeal from the denial of your motion, petition, or application? N/A

      Yes [ ]   No [ ]

   (5) If your answer to Question (c)(4) is "Yes," did you raise the issue in the appeal? N/A

      Yes [ ]   No [ ]

   (6) If your answer to Question (c)(4) is "Yes," state:

   Name and location of the court where the appeal was filed:

   N/A

   Docket or case number (if you know):

   Date of the court's decision:

   Result (attach a copy of the court's opinion or order, if available):

(7) If your answer to Question (c)(4) or Question (c)(5) is "No," explain why you did not appeal or raise this issue:

This is a step in an ongoing litigation that is not yet final.

App - 24

136

13. Is there any ground in this motion that you have <u>not</u> previously presented in some federal court? If so, which ground or grounds have not been presented, and state your reasons for not presenting them:

No

14. Do you have any motion, petition, or appeal <u>now pending</u> (filed and not decided yet) in any court for the ground you are challenging?   Yes [X]   No [ ]

If "Yes," state the name and location of the court, the docket or case number, the type of proceeding, and the issues raised.

This amended motion is in continuation to the original §2255 proceeding initiated on November 10, 2015, in Case No.: 2:15-CV-8043-KOB

15. Give the name and address, if known, of each attorney who represented you in the following stages of the proceedings you are challenging:

(a) At the preliminary hearing:

Jeffrey Bramer and David Luker

(b) At the arraignment and plea:

Glennon Threatt and Allison Case

(c) At the trial:

N/A

(d) At sentencing:

Brett Bloomston

(e) On appeal:

Brett Bloomston

(f) In any post-conviction proceeding:

Pro Se

(g) On appeal from any ruling against you in a post-conviction proceeding:

N/A

App - 25

137

16. Were you sentenced on more than one court of an indictment, or on more than one indictment, in the same court and at the same time? Yes [X] No [ ]

17. Do you have any future sentence to serve after you complete the sentence for the judgment that you are challenging? Yes [ ] No [X]

    (a) If so, give name and location of court that imposed the other sentence you will serve in the future:

    N/A
    _____

    (b) Give the date the other sentence was imposed: N/A
    _____
    (c) Give the length of the other sentence: N/A
    _____
    (d) Have you filed, or do you plan to file, any motion, petition, or application that challenges the judgment or sentence to be served in the future? N/A Yes [ ] No [ ]

18. TIMELINESS OF MOTION: If your judgment of conviction became final over one year ago, you must explain why the one-year statute of limitations as contained in 28 U.S.C. § 2255 does not bar your motion.*

    This amended motion is timely because all claims relate back to claims in Mr. Riggs' original §2255, and amendment was authorized by an order of the district court.

_____

* The Antiterrorism and Effective Death Penalty Act of 1996 ("AEDPA") as contained in 28 U.S.C. § 2255, paragraph 6, provides in part that:
   A one-year period of limitation shall apply to a motion under this section. The limitation period shall run from the latest of –
       (1) the date on which the judgment of conviction became final;
       (2) the date on which the impediment to making a motion created by governmental action in violation of the Constitution or laws of the United States is removed, if the movant was prevented from making such a motion by such governmental action;
       (3) the date on which the right asserted was initially recognized by the Supreme Court, if that right has been newly recognized by the Supreme Court and made retroactively applicable to cases on collateral review; or
       (4) the date on which the facts supporting the claim or claims presented could have been discovered through the exercise of due diligence.

App - 26

138

Therefore, movant asks that the Court grant the following relief: Mr. Riggs asks this court to vacate his sentence and conviction. Thus, returning him to the pre plea stage of his trial process.

or any other relief to which movant may be entitled.

_____ N/A _____
Signature of Attorney (if any)

I declare (or certify, verify, or state) under penalty of perjury that the foregoing is true and correct and that this Motion under 28 U.S.C. § 2255 was placed in the prison mailing system on _____
(month, date, year)

Executed (signed) on _____ (date)

_____
Signature of Movant

If the person signing is not movant, state relationship to movant and explain why movant is not signing this motion.

IN THE UNITED STATES DISTRICT COURT
FOR THE NORTHERN DISTRICT OF ALABAMA
SOUTHERN DIVISION

KELLY PATRICK RIGGS,	]	
	]	
Plaintiff,	]	
	]	
v.	]	2:15-cv-08043-KOB
	]	
UNITED STATES OF AMERICA	]	
	]	
Defendant.	]	

MEMORANDUM OPINION

The movant Kelly Patrick Riggs pled guilty to one count of attempted enticement of a minor to engage in sexual activity, in violation of 18 U.S.C. § 2422(b), and one count of transfer of obscene material to a minor, in violation of 18 U.S.C. § 1470. (Cr. Doc. 89).[1] The court sentenced him to 120 months imprisonment on each count, to run concurrently. (*Id.*). Mr. Riggs moved, under 28 U.S.C. § 2255, to vacate his sentence. (Doc. 1). After the government responded (doc. 13), Mr. Riggs moved to amend his § 2255 motion. (Doc. 59). The court granted the motion to amend, and Mr. Riggs filed an amended § 2255 motion and a motion for appointment of counsel. (Docs. 63, 67). The Government responded to the amended § 2255 motion and Mr. Riggs replied. (Docs. 72, 75).

In his amended § 2255 motion, Mr. Riggs contends that (1) his guilty plea was not intelligent, knowing, and voluntary; (2) counsel was ineffective because he had a conflict of interest; and (3) he is actually innocent. (Doc. 63). The court WILL DENY Mr. Riggs' § 2255 motion because the record confirms that Mr. Riggs' challenge to his guilty plea is procedurally barred and procedurally defaulted; Mr. Riggs waived the alleged conflict of interest; and

---

[1] The court cites documents from Mr. Riggs' underlying criminal case, *United States v. Riggs*, 2:12-cr-00297-KOB-JEO, as "Cr. Doc. __."

Mr. Riggs' freestanding claim of actual innocence is not cognizable in a § 2255 motion. The court WILL DENY AS MOOT Mr. Riggs' request for appointment of counsel.

I. BACKGROUND

In 2012, a grand jury charged Mr. Riggs with one count of enticing a minor to engage in criminal activity in violation of 18 U.S.C. § 2422(b) and one count of transfer of obscene material to a minor in violation of 18 U.S.C. § 1470. (Cr. Doc. 6). The court appointed Jeffrey Bramer as his defense attorney. (Cr. Doc. 3). Mr. Bramer, however, quickly withdrew as counsel based on an undisclosed "ethical issue." (Cr. Doc. 18 at 2; Cr. Doc. Minute Entry, Oct. 9, 2012).

Next, the court appointed David Luker as Mr. Riggs' defense attorney. (Cr. Doc. 20). While represented by Mr. Luker, Mr. Riggs filed a *pro se* motion seeking to represent himself. (Cr. Doc. 28). A magistrate judge held a hearing, at which he allowed Mr. Luker to withdraw and appointed the Federal Public Defender to represent Mr. Riggs. (Cr. Doc. 100 at 16–17).

Allison Case and Glennon Threatt entered appearances as Mr. Riggs' public defenders. (Cr. Docs. 35, 36). While they were representing him, Mr. Riggs filed a *pro se* motion seeking subpoenas for various witnesses, including seven alleged alibi witnesses and three character witnesses. (Cr. Docs. 45, 105). After holding a hearing on the motion, the magistrate judge issued all of the requested subpoenas. (Cr. Docs. 46, 105).

Mr. Riggs next filed a *pro se* motion requesting that the court hold a hearing on whether Mr. Threatt had a conflict of interest. (Cr. Doc. 51). Mr. Riggs alleged that members of a prison gang had threatened to harm or kill Mr. Threatt and his family, and stated that he had also told Mr. Threatt about "a confession to killing a co-conspirator and the intent to kill witnesses of that event." (*Id.* at 2). Although that *pro se* motion itself did not state who the alleged co-conspirator was, who made the alleged confession, or what its relation to Mr. Riggs' criminal case was, Mr. Riggs' current § 2255 motion makes it apparent that Mr. Riggs was referring to another of Mr. Threatt's clients, a man named Alvin Johnson, who Mr. Riggs says confessed to killing another man named DeAndre Washington. (*See* Doc. 63 at 6–8).

On September 5, 2013, the magistrate judge held a hearing on Mr. Riggs' allegation about Mr. Threatt's alleged conflict of interest. (Cr. Doc. 109). The magistrate judge indicated that Mr. Threatt "was aware of [the threat against Mr. Threatt] and [he] has already discussed it with the Federal Defender, Mr. Butler, and they reached the conclusion that no further action would be taken on their part at the present time . . . . And they also did make their own independent inquiry as to whether or not there's a conflict issue. And . . . Mr. Threatt . . . and Mr. Butler did not believe there was a conflict." (*Id*. at 7). Mr. Riggs then told the magistrate judge that he had discussed the issue with Mr. Threatt several days earlier and they had "determined that it was not going to be an issue," but by then, he had already mailed the motion. (*Id*.). After the hearing, the magistrate judge entered an order stating that he was "convinced there is no conflict in the representation of the defendant by present counsel." (Cr. Doc. Minute Entry, Sept. 5, 2013).

At the same hearing, Mr. Riggs stated that when he mailed the motion requesting a hearing on Mr. Threatt's alleged conflict, he also mailed two other pleadings, one of which was a notice of alibi. (Doc. 109 at 3–5). The magistrate judge noted that the court had not yet received those filings. (*Id*. at 3–4). Mr. Riggs stated that, since mailing the notice of alibi, he had spoken with Mr. Threatt and they had "come to a point." (*Id*. at 5). Neither Mr. Riggs nor Mr. Threatt disclosed the content of their discussion, but Mr. Riggs indicated that he was "satisfied with the results of [that] conversation," and Mr. Threatt indicated that he was not planning to file a notice of alibi. (*Id.* at 5–6).

Mr. Riggs requested to withdraw the two pleadings that he had mailed. (*Id.* at 13–14). The magistrate judge stated that he would review them before allowing Mr. Riggs to withdraw them. (*Id.*). The record does not include an order permitting withdrawal, nor does it contain the two pleadings.

The day after the conflict hearing, Mr. Riggs entered a plea agreement with the Government, in which he agreed to plead guilty to both counts against him. (Cr. Doc. 55). The plea agreement described the factual basis of the crime. (*Id.* at 3–5). It stated that, on May 23, 2012, Mr. Riggs responded to an internet advertisement and emailed an undercover law enforcement officer whom he believed to be a 14 year old girl. (*Id.* at 2–3). Over the next few days, he emailed and texted with the undercover officer, sending her nude pictures of an adult man's body and asking for nude pictures in return. (*Id.* at 3–4). He eventually arranged to meet the purported 14 year old girl at a bowling alley around 10:00 am on May 26, 2012, but when he arrived there at 10:20 am, law enforcement officers arrested him. (*Id.* at 4–5).

At Mr. Riggs' change of plea hearing, Mr. Riggs stipulated that the factual basis set forth in the plea agreement was accurate. (Cr. Doc. 62 at 25–26). The court asked Mr. Riggs: "Has anyone promised you anything or threatened you in any way to encourage you to enter this plea of guilty?" (*Id.* at 16). Mr. Riggs responded, "No." (*Id.*). The court also asked Mr. Riggs if he was "satisfied with Mr. Threatt and the work that he has done," to which Mr. Riggs responded, "Yes." (*Id.* at 24).

The next month, Mr. Riggs filed a *pro se* motion to withdraw his guilty plea and to replace his attorney. (Cr. Doc. 57). In the motion, he stated that he had entered the plea agreement under duress because (1) a gang had threatened his family, and (2) Mr. Threatt had told him the only way to get a reduction in his sentence was to plead guilty. (*Id.* at 1–2). He explained that, on the day of the prior conflict hearing, he had given a statement against Mr. Threatt's other client, Alvin Johnson, because Mr. Johnson had made a jailhouse confession to the murder of DeAndre Washington and had threatened Mr. Threatt and Mr. Threatt's family. (*Id.* at 2, 6, 8). According to Mr. Riggs, after he notified Mr. Threatt of those matters, Mr. Threatt told Mr. Johnson that Mr. Riggs "was a problem to [Mr. Johnson's] case." (*Id.* at 6). Mr. Riggs also alleged that Mr. Threatt had told a United States marshal that "this was a conflict." (*Id.*).

The magistrate judge held a hearing on the portion of the motion seeking to discharge counsel. (Cr. Doc. 111). Expressing concern about potentially breaching attorney-client privilege and revealing defense strategy, the magistrate judge told Mr. Riggs not to reveal any confidential communications between his attorney and himself. (*Id.* at 7–8). But when the magistrate judge asked Mr. Threatt if he opposed Mr. Riggs' motion for a new attorney, Mr. Threatt said he did not. (*Id.* at 6).

After that hearing, the magistrate judge entered an order stating that "the interests of justice warrant the release of the Federal Defender and the appointment of new counsel. The court notes that the decision in no way reflects on the performance of counsel, but is indicative of the defendant's narcissistic personality." (Cr. Doc. 59 at 4). The magistrate judge appointed Brett Bloomston as Mr. Riggs' fifth appointed attorney. (Cr. Doc. 60).

The court then held a hearing on the motion to withdraw Mr. Riggs' guilty plea. (Cr. Doc. 114). Mr. Riggs told the court that after the first conflict hearing on September 5, 2013, at which the court had ruled that Mr. Threatt had no conflict, Mr. Riggs met with a United

States deputy marshal about Mr. Johnson's statements. (*Id.* at 4–5). At that time, Mr. Threatt told the marshal that because Mr. Johnson was another of his clients, he could not represent Mr. Riggs during the marshal's interview of Mr. Riggs. (*Id.* at 5). The court asked if Mr. Riggs understood that "the conflict that Mr. Threatt was referring to had to do with your conversation with the marshal about Mr. Johnson . . . [h]ad nothing to do about his continued representation with you at trial or at your plea." (*Id.* at 6). Mr. Riggs stated that he understood the difference. (*Id.*).

The court pointed out that Mr. Riggs' change of plea hearing took place after the meeting with the United States marshal about Mr. Johnson, but Mr. Riggs had not mentioned the conflict at that time, despite testifying under oath that he was satisfied with Mr. Threatt's representation. (Cr. Doc. 114 at 6–8). And the court asked Mr. Riggs about his testimony that he had not been threatened into entering the plea agreement. (*Id.* at 11). Mr. Riggs stated that he had lied to protect his family. (*Id.*).

The Government called Mr. Threatt to testify at the hearing on Mr. Riggs' motion to withdraw. (Cr. Doc. 114 at 37). Mr. Threatt testified that, at Mr. Riggs' meeting with the United States deputy marshal on September 5, he had told Mr. Riggs that the interview should take place "outside [his] presence because [he] believed that [Mr. Riggs] was going to give information about a client of [his] at the time." (*Id.* at 39–40). He testified that Mr. Riggs never told him he was entering the plea agreement because of fear for himself and his family. (*Id.* at 43). And he testified that he and Mr. Riggs had, on at least three occasions, watched a videotaped confession in which Mr. Riggs admitted to sending the emails and text messages, including the obscene photographs. (*Id.* at 45). Mr. Threatt testified that Mr. Riggs had never refuted that confession. (*Id.*).

After the Government and defense counsel questioned Mr. Threatt, the court permitted Mr. Riggs to question Mr. Threatt directly. (Cr. Doc. 114 at 55–84). In response to Mr. Riggs' questions, Mr. Threatt testified that he "spoke to at least eight of [ten people who Mr. Riggs wanted to subpoena] on the phone about the matters that [Mr. Riggs] had asked [him] about." (*Id.* at 55). He also testified that he and Mr. Riggs had several conversations about an alibi defense, and Mr. Riggs had filed a *pro se* notice of alibi defense. (*Id.* at 74). Mr. Threatt testified that he told Mr. Riggs he would not file the notice because "alibi means that an individual is asserting that they were at a place other than the place that a crime was committed. When an individual—when the criminal allegation is that you were sending text messages from a phone, it does not matter whether you were doing that in this building or across the street. That's the conversation we had." (*Id.* at 74–75). In addition, Mr. Threatt testified that he felt an alibi defense would be inconsistent with Mr. Riggs' confession. (*Id.* at 75).

The court found that Mr. Riggs' plea was knowing and voluntary, and that sufficient evidence existed to justify a finding of guilt. (Cr. Doc. 114 at 88). The court also found that Mr. Threatt and his predecessor attorneys had provided Mr. Riggs with effective assistance. (*Id.* at 88–90). As a result, the court denied the motion to withdraw the guilty plea. (*Id.* at 90).

The court sentenced Riggs to two concurrent 120-month sentences. (Cr. Doc. 89). Mr. Riggs appealed. On appeal, Mr. Bloomston filed a brief under *Anders v. California*, 386 U.S. 738 (1967), stating that he believed no issues of arguable merit existed. (Doc. 13-2 at 55–72). In response, Mr. Riggs filed a *pro se* brief, contending, among other things, that all of his attorneys had provided ineffective assistance, that his guilty plea was invalid because Mr. Threatt and other federal public defenders coerced him to enter that plea, and that he was actually innocent. (Doc. 13-2 at 75–93). Specifically, Mr. Riggs argued that Mr. Threatt "knowingly and willingly hamper[ed] the prosecution of the murder of one DeAndre Washington . . . reported by the accused." (*Id.* at 85). He also argued that the plea agreement was void because he entered it based on Mr. Johnson's threats against his family and his erroneous impression that it was the only way to protect them. (*Id.* at 89–91).

After an independent review of the record, the Eleventh Circuit affirmed Mr. Riggs' convictions and sentences. *United States v. Riggs*, 589 F. App'x 523 (11th Cir. 2015).

II.   DISCUSSION

Mr. Riggs primarily raises three issues in his § 2255 motion: (1) Mr. Riggs' guilty plea was not knowing and voluntary; (2) trial counsel was ineffective because of his conflict of interest; and (3) he is actually innocent.[2] (Doc. 63).

1. Invalid Guilty Plea

Mr. Riggs' first claim is that his guilty plea was involuntary. He asserts that after he gave a statement against Mr. Johnson and before he entered the plea agreement, he told Mr. Threatt that Mr. Johnson had threatened Mr. Riggs' wife and children. (Doc. 63 at 4). According to Mr. Riggs, Mr. Threatt told him that the United States Marshals Service would protect Mr. Riggs' family only if he pled guilty. (*Id.*). Mr. Threatt allegedly also told Mr. Riggs that, if

---

[2] Mr. Riggs states at various points throughout his § 2255 motion and in his briefs that counsel's alleged conflict of interest resulted in the *denial* of counsel at each of the conflict-of-interest hearings. (Doc. 63 at 8–9, 14, 17–19; Doc. 75 at 2–5). To the extent that Mr. Riggs attempts to raise a denial-of-counsel claim, the court denies it because the record confirms that Mr. Riggs was represented by counsel at every stage of his criminal proceedings.

Mr. Riggs also alleges that another federal public defender, Sabra Barnett, who was not representing him, shared information about him with one of her clients. (Doc. 63 at 18–19; 75 at 7). But an attorney who was not representing him cannot have provided him with ineffective assistance. To the extent that Mr. Riggs attempts to assert a claim of ineffective assistance about Ms. Barnett's actions, the court denies that claim as well.

App - 35

147

he pled guilty, he would receive a sentence of time served for substantially assisting the Government. (*Id.* at 14–15).

Of relevance to Mr. Riggs' § 2255 motion, a movant seeking to challenge his sentence faces two procedural hurdles to raising a claim. First is the procedural bar, which provides that "once a matter has been decided adversely to a defendant on direct appeal it cannot be re-litigated in a collateral attack under section 2255." *United States v. Nyhuis*, 211 F.3d 1340, 1343 (11th Cir. 2000) (quotation marks omitted). The other is the doctrine of procedural default, which precludes any claim that the defendant could have, but did not, raise on direct appeal. *Lynn v. United States*, 365 F.3d 1225, 1234 (11th Cir. 2004).

The procedural bar and procedural default rules—the first prohibiting claims that the movant raised on direct appeal and the second prohibiting claims that the movant did *not* raise on direct appeal—may seem to place the movant in an impossible position. The movant may navigate the narrow passage between those two rules by raising in his § 2255 motion a claim that he *could not have raised* in his direct appeal—for example, a claim of ineffective assistance or a claim based on newly discovered evidence. *See, e.g., Bousley v. United States*, 523 U.S. 614, 621–22 (1998) (noting the "exception to the procedural default rule for claims that could not be presented [on direct appeal] without further factual development"); *Brown v. United States*, 688 F. App'x 644 (11th Cir. 2017) ("One example of a claim typically requiring further factual development through a § 2255 proceeding is a claim based on ineffective assistance of counsel.").

But Mr. Riggs' claim challenging the validity of his guilty plea does not rest on the ineffectiveness of his attorney or on evidence that he discovered *after* his appeal. Instead, Mr. Riggs' claim is simply that his guilty plea was invalid because (1) he entered the guilty plea based on his belief that pleading guilty was the only method to protect his family from Mr. Johnson, who had threatened them; and (2) Mr. Threatt told him that was the only way to get a lower sentence for substantially assisting the Government. (Doc. 63 at 4, 14–15).

The court finds that his claim is procedurally barred in part and procedurally defaulted in part. As to the part of his claim relating to Mr. Johnson's alleged threats against Mr. Riggs' family, the claim is procedurally barred. In his *pro se* brief on appeal to the Eleventh Circuit, Mr. Riggs argued that his guilty plea was invalid because he entered the plea agreement under the erroneous impression that it was the only way to protect his family. (Doc. 13-2 at 90–91). The Eleventh Circuit, in affirming his convictions, rejected that argument. *Riggs*, 589 F. App'x 523.

The Eleventh Circuit has held that a *pro se* brief filed in response to counsel's *Anders* brief triggers the procedural bar because "an issue presented is presented, even if raised only in the *pro se* response to an *Anders* brief." *Stoufflet v. United States*, 757 F.3d 1236, 1242 (11th Cir. 2014) (quotation marks, alteration, and citation omitted). Because Mr. Riggs challenged the validity of his guilty plea based on the alleged threats by Mr. Johnson against his family, and the Eleventh Circuit rejected that challenge, the procedural bar prevents this court from considering that claim on collateral review.

Less clear is whether the portion of Mr. Riggs' claim relying on Mr. Threatt's alleged promise of a sentence reduction is also procedurally barred. Mr. Riggs' *pro se* brief on appeal did not mention any promise of a sentence reduction, even though Mr. Riggs had already raised that alleged promise in the district court as a ground to withdraw his guilty plea. (*See* Cr. Doc. 57 at 1–2; Doc. 13-2 at 90–91). But the court need not decide whether that portion of the claim is procedurally barred because, even if it is not, Mr. Riggs procedurally defaulted it.

App - 37

Mr. Riggs' motion to withdraw his plea alleged that Mr. Threatt had induced him to plead guilty by telling him that such a plea was the only way to get a reduction in his sentence. (Cr. Doc. 57 at 1–2). He *could have* raised that argument in his *pro se* brief on appeal—he had already raised it in the district court by that point—but his *pro se* brief on appeal challenged his guilty plea only on the basis that he entered the plea to protect his family. (*See* Doc. 13-2 at 90–91). And his § 2255 motion does not allege any newly discovered evidence supporting the claim; it does not bring to light any information that was not already in the record of the trial proceedings. As a result, he procedurally defaulted his challenge to the guilty plea based on Mr. Threatt's alleged promise of a sentence reduction.

Two exceptions to the procedural default rule exist. Under the first exception, "a defendant must show cause for not raising the claim of error on direct appeal *and* actual prejudice from the alleged error." *Lynn*, 365 F.3d at 1234. Mr. Riggs has not alleged any facts that could support a showing of cause or prejudice. Under the second exception, a court may excuse the movant's procedural default "if a constitutional violation has probably resulted in the conviction of one who is actually innocent." *Id.* (quotation marks omitted). Mr. Riggs relies on the second exception by arguing that he is innocent of his crimes of conviction. (Doc. 63 at 5).

To establish actual innocence, a § 2255 movant must demonstrate that, in light of all the evidence, "it is more likely than not that no reasonable juror would have convicted him." *Bousley v. United States*, 523 U.S. 614, 623 (1998) (quotation marks omitted). Mr. Riggs makes two arguments in support of his allegation that he is actually innocent. First, he alleges that, unbeknownst to him, his housemate at the time of the crimes was a confidential informant named Joy Brown, using the alias Laney Jones, who was working with police in exchange for a lighter sentence. (Doc. 63 at 22–23). Mr. Riggs contends that she used a SIM card from one of his broken cellphones to send the texts and explicit photographs to the other undercover agent who was posing as a young girl, all in a scheme to frame him and stop his work as an informant exposing the involvement of public officials in the drug trade. (*Id.* at 4–5, 22). He states that, while he was in jail, Ms. Brown admitted to him that she sent the nude pictures of him from her cellphone. (*Id.* at 22). Second, he alleges that ten alibi witnesses would have proved that he was not "even present when the alleged conduct occurred." (*Id.* at 12, 23).

Mr. Riggs has not established that, "more likely than not . . . , no reasonable juror would have convicted him." *Bousley*, 523 U.S. at 623. Law enforcement officers arrested Mr. Riggs on the date and at the time and place that he had arranged to meet with someone he believed was 14 years old, after he had sent numerous explicit text messages and emails, including nude photographs of himself, to that person. (*See* Doc. 55 at 4–5). Furthermore, at the hearing on Mr. Riggs' motion to withdraw his guilty plea, Mr. Threatt testified that Mr. Riggs had made a videotaped confession to the police in which he admitted to sending the emails, text messages, and nude photographs.[3] (Cr. Doc. 114 at 45). Although the Government did not submit that confession during Mr. Riggs' criminal proceedings, it would be entitled to do so now. *See Bousley*, 523 U.S. at 624 ("[T]he Government is not limited to the existing record to rebut any showing [of actual innocence] that petitioner might make. Rather, on remand, the Government should be permitted to present any admissible evidence of petitioner's guilt even if that evidence was not presented during petitioner's plea colloquy . . . .").

In contrast to that evidence, Mr. Riggs presents his own allegation that Ms. Brown was an informant who framed him. Because he does not include any affidavit from Ms. Brown or any

---

[3] In his reply brief, Mr. Riggs mentions in passing that Mr. Threatt "presented an edited version of the videotaped interview," but he does not explain that statement any further. (*See* Doc. 75 at 7).

other witness, the court can only assume that he is proffering his own testimony in support of that allegation. Even if Mr. Riggs had taken the stand at trial and testified about the alleged conspiracy to frame him, the court cannot find it more like than not that his testimony would have overcome the strong evidence against him such that "no reasonable juror would have convicted him." *Bousley*, 523 U.S. at 623.

As for Mr. Riggs' assertion of an alibi defense, the court notes that an alibi is "[a] defense based on the physical impossibility of a defendant's guilt by placing the defendant in a location other than the scene of the crime at the relevant time." *Alibi*, Black's Law Dictionary (10th ed. 2014). Mr. Riggs does not set out how his ten alibi witnesses would have proved the "physical impossibility" of him using his phone to send text messages, emails, and photographs to the undercover agent. (*See generally* Doc. 63; Doc. 75 at 6). The court notes that, at the hearing on Mr. Riggs' motion to withdraw his plea, Mr. Threatt testified that he spoke to "at least" eight of the witnesses Mr. Riggs said would provide him with an alibi, but he had declined to file an alibi because "when the criminal allegation is that you were sending text messages from a phone, it does not matter whether you were doing that in this building or across the street." (Cr. Doc. 114 at 55, 74–75). And, as discussed above, police arrested Mr. Riggs at the appointed time of an arranged encounter with a girl he believed to be underage, after exchanging multiple text messages and emails from his phone. Again, the court cannot find that, more likely than not, "no reasonable juror would have convicted" Mr. Riggs if he had presented his alibi defense. *See Bousley*, 523 U.S. at 623.

Mr. Riggs' claim that his guilty plea is invalid because he entered it under duress is procedurally barred in part and procedurally defaulted in part. And Mr. Riggs cannot excuse the procedural default because he cannot establish his actual innocence. As a result, the court WILL DENY this claim.

2. Ineffective Assistance Based on Conflict of Interest

Mr. Riggs' second claim is that Mr. Threatt provided ineffective assistance because he was operating under a conflict of interest by representing both Mr. Johnson—who allegedly confessed to Mr. Riggs that he had committed an unsolved murder—and Mr. Riggs. (Doc. 63 at 7, 12). Mr. Riggs contends that, to protect Mr. Johnson, Mr. Threatt had to "silence" Mr. Riggs. (*Id.*). This claim fails because, even if Mr. Threatt had a conflict of interest, Mr. Riggs waived the conflict on the record.

In a typical claim of ineffective assistance of counsel, the movant must demonstrate that (1) his counsel's performance fell below an objective standard of reasonableness; *and* (2) he suffered prejudice because of that deficient performance. *Strickland v. Washington*, 466 U.S. 668, 684–91 (1984). But the standard is different when a movant alleges ineffective assistance based on a conflict of interest. A movant who can "show[ ] that a conflict of interest actually affected the adequacy of his representation need not demonstrate prejudice in order to obtain relief." *Cuyler v. Sullivan*, 446 U.S. 335, 349–50 (1980). To obtain the presumption of prejudice in this type of case, the movant must "demonstrate[ ] that counsel actively represented conflicting interests and that an actual conflict of interest adversely affected his lawyer's performance." *Strickland*, 466 U.S. at 692. But a defendant can waive the right to conflict-free counsel. *United States v. Garcia*, 517 F.2d 272, 276–78 (5th Cir. 1975),[4] *abrogated on other grounds by Flanagan v. United States*, 465 U.S. 259 (1984).

---

[4] In *Bonner v. City of Prichard*, 661 F.2d 1206, 1207 (11th Cir. 1981) (en banc), the Eleventh Circuit adopted as binding precedent all decisions of the former Fifth Circuit handed down before October 1, 1981.

During Mr. Riggs' criminal proceedings, a magistrate judge found that Mr. Threatt did not have a conflict based on his concurrent representation of Mr. Riggs and Mr. Johnson, and the court found that Mr. Threatt had provided effective assistance despite Mr. Riggs' charge of a conflict. (Cr. Doc. Minute Entry, Sept. 5, 2013; Cr. Doc. 114 at 88–90). Mr. Riggs did not challenge those findings in his direct appeal. (*See* Doc. 13-2 at 55–72).

Nevertheless, because Mr. Riggs' current claim is one of ineffective assistance based on the alleged conflict, the court will not deny the claim as procedurally defaulted. *See Massaro v. United States*, 538 U.S. 500, 509 (2003) ("We . . . hold that failure to raise an ineffective-assistance-of-counsel claim on direct appeal does not bar the claim from being brought in a later, appropriate proceeding under § 2255."). But the court also will not reevaluate the underlying finding that Mr. Threatt had no conflict, because Mr. Riggs had the opportunity to challenge that finding and failed to do so.

In light of the magistrate judge's and the court's earlier findings that Mr. Threatt had no conflict, Mr. Riggs cannot now establish ineffective assistance based on a conflict of interest. *See Cuyler*, 446 U.S. at 349–50 (requiring the movant to show *both* an *actual* conflict of interest and that the conflict affected the adequacy of his representation).

And even if the magistrate judge had not made a finding that Mr. Threatt had no conflict, or if that finding were somehow wrong, Mr. Riggs would not be able to demonstrate that Mr. Threatt's representation of him violated the Sixth Amendment, because Mr. Riggs waived the right to conflict-free counsel. To establish waiver, the record must demonstrate "that the defendant was aware of the conflict of interest; realized the conflict could affect the defense; and knew of the right to obtain other counsel." *United States v. Rodriguez*, 982 F.2d 474 (11th Cir. 1993).

The record demonstrates each of those requirements. Mr. Riggs was clearly aware of the alleged conflict of interest, aware that a conflict could affect his defense, and aware of the right to obtain other counsel, because he filed not one, but two *pro se* motions based on the alleged conflict, expressly seeking a new attorney in one of those motions. (*See* Cr. Doc. 51; Cr. Doc. 57 at6). Yet at the hearing on his first motion about the conflict, he told the magistrate judge that, after he had placed his motion in the mail, he had discussed the alleged conflict with Mr. Threatt and they had "determined this was not going to be an issue." (Cr. Doc. 109 at 7). Finally, the court notes that, at his change of plea hearing, which took place *after* the conflict hearing, Mr. Riggs responded "yes" when the court asked if he was satisfied with Mr. Threatt's representation of him. (Cr. Doc. 62 at 24).

The court finds that, even *assuming* that Mr. Threatt had an actual conflict of interest—an assumption that the court doubts—Mr. Riggs validly waived that conflict. And to the extent that Mr. Riggs asserts that his other attorneys had conflicts of interest, he has not explained what the conflict of interest was or how it adversely affected their representation of him. *See Cuyler*, 446 U.S. 335, 349–50 (requiring both an actual conflict of interest and that the conflict affected the adequacy of counsel's representation). As a result, he cannot establish that he received ineffective assistance of counsel. *See McCorkle v. United States*, 325 F. App'x 804, 807–08 (11th Cir. 2009) (concluding that the movant did not receive ineffective assistance of counsel because he waived his trial attorney's conflict of interest). As a result, the court WILL DENY this claim.

3. Actual Innocence

Mr. Riggs contends that a confidential informant, Joy Brown, sent the explicit text and email messages that formed the basis for his convictions. (Doc. 63 at 5). As the court discussed above, Mr. Riggs cannot establish that he is actually innocent. But even if he could, a freestanding claim of actual innocence is not cognizable in a § 2255 motion. *Jordan v. Sec'y Dep't of Corr.*, 485 F.3d 1351, 1356 (11th Cir. 2007) ("[O]ur precedent forbids granting habeas relief based upon a claim of actual innocence, anyway, at least in non-capital cases."); *see also Herrera v. Collins*, 506 U.S. 390, 400 (1993) ("Claims of actual innocence based on newly discovered evidence have never been held to state a ground for federal habeas relief absent an independent constitutional violation . . . ."). As a result, the court WILL DENY this claim.

4. Certificate of Appealability

Rule 11 of the Rules Governing § 2255 Cases requires the court to "issue or deny a certificate of appealability when it enters a final order adverse to the applicant." Rule 11(a), Rules Governing § 2255 Cases. The court may issue a certificate of appealability "only if the applicant has a made a substantial showing of the denial of a constitutional right." 28 U.S.C. § 2253(c)(2). To make such a showing, a "petitioner must demonstrate that reasonable jurists would find the district court's assessment of the constitutional claims debatable or wrong," or that "the issues presented were adequate to deserve encouragement to proceed further." *Miller-El v. Cockrell*, 537 U.S. 322, 336, 338 (2003) (quotation marks omitted). This court finds that Mr. Riggs' claims do not satisfy either standard. The court WILL DENY a certificate of appealability.

III. CONCLUSION

The court WILL DENY Mr. Riggs' § 2255 motion. The court WILL DENY AS MOOT Mr. Riggs' motion for appointment of counsel. The court WILL DENY Mr. Riggs a certificate of appealability.

The court will enter a separate order consistent with this opinion.

App - 44

DONE and **ORDERED** this 2nd day of May, 2018.

KARON OWEN BOWDRE
CHIEF UNITED STATES DISTRICT JUDGE

**IN THE UNITED STATES DISTRICT COURT
FOR THE NORTHERN DISTRICT OF ALABAMA
SOUTHERN DIVISION**

KELLY PATRICK RIGGS,	]	
	]	
Plaintiff,	]	
	]	
v.	]	2:15-cv-08043-KOB
	]	
UNITED STATES OF AMERICA	]	
	]	
Defendant.	]	

FINAL ORDER

This matter comes before the court on Kelly Patrick Riggs' amended 28 U.S.C. § 2255

motion to vacate sentence (doc. 63) and his motion for appointment of counsel (doc. 67). For the

reasons set out in the accompanying memorandum opinion, the court DENIES Mr. Riggs'

§ 2255 motion; DENIES AS MOOT Mr. Riggs' motion for appointment of counsel; and

DENIES Mr. Riggs a certificate of appealability.

DONE and **ORDERED** this 2nd day of May, 2018.

Karon O. Bowdre
KARON OWEN BOWDRE
CHIEF UNITED STATES DISTRICT JUDGE

UNITED STATES DISTRICT COURT
NORTHERN DISTRICT OF ALABAMA
SOUTHERN DIVISION

KELLY PATRICK RIGGS   :

      :   CASE NO.: 2:15-CV-8043-KOB

V.   :

      :

      :

UNITED STATES OF AMERICA   :

      :

NOTICE OF APPEAL

Mr. Riggs gives notice of appeal from this Courts final judgment to deny him a certificate of appealability and/or denial of evidentiary hearing to settle contested factual issues.

Mr. Riggs shows that the district judges's ruling is in direct contradiction with Clisby v. Jones, 960 F.2d. 925(11th Cir. 1992) (en banc). The order handed down by the Court addresses only three of Mr.Riggs' four claims and the three it did address are incomplete. In Mr. Riggs' petition, to request a certificate of appealability will particularize that the district court left unanswered the following:

1) his claim of Conflict of Interest with the Federal Public Defenders office as a whole.

2) his claim of outright denial of counsel at a critical stage of the criminal proceeding. (Ground Three)

3) his claim that Glennon F. Threatt and Sabra Barnett conspired to murder Mr. Riggs in a jail cell by discussing his case with cartel associate Lois Rodriguez.

4) his claim that Brett Bloomston provided ineffective assistance of trial counsel by failing to refine and/or clarify Mr. Riggs' claims in his motion to withdraw his plea agreement.

5) his claim that Glennon Threatt failed to provide effective

assistance of counsel by presenting a version of a police video, edited to appear to be a confession, rather than challenging the governments evidence.

6) that Glennon Threatts representation was in fact a constructive denial of counsel where he "testified that he felt an alibi defense would be inconsistent with Mr. Riggs confession." Thus, failing to provide adversarial testing of governments evidence.

7) Mr. Riggs expressly moved for the appointment of conflict free counsel, yet the Court dispatched Glennon Threatt to counsel Mr. Riggs concerning the conflict of interest. Thus, Mr. Riggs did not know, "of the right to obtain other counsel" where the Court failed to advise him and failed to appoint unconflicted counsel. Moreover, Mr. Threatt counseled, likely at the behest of the Court, that Mr. Riggs wouldn't get new counsel because he was getting time served for his assistance anyway.

8) The claim that Brett Bloomston abandoned Mr. Riggs at appeal, making it highly unlikely that Mr. Riggs could articulate meaningful appeal claims on his own. An inability the Court now relys on to deny Mr. Riggs his right to an evidentiary hearing. §2255(b).

9) In this action its the Court itself that obstructs justice by concealing the contested video confession, the alibi witnesses, and the presiding judges personal and church relationship with Brad Taylor and the Hazelrig family. Researching the murder of Sambo Hazelrig and the attempted murder of Mr. Riggs in 2011.

10) The district court committs fraud on the American people of the Northern District of Alabama by falsifying established Court record in her memorandum. The record reflects that on December 20, 2013 Id at 74, states "we actually filed a Notice of Alibi" and "we subpoenaed at least ten people in the case." Id at 55

App - 48

160

11) That Mr. Riggs claims that the ineffectiveness of counsel has facilitated the conviction of someone who is actually innocent. The facts of the criminal case show that Mr. Riggs was in a pool with his wife and children at the time the Court has testified that Mr. Riggs answered agents messages.

12) Mr. Riggs will show that neither the government nor the Court has provided a single affidavit from anyone on anything the Court currently is testifying to.

13) Mr. Riggs' claim that he was not appointed unconflicted counsel at a conflict of interest hearing. The Court tries to dismiss the claim by not addressing Mr. Riggs' Ground Three and addressing the claim, in part, in a foot note on page eight of the Courts memorandum. The facts are:

A) Mr. Riggs has filed no briefs and set his claim out clearly in Ground Three of his amended § 2255 Motion.

B) The Court refuses to "re-evaluate the underlying finding that Mr. Threatt had no conflict, because Mr. Riggs had the opportunity to challenge that finding and failed to do so." But, the Court fails to state that Mr. Riggs' only opportunity to challenge the finding was while he was deprived of counsel.

C) Mr. Riggs challenged Mr. Threatts loyalties in a pro se motion.

D) The Court dispatched Mr. Threatt, to address Mr. Riggs' motion with Mr. Riggs, rather than unconflicted counsel.

E) The Court failed to advise Mr. Riggs of his right to un-conflicted counsel at the conflict hearing and failed to ap-point unconflicted counsel to advise Mr. Riggs concerning his right to conflict free counsel at the conflict hearing.

F) At the hearing Mr. Riggs interest was to prove that counsel was conflicted, Glennon Threatts interest was to prove there was no conflict. This represents a second independant conflict of interest where Mr. Riggs was without counsel.

G) The Court did not advise Mr. Riggs of his right to unconflicted counsel to assist him in deciding to waive the conflict of counsel. Nor, did the Court conduct a Ferretta hearing to decide if Mr. Riggs could represent his own interests or understand the impact of his decision to represent himself in waiving his right to conflict free counsel.

14 Finally, the Court has rushed Mr. Riggs to judgment where the Court issued an "order regarding summary disposition", in which it "gives Mr. Riggs until May 15, 2018... to supply any additional evidentiary materials or legal arguments...", but yet issued a "Final Order" to deny Mr. Riggs § 2255 on May 2, 2018. Mr. Riggs moves this Court to designate the record for appeal.

Submitted on May 14, 2018, By:

Kelly Patrick Riggs
Register No.:
FCC Coleman Low Unit A-4
PO Box 1031
Coleman, FL 33521

Certificate of Service

I have served a copy of this notice on the clerk of this Court, the United States of America, the 11th Circuit Court Clerk, and the Release of Innocent Prisoners Effort, Inc. All in the interest of justice and publication on social media. "What we do in the dark will come to the light."

Submitted on May 14, 2018, By:

Kelly Pátrick Riggs
Register No.:
FCC Coleman Low   Unit A-4
PO Box 1031
Coleman, FL 33521

KELLY PATRICK RIGGS

UNITED STATES COURT OF APPEALS
FOR THE ELEVENTH CIRCUIT

APPEAL NO.: 18-12111-F

KELLY PATRICK RIGGS

VS.

UNITED STATES OF AMERICA

On appeal from the US District Court
for the Northern District of Alabama

Civil No.: 2:15-CV-8043-KOB
Criminal No.: 2:12-CR-297-KOB-JEO

Judge Karen Owen Bowdre

MOTION FOR ISSUANCE OF A CERTIFICATE OF APPEALABILITY

KELLY PATRICK RIGGS
REGISTER NO.: 29821-001
FCC COLEMAN LOW   UNIT A-4
PO BOX 1031
COLEMAN, FL 33521

App - 52

IN THE

UNITED STATES COURT OF APPEALS

FOR THE ELEVENTH CIRCUIT

KELLY PATRICK RIGGS,	:	Appeal No.: 18-12111-F
	:	
Appellant,	:	
	:	(Appealed from the
	:	
v.	:	UNITED STATES DISTRICT COURT
	:	
	:	NORTHERN DISTRICT OF ALABAMA
UNITED STATES OF AMERICA,	:	
	:	Crim. No.: 2:12-cr-297-KOB-JEO-1)
Appellee,	:	
	:	Civil No.: 2:15-cv-8043-KOB

CERTIFICATE OF INTERESTED PERSONS

AND CORPORATE DISCLOSURE STATEMENT

Pursuant to the Eleventh Circuit Rule 26.1, the Appellant, KELLY PATRICK RIGGS, certifies that the following persons may have and interest in the outcome of this case:

1) Manu K. Balachandran, A.U.S.A.

2) Brett Bloomston, Former Appellate Counsel

3) Karen Owen Bowdre, Chief District Judge

4) Jeffrey D. Braemer, Former Defense Counsel

5) Kevin L. Butler, Former Defense Counsel

6) Allison Case, Former Defense Counsel

7) Staci Cornelius, Former A.U.S.A.

8) Daniel Fortune, A.U.S.A.

9) John D. Lloyd, Conspirator with Defense Counsel

10) Davis S. Luker, Former Defense Counsel

11) John E. Ott, Magistrate Judge

12) Robert Posey, Acting US Attorney

13) Kelly Patrick Riggs, Appellant

14) Jennifer Murnaham Smith, A.U.S.A.

15) Michael B. Billingsley, A.U.S.A.

16) Glennon F. Threatt, Jr., Former Defense Counsel

17) Jay E. Town, US Attorney

App – 54

UNITED STATES COURT OF APPEALS
FOR THE ELEVENTH CIRCUIT

APPEAL NO.: 18-12111-F

KELLY PATRICK RIGGS

VS.

UNITED STATES OF AMERICA

On appeal from the US District Court
for the Northern District of Alabama

Civil No.: 2:15-CV-8043-KOB
Criminal No.: 2:12-CR-297-KOB-JEO

Judge Karen Owen Bowdre

MOTION FOR ISSUANCE OF A CERTIFICATE OF APPEALABILITY

Mr. Riggs moves this Court to issue a certificate of appealability (C.O.A. hereafter) He seeks the issuance of a C.O.A. pursuant to 28 USC § 2253(c)(2) authorizing him (Mr. Riggs) to appeal the denial of his 28 USC § 2255 Motion to Vacate, set aside or correct sentence. See Buck v. Davis, 137 S.Ct. 759 (2017); Slack v. McDaniel, 529 US 473 (2000); Miller -El v. Cockrell, 537 US 322; Prozer v. US, 696 Fed. Appx. 977(11th Cir 2017); Termitus v. Secretary, Florida Dept. of Corr., 667 Fed. Appx. 303 (11th Cir. 2016); and Mitchell v. US, 612 Fed. Appx. 542 (11th Cir. 2015).

I.

STATEMENT OF JURISDICTION

Jurisdiction to issue a C.O.A. is given to this Court of Appeals pursuant to 28 USC §§§ 1291; 2253(c)(2); and 2255.

App - 55

II.

STATEMENT OF THE CASE

Following Mr. Riggs' criminal case he filed an instant motion pursuant to 28 USC § 2255, in which he raised several contested factual issues that go unresolved. See Clisby v. Jones, 960 F.2d 925 (11th Cir 1992)(en banc).

1) On or bout November 16, 2015, the Clerk of the District Court received Mr. Riggs' 28 USC § 2255 Motion.

2) On or about December 11, 2015, the United States Attorneys Office filed its response.

3) On or about December 22, 2015, Mr. Riggs concluded the substantive pleading by filing his reply. After which Mr. Riggs filed a number of poorly drafted Motions that served to hinder the district Court.

4) On or about March 17, 2016 the district Court issued its "ORDER REGARDING SUMMARY DISPOSITION."

5) On or about March 30, 2016, Mr. Riggs filed his opposition to the Courts intentions.

6) On or about June 13, 2017, Mr. Riggs filed his "Motion For Leave To Amend."

7) On or about January 2, 2018, Mr. Riggs filed his "PETITION FOR A WRIT OF MANDAMUS", with the Eleventh Circuit Court of Appeals and serving a copy on Judge Karen Owen Bowdre.

8) On or about January 12, 2018, the district Court issued its order granting Mr. Riggs' Motion For Leave To Amend. The order providing that, "Mr. Riggs may file his amended § 2255 Motion on or by February 17, 2018."

9) On or about February 14, 2018, the District Court Clerk received for filing Mr. Riggs' amended § 2255 Motion. USPS Tracking Number, 9114-9012-3080-1329-5910-88.

10) On or about March 2, 2018, the Court issued an "ORDER TO SHOW CAUSE."

App - 56

168

11) On or about March 9, 2018, Mr. Riggs filed a Motion to Appoint Counsel.

12) On or about March 20, 2018, the government filed its response but failed to provide Mr. Riggs with service.

13) On or about April 2, 2018, Mr. Riggs filed a Motion seeking an order requiring the government to provide service.

14) On or about April 23, 2018, Mr. Riggs filed his "Reply To 'United States'" belated response.

15) On or about April 24, 2018, the district Court issued its "ORDER REGARDING SUMMARY DISPOSITION." In the Courts order it provides, "Mr. Riggs until May 15, 2018, twenty days after the date of this order, to supply any additional evidentiary materials or legal arguments he may wish to offer regarding whether the motion is subject to summary disposition."

16) On or about May 2, 2018, the Court issued its "FINAL ORDER" in which the Court "Denies Mr. Riggs' § 2255 Motion." Identifying a 'Rush To Judgment'.

17) On or about May 3, 2018, Mr. Riggs filed his "objection and opposition to the Courts order Regarding summary disposition" in good faith. Additionally, Mr. Riggs filed a motion for judicial notice on that same day.

18) On or about May 14, 2018, after Mr. Riggs received the Courts order to deny and before the date in which the Court set for Mr. Riggs' filing additional materials, Mr. Riggs filed his Notice of Appeal.

19) On or about May 17, 2018, the Court "Denied as Moot" Mr. Riggs additional evidentiary materials.

III.

STATEMENT OF THE FACTS

Due in large part to Mr. Riggs ignorance of complex habeas corpus law and his legal disability; he files his motion, for issuance of Certificate of Appealability, with an abundance of caution. He files this motion for

C.O.A. believing that the Court, more likely, should vacate the district Courts denial and remand for consideration of all Constitutional claims raised.

The Eleventh Circuit has long held that a district Court must resolve all claims for relief raised in a § 2255 Motion. Regardless of whether habeas relief is granted or denied. See Clisby, 960 F.2d at 936. A claim for relief is "any allegation of a Constitutional violation." Clisby, 960 F.2d 936. The Court of Appeals cannot consider claims not resolved by the district Court in the first instance. See id. at 935. Instead, when a district Court fails to address all claims in a Motion to Vacate, the Eleventh Circuit "Will vacate the district Courts judgment without prejudice and remand the case for consideration of all remaining claims." Id. at 938. Ineffective assistance of counsel is a violation of a defendants' Sixth Amendment rights and, as a result, is a claim of a constitutional violation. Strickland v. Washington, 466 US 668, 685-86, 104 S.Ct. 2052, 2063-64, 80 L.Ed. 2d 674 (1984). See Prozer v. United States, 696 Fed. Appx. 977 (11th Cir. 2017).

In Mr. Riggs' Amended § 2255 Motion he raised four grounds for relief (Appended hereto). In the district Courts "Memorandum opinion," however, it only addressed three of the four grounds. Page 1 of 18 DE-76-1.(Appended hereto). In addition Mr. Riggs raised a detailed claim of ineffective assistance of counsel against Brett M. Bloomston, appointed counsel. See § 2255 Ground One, at ¶32; and Ground Three, at ¶10. The district Court in its memorandum opinion makes no mention of the claim against Mr. Brett Bloomston.

IV.

UNADDRESSED CLAIMS

1) Mr. Riggs was deprived of his Sixth Amendment right to counsel at

a critical stage of the criminal proceeding. Ground Three.

2) Brett Bl;oomston was ineffective for failing to refine or clarify Mr.Riggs Motion to Withdraw his plea agreement.

3) Brett Bloomston abandoned Mr. Riggs at appeal, leaving an alibi defense unexplored.

4) Glennon Threatt and Sabra Barnett conspired together to intimidate and/or attempt to murder Mr. Riggs by discussing details concerning Mr. Riggs with Mexican National Lois Rodriguez. See attached letter to the Alabama Bar Association.

5) Denial of Mr. Riggs' right to an evidentiary hearing, pursuant to 28 USC § 2255(b), leaves open the contested factual issue of whether an edited version of a police interview serves as proof of Glennon Threatts ineffectiveness.

CONCLUSION

Wherefore, Mr. Riggs moves this Court to vacate the district Courts denial of his § 2255 Motion in compliance with standing Eleventh Circuit precedent. In the alternative this Court could grant Mr. Riggs request for C.O.A. and remand for further proceedings.

Submitted on June 6, 2018, By:

Kelly Patrick Riggs, Pro se
Register No.: 29821-001
FCC Coleman Low   Unit A-4
PO Box 1031
Coleman, FL 33521

KELLY PATRICK RIGGS

CERTIFICATE OF SERVICE

I have served a copy of this petition on the US Attorney's Office,

mailing it to:

    1801 4th Avenue N.
    Birmingham, AL 35203

Submitted on June 6, 2018, By:

_____
Kelly Patrick Riggs, Pro se
Register No.: 29821-001
FCC Coleman Low   Unit A-4
PO Box 1031
Coleman, FL 33521

IN THE UNITED STATES COURT OF APPEALS
FOR THE ELEVENTH CIRCUIT

KELLY RIGGS,	)
	)
Petitioner-Appellant,	)
	)
v.	) Case No. 18-12111-F
	)
UNITED STATES OF AMERICA,	)
	)
Respondent-Appellee.	)

CERTIFICATE OF INTERESTED PERSONS
AND CORPORATE DISCLOSURE STATEMENT

In compliance with Fed. R. App. P. 26.1, 11th Cir. R. 26.1-1, and 11th Cir. R. 26.1-2(a), the undersigned hereby certifies that, the following persons may have an interest in the outcome of the case:

1. Balachandran, Manu, Assistant United States Attorney, represented the Respondent-Appellee in the district court;

2. Billingsley, Michael B., Assistant United States Attorney, Chief of the Appellate Division;

3. Bloomston, Brett, defense counsel in the district court;

4. Bowdre, Hon. Karen O., United States District Judge for the Northern District of Alabama;

5. Bramer, Jeffrey, defense counsel in the district court;

C1 of 3

No. 18-12111-F

Riggs v. United States

Certificate of Interested Persons and
Corporate Disclosure Statement *(cont'd)*

6. Butler, Kevin, Federal Public Defender, represented Defendant-Appellant in the district court;

7. Case, Allison, Assistant Federal Public Defender, represented Defendant-Appellant in the district court;

8. Cornelius, Hon. Staci G., United States Magistrate Judge for the Northern District of Alabama;

9. Fortune, Daniel J., former Assistant United States Attorney, represented the Respondent-Appellee in the district court;

10. Greene, Hon. Paul W., United States Magistrate Judge for the Northern District of Alabama;

11. Luker, David, defense counsel in the district court;

12. Murnahan, Jennifer Smith, former Assistant United States Attorney, represented the Respondent-Appellee in the district court;

13. Ott, Hon. John E., United States Magistrate Judge for the Northern District of Alabama;

14. Riggs, Kelly, Petitioner-Appellant;

No. 18-12111-F

Riggs v. United States

**Certificate of Interested Persons and
Corporate Disclosure Statement** *(cont'd)*

15. Threatt, Jr., Glennon, Assistant Federal Public Defender, represented

    Defendant-Appellant in the district court;

16. Town, Jay E., United States Attorney for the Northern District of

    Alabama; and

17. Ward, John B., Assistant United States Attorney, represented the

    Respondent-Appellee in the district court.

/s/ Michael B. Billingsley
Michael B. Billingsley
Assistant United States Attorney

C3 of 3

App - 63

CHAPTER SIX

TIPS FOR QUESTION CONSTRUCTION

Personally, I hate to harp on anything, but repetition is a great teaching tool. I cannot stress to you enough the importance of the questions you present to The Supreme Court. The reality of this is that your petition lives or dies by the implication of your questions. Even great questions that do not have a national impact on the administration of federal law or Constitutional rights have been passed over throughout the history of The Supreme Court. To compound this issue is the fact that the person most dangerous to your great questions is not even a judge but only a clerk. That clerk, or law clerks as some call themselves, need only to write a negative memorandum, and your petition will never be read by one of the nine justices. Again, the best way to get past the clerk and into the hands of a justice is in the quality of your questions.

The questions that get the greatest amount of attention are the ones that challenge the validity of a rule, a right, or a law. Even then, you risk rejection based simply on the number of petitions received in The Supreme Court each month. Although there is no defined science of question selection, history is a great teacher. One constant remains true: if you challenge The Supreme Court with the influence of politics, the likelihood of getting a review improves exponentially.

One example of this phenomenon was the case of *Planned Parenthood v. Casey*, 505 U.S. 833 (1992). The case was filed by Kathryn Kolbert, an A.C.L.U. attorney, who was concerned for the future of legalized abortion. After the loss in the Third Circuit, of the Court of Appeals, Ms. Kolbert decided that the protections of *Roe v. Wade*, 410 U.S. 113 (1973), had eroded to such a point as to be better off to be overturned entirely. The most important implication of her choice in questions was a two-prong issue:

1) at that time, legalized abortion was a huge social issue in 1991; and

2) 1992 was an election year. Ms. Kolbert's only assurance of getting her case before The Supreme Court was in her choice of questions. She opted to present only one question to The Supreme Court. In her question, she challenged The Courts own precedent in *Roe v. Wade* and fashioned her question in a way that would affect voters in an election year. She knew that the art of writing the questions was to frame the issue in a way that would get the attention of at least four justices who would vote to take the case. Her single question was stated in simple terms:

> "Has The Supreme Court overruled *Roe v. Wade*, holding that a woman's right to choose abortion is a fundamental right protected by the United States Constitution?"

In reality, Ms. Kolbert's only challenge was to a small portion of the Pennsylvania statute. She also knew that The Supreme Court would have likely passed over her petition in favor of a more meaningful case. Thus, Ms. Kolbert did the unthinkable; instead of claiming that the Pennsylvania statute was unconstitutional over a small portion of it, she decided to challenge the Court's position on the issue of legalized abortion as a whole. Had the Court decided against ruling on her case, their workload would have exploded overnight.

Another example was *Johnson v. United States*, 576 U.S.____ , (2015). The Johnson case was filed during the Obama era, right after the long controversy over the two-point reduction for low-level drug offenders. The drive had started to correct the racial disparity in the federal criminal justice system. Again, Johnson attacked the validity of a law, 18 U.S.C. §924(e) and The Armed Career Criminal Act; he did so during a time of social outrage; and in a year proceeding an election year. The Court did not want to seem unsympathetic, doing so would have driven the voters to the polls with the criminal justice system on their minds.

If you paid attention to the last chapter, you would have noticed that I challenged the constitutionality of 28 U.S.C. §2255(b) as being unconstitutionally void for vagueness. I did so not only to have my grounds ruled on in their entirety but also because every court in America takes advantage of Pro Se litigants by exploiting the lack of clarity in the statute. It's hard to say how this claim will turn out, but my case will get resolved to kill the claim. Those of you who follow me must do the same to get an "expeditious remedy" in your own case.

As you have likely noticed, I target statutes that seem unclear. My favorite method of doing this is to give the court a choice between invalidating one of two statutes. Think about this example, 18 U.S.C. §2422(b) states that:

> "whoever, using the mail or any facility or means of interstate or foreign commerce or within the special maritime and territorial jurisdiction of The United States, knowingly persuades, induces, entices, or coerces any individual who has not attained the age of 18 years, to engage in prostitution or any sexual activity for which any person can be charged with a criminal offense, or attempts to do so, shall be fined under this title and imprisoned not less than 10 years or for life."

Additionally, 18 U.S.C. §2427 states that:

> "inclusion of offenses relating to child pornography in the definition of sexual activity for which any person can be charged with a criminal offense."

In this chapter [18 U.S.C.S. §§2421 et. Seq.], the term "sexual activity for which any person can be charged with a criminal offense" includes the production of child pornography, as defined in section 2256(8)."

I raise this particular statute as an example for a number of reasons. The most important reason is it's residual clause, defined in 18 U.S.C.§2427. The clause, as you can see here, is defined to include the production of child pornography. But, it is most commonly used as an all-purpose sexual abuse statute. This is done because Congress did not establish a bright line limitation that makes clear what conduct is unlawful under the residual clause. Thus, the residual clause in 18 U.S.C. §2442(b) is unconstitutionally void- for-vagueness.

I say all this to draw your mind away from issues that have little relevance. You should always scrutinize the convicting statute in your case before you assume that it is Constitutional. As of today, a number of residual clauses have been found to be unconstitutional. Think of it this way; any time a judge, a police officer, or a prosecutor has to make a decision as to whether your conduct was unlawful, then the statute is questionable. In the case of a residual clause, or catch all phrase as I call them, I always question the Constitutionality of the clause as void- for-vagueness. My other favorite, as you saw in the previous chapter, is "has Congress delegated it's legislative authority to the executive branch of government"? The implications of that question are limitless.

In a more recent case, is another sample of wise development. In *McCoy v. Louisiana*, attorneys Richard Bourke and Meghan Shapiro, from the Louisiana Capital Assistance Center, petitioned The Supreme Court for a writ of certiorari on behalf of Robert McCoy, a death row inmate. During Mr. McCoy's trial and/or Capital Sentencing hearing, his retained counsel, Larry English, violated his client's trust by conceding guilt against his client's wishes and his alibi defense. Moreover, Mr. McCoy was alleged by alibi witnesses to be in another state at the time of the offense.

Ordinarily Mr. McCoy's case would have been viewed as either a case of ineffective assistance of counsel or of structural error. Either of which is a case of individual relief, thus affecting only Mr. McCoy. It's my opinion that Mr. McCoy was granted certiorari based on only one thing, his attorneys from the Capital Assistance Center employed a great deal of wisdom in drafting their two questions. Their questions presented to The Supreme Court included:

1) Is it unconstitutional for defense counsel to concede an accused's guilt over the accused's express objection?

2) Whether Louisiana's rule, that a prosecutor's strike of an African-American juror is irrelevant to the prosecutor's strikes of other African-American jurors if the defense simultaneously struck the same juror, violates this court's holding in Foster, Miller - El and Batson requiring consideration of all relevant circumstances.

Notice that question one is the only question that is actually relevant. And if you read the case in the law library you find that both the Supreme Court and the lawyers spend most of their time addressing question one.

In the opinion delivered by Justice Ginsburg, the Court said:

> "We granted certiorari in view of a division of opinion among state courts of last resort on the question whether it is unconstitutional to allow defense counsel to concede guilt over the defendant's intransigent and unambiguous objection. 582 U.S.____, 138 S. Ct. 53, 198 A. 2d 803, 842-846 (Del. 2009)(counsel's pursuit of a 'guilty but mentally ill' verdict over defendant's 'vociferous and repeated protestations' of innocence violated defendant's 'Constitutional right to make the fundamental decision regarding his case'); *State v. Carter*, 270 Kan. 426, 440, 14 P. 3d 1138, 1148 (2000)(counsel's admission of client's involvement in murder when client adamantly maintained his innocence contravened sixth amendment right to counsel and due process right to a fair trial)." *McCoy v. Louisiana*, 584 U.S., 138 S. Ct. , 200 L. Ed. 2d 821 (2018).

If you remember back to the beginning of 2019, you will remember a number of cases that were recalled to The Supreme Court involving A.C.C.A. claims. They were all recalled because of the political climate concerning the injustice that plagues the criminal justice system. One of those cases that went nearly unnoticed also involved the split between McCarthan in the Eleventh Circuit and Wheeler in the Fourth Circuit.

As an additional example of possible Supreme Court questions, these are the ones I presented in the Anderson case:

QUESTION PRESENTED

This petition presents two important issues concerning the proper interpretation of the Saving Clause, 28 U.S.C. §2255(e); and the appropriate application of the Armed Career Criminal Act, 18 U.S.C. §924(e) after this Court's decision in *Johnson v. United States*, 135 S. Ct. 2251 (2015).

Since this Court's decision, in *Johnson v. United States*, id., striking down the ACCA's residual clause as unconstitutionally vague. Circuit Courts of Appeals have issued published decisions on whether various state-controlled substance offenses qualify as predicate offenses to trigger 18 U.S.C. §924(e) enhancements. As a result of the differing conclusions these courts have reached, a direct conflict has emerged about whether state statutes are divisible and subject to categorical analysis, or are they broader than a never-existed federal common law. Thus*, Descamps v. United States*, 133 S.Ct. 2276 (2013); and *Mathis v. United States*, 136 S.Ct. 2243 (2016) have redefined which prior convictions qualify as predicate enhancement offenses.

In the ordinary case where someone has already filed for this first round of collateral relief this question would be raised in a request for second and successive authorization, see 28 U.S.C.§2244, and §2255. In the odd set of circumstances where an defendant has been found guilty of being a felon in possession of a firearm and then enhanced under the Armed Career Criminal Act he is authorized to seek relief in collateral review only when the law has been changed and The Supreme Court holds that relief should apply retroactively.

In Mr. Anderson's case he plead guilty and was enhanced under the ACCA. After he had filed for collateral relief this Court ruled in *Mathis v. United States*, 136 S.Ct. 2243 (2016). Mr. Anderson was denied second and successive authorization by the Eleventh Circuit, an order that is unappealable. Thus, Mr. Anderson's only recourse, for correcting a sentence found to be unconstitutional, is found in 28 U.S.C. §2241.

After Mr. Anderson was denied second and successive authorization and before he was able to articulate himself in petition for Habeas Corpus, the Eleventh Circuit issued its ruling *in McCarthan v. Director of Goodwill Industries – Suncoast, Inc.*, 851 F.3d 1076, (11th Cir. 2017) (*en banc*), effectively suspending the writ in the Eleventh Circuit.

On or about April 2, 2018, the Fourth Circuit Court of Appeals visited the very same issue – saving clause interpretation – as did the Eleventh Circuit, in *United States v. Wheeler*, ____F.3d___, 2018 WL 1514418 (4th Cir. 2018). The Fourth Circuit deciding that the Saving Clause is available – if sentencing was carried out in accordance with the law, the law was retroactively changed after direct appeal and first habeas petition, and the sentence presents an error grave enough to be deemed a fundamental defect- putting the Fourth Circuit at odds with the Eleventh Circuit which recently held that a change in circuit sentencing law didn't qualify for the saving clause. Thus, Mr. Anderson presents, for resolution, the questions that follows:

1) Has the Eleventh Circuit of appeals effectively suspended the writ of Habeas Corpus, without authorization, where the court has overruled its entire line of Saving Clause precedent to narrow the circumstances under which a federal prisoner can proceed under 28 U.S.C. § 2241?

2) Does the difference between the Fourth and Eleventh Circuit decisions concerning the Saving Clause interpretation call for the exercise of this Court's supervisory power to the end that it may secure uniformity in the court of appeals?

3) Has the Eleventh Circuit established a procedural framework, by reason of its operation, that made it highly unlikely in a typical case that a prisoner would have a meaningful opportunity to challenge a sentence, later determined to be unconstitutional?

4) Does 28 U.S.C. § 2241 provide relief from a sentence that this court has determined is unconstitutional in a decision subsequent to his being denied post-conviction relief?

CHAPTER SEVEN

PETITION CONSTRUCTION

As you can see, I don't use the forms provided by The Supreme Court. If you choose to follow my lead, which I do not recommend, you must follow the rules. Thus, I would suggest that you study the information provided in Chapter One. Read the guides provided to you at the end of Chapter One.

Not only should you glance over what is provided, but you should study the pertinent material while you are preparing each individual part of your petition. Individualize every step of your petition. While you are working on your questions, for example, give no consideration or thought to anything else.

By now, I trust you have read and/or studied Chapter One of this book and *Post-Conviction Relief: Advancing Your Claim*. Therefore, I will not be going into the finer elements of claims preparation. What I will be doing is providing a clear and concise list of elements you should provide to the clerk of The Supreme Court.

AUTHOR'S NOTE

In Chapter Five, I included a copy of a petition I recently filed in The Supreme Court. In that petition, you will discover that it does not include a section titled "Opinions Below." This was done on purpose. What I filed was a petition seeking a writ of mandamus rather than a writ of certiorari. A petition for a writ of mandamus is what is filed when a court refuses to provide its honest service. Thus depriving a litigant of an "opinion below."

Realizing that to have come this far in the post-conviction process, those who are preparing a petition for a writ of certiorari have filed a number of briefs, motions, and petitions in the past. But I assure you that you, just as I, don't know as much as we may believe. The biggest problem I have encountered, with most Pro Se litigants and a small number of professional lawyers, is what I refer to as "bad background." It is relatively simple and much like programming an old-style computer; if you put crap in, you will get crap out. Thus, if you trust what you believe to be true rather than follow the rules of The Supreme Court, you hurt your chances of relief rather than help them. Please, forget everything you think you know and follow the rules. Apply some critical word usage as you read and follow the steps that are set out, and please don't take my word for anything, check it out for yourself.

PETITION FIRST

When I prepared my petition, which you see in this book, I consulted the Rules of The Supreme Court the whole way. I started with Rule 10 to determine if the Court would consider my claim. My claim is that I am actually innocent; the Courts, both District and Appellate, outright denied me counsel, and they are now trying to stall the claims until my sentence has been served.

After reading Rule 10, I discovered that not only do I not qualify for review because I have no decision, but also because my case only affects my case. Therefore, it was time to reconsider my position. I am suffering harm because of what the courts are not doing. But, what is important is what does or does not give them the authority to stall my case for years on end, and do the same circumstances affect other cases beyond the facts and parties in my case.

When I discovered that my case represented a national issue, I began to seek out how the public viewed the particular problem. Don't misunderstand, most of the American public would draw a blank if you mentioned inordinate delay or mandamus. But, if you ask someone about Mass Incarceration, Tax dollars, or The First Step Act, then you get people's attention. I hope you can see the shift, which allowed me to frame questions that challenged an Act of Congress. Once I had questions that put the law square in the face of The Supreme Court, I started to draft my petition first.

Cover – Of course, you can use the format provided by The Supreme Court, which is identical to the one provided at the end of Chapter One, or you can type your own. The cover that you see on my own personal petition is specifically designed for an extraordinary writ under Rule 20 and will not work for a writ of certiorari. For seeking certiorari, your cover sheet must comply with Supreme Court Rule 34. Again, copy or use the cover provided by The Supreme Court of the United States.

Question Presented – This is where your petition begins. First, go back to Supreme Court Rule 14, and read along step by step. Rule 14.1(a) states in part that: "The question shall be set out on the first page following the cover. …" I want you to note the mandatory language, "shall …" and ."..following the cover. …" This does not mean on the back of the cover. Although the format of the petitions in this book may suggest otherwise, Petitions to the Supreme Court that are prepared on plain paper, under Rule 33.2, are recommended to be printed on one side only. Let me say this once again, your petition lives and dies in your questions. Remember provocative national issues, if your questions are not bigger than you and the facts of your case you are not likely to get review.

<h2 style="text-align:center">QUESTIONS PRESENTED</h2>

1) Did the panel of the Eleventh Circuit err by deciding the merit of an appeal not properly before the court to justify the denial of a certificate of appealability.

2) Has The Supreme Court of the United States overturned its own precedent in *Buck v. Davis*, 137 S.Ct. 759 (2017); *Trevino v. Thaler*, 133 S.Ct. 1911 (2013); and *Martinez v. Ryan*, 566 U.S. 1 (2012). Where this court decided that a procedural default would not bar a claim of ineffective assistance of trial counsel, when collateral proceeding was the first place to challenge a conviction on a ground of ineffective assistance.

3) Does the Supreme Court decision in *Buck v. Davis* violate the equal protection of law, where it allows a different standard of review for state prisoners as compared to federal prisoners who are similarly situated.

List of Parties – Rule 12.6 sets out that "All parties to the proceeding in the court... are deemed parties. …" This does not include the court. People often get mislead on this issue because the petition for the writ is to a particular court. Again I would use the form provided by The Supreme Court which is identical to what you find in Chapter One. If you are truly filing for certiorari concerning a certificate of appealability your parties are listed on the cover you just finished. Thus, "All parties appear in the caption of the case on the cover page."

<h2 style="text-align:center">AUTHOR'S NOTE</h2>

Please notice that you cannot complete a table of contents until you finish the writ, list the items in your appendix, and number the pages. Don't panic, you can come back to this step of the process. When you do, remember that the most often overlooked part of the table of contents is the index of appendices. This part is important, so don't forget it.

Table of Authorities – The table of authorities is nothing more than a list of the laws, the rules, the cases, and any other authorities you might have relied on for guidance. This table is probably the second most important element of your petition during the initial review. Once a clerk opens the cover of your petition and finds compelling questions, he or she is going to your list of authorities next. That clerk is going to want to know what decisions and laws are going to be called into question and what assumptions the public can make based on the court's decision to entertain the case. Therefore, use the courts pre-printed form for guidance.

Remember to start with your cases first listed in alphabetical order; you can view the table in Chapter Five for guidance. You should wait to prepare this table until after you have prepared your petition, as well.

Petition for a Writ of Certiorari – Notice that neither the instructions from the Supreme Court, found in Chapter One, or The Rules of The Supreme Court, Rule 14.1, include this element as required. Make no mistake, this element is required.

AUTHOR'S NOTE

It is my personal belief that this element has been left out on purpose. Lawyers already know that all motions and petitions require the requesting party to make his desires known to the court. For those required to proceed in Pro Se, a form is provided for you. If you look at the top of page one of the form provided, it has the request for certiorari printed above the "Opinions Below" preprinted for you.

Let me say again that anyone who can afford competent counsel should be represented. I do not recommend that anyone represent themselves in court, especially a layman of law in The Supreme Court of the United States. That said, the remainder of this chapter is for guidance for those of us who have no other choice. As I indicated in Chapter Five, I was deprived of judgment and, therefore, not authorized to seek a petition for certiorari. Therefore, the examples that follow have not been filed in any court and serve only as a model for those of you who are not using the court's pre-printed form. Here is an example:

PETITION FOR WRIT OF CERTIORARI

Petitioner Kelly Patrick Riggs respectfully requests that the court grant a writ of certiorari. He seeks a review of the decision of the Eleventh Circuit Court of Appeals denying his motion for a certificate of appealability.

Mr. Riggs is the movant and the movant-appellant in the courts below. The respondent is the United States, the plaintiff, and plaintiff-appellee in the courts below."

Opinions Below – As you can see, many of the elements that make up the petition are relatively short. Even when typing in ten pitch, double space, and maintaining a minimum one-inch margin from all sides of the paper, the elements take up little space on a page. Therefore, if you are typing your petition on plain typing paper, follow my lead and type more than one element per page, starting on page one of the "PETITION FOR WRIT OF CERTIORARI. The Supreme Court, like all others, appreciates the economy. The Opinions Below section provides guidance as to what decision you want revised; thus, only a short description is required. Example:

OPINIONS BELOW

The opinion of the Eleventh Circuit of the Court of Appeals, denying Mr. Riggs's motion for a certificate of appealability, was recorded in a digest unknown to Mr. Riggs (2019). A copy of the panel's judgment is made a part of the appendix on App-1.

Jurisdiction – The reason this section is required in a petition is because the court needs information. It's not because the clerks don't know the extent of the court's authority but because they don't know the posture of your particular case. This becomes especially important because the rules of the court set a firm time limitation. Thus, if the petition is late, the Supreme Court is divested of its jurisdiction. Additionally, you cannot use the jurisdictional statement from Chapter Five in a petition for a writ of certiorari. If you are using the form provided by the court, you need only to fill in the blanks. For those of you who are typing your own, here is an example:

JURISDICTIONAL STATEMENT

Mr. Riggs invokes this court's jurisdiction to grant the petition for a writ of certiorari to the Eleventh Circuit of the United States Court of Appeals on the basis of 28 U.S.C. §1254(1). The court of appeals denied Mr. Riggs motion for the issuance of a certificate of appealability on February 20, 2019. Mr. Riggs did not file for a rehearing in the court of appeals. This petition is timely filed in accordance with the Rules of The Supreme Court, Rule 13.1."

Relevant Constitutional and Statutory Provisions – I'm sure by now, you have discovered how dry the court rules and its guide are on this subject.

This should be more than just a list of the laws and rules involved in your case. This should be a list of laws, rights, rules, and other authorities that are implicated by the questions that you have presented. If you remember the suggestions for question development in Chapter Six, you will remember that it was suggested that you challenge the Constitutionality of a statute, etc. This is the place where you provide a reading of the statutes involved. Example:

RELEVANT CONSTITUTIONAL AND STATUTORY PROVISIONS

The questions presented implicate the following provisions of the Constitution of the United States and the United States Code.

THE FIFTH AMENDMENT: No person shall be held to answer for a Capital or otherwise infamous crime unless on a presentment or indictment of a Grand Jury, except in cases arising in the land or naval forces or in the Militia, when in actual service in time of War or public danger; nor shall any person be subject for the same offense to be twice put in jeopardy of life or limb; nor shall be compelled in any criminal case to be a witness against himself, nor be deprived of life, liberty, or property, without due process of law; nor shall private property be taken for public use, without just compensation.

28 U.S.C. §2253(c)(1)(B): "Unless a circuit justice or judge issues a certificate of appealability, an appeal may not be taken to the court of appeals from... the final order in a proceeding under Section 2255."

28 U.S.C. §2255(a): "A prisoner in custody under sentence of a court established by Act of Congress claiming the right to be released upon the ground that the sentence was imposed in violation of the Constitution or laws of the United States, or that the court was without jurisdiction to impose such sentence, or that the sentence was in excess of the maximum authorized by law, or is otherwise subject to collateral attack, may move the court which imposed the sentence to vacate, set aside or correct the sentence."

Statement of the Case – This is a good time to remember that you want something from the court, as opposed to them wanting something from you. I can't stress to you enough how important it is to give them all the information they need to review your case. If you read Rule 14.1(g) of The Supreme Court rules, you find a detailed description of what they require. In Chapter Five, you find an example of this element in my own petition, which, of course, gives some guidance as to how yours should look. What I think is most important about this element is the reality check that it provides to you, the petitioner.

Again, your chances of review are hanging on the national impact of deciding your case. Obviously, if the clerk is reading your "Statement of the Case," you have presented some good questions. But now, you must present facts and material to the consideration of the questions you presented. Your "Statement of the Case" must also specify each stage in the proceedings at which your questions for review were raised. In a case for a certificate of appealability to the court of appeals, you should also set out the method in which you raised the claim, i.e., "Motion for Issuance of a Certificate of Appealability," and the way the court decided your request.

Your "Statement of the Case" represents two situations in which The Supreme Court commonly rejects petitions for writs of certiorari. The first, of course, is where the certiorari petition fails to include material facts.

The second is where the "Statement of Facts" fails to present the facts in a concise manner.

The reason for being concise is clarity. The most common failure to be clear in a "Statement of the Case" is argument. Yes, many people start to argue in the "Statement of the Case" that this is a major mistake. The clerk's review, upon which they base their memorandum, should be easy and quick.

Give them compelling questions, current supporting citations, and above all, a clear and concise "Statement of the Case." I wish I could provide you with an all-encompassing "Statement of the Case" for you to use. But that just isn't possible; this is all about you. your case and your facts that support your questions.

Reasons to Grant the Writ – My explanation here is in addition to the instruction provided in Chapter One. Simply put, this is where you explain that deciding your case will resolve a national problem that will affect many cases that are pending or that will follow. Another issue that I find interesting is that Rule 14, of The Supreme Court rules, makes no mention of a section titled "Reasons to Grant the Writ." You will find that Rule 14.1(h) states, "A direct and concise argument amplifying the reasons relied on for allowance of the writ, see Rule 10." Therefore, I follow the lead of a large number of professionals who practice law before The Supreme Court regularly. I do this by being concise even in the title of this section. I provide the court with my "REASONS TO GRANT THE WRIT."

Getting past the title, the next and most important aspect is to provide an explanation to the court. I, following the lead of many professional lawyers, start out by addressing the questions that I presented to the court. Remember, the first thing in the petition you presented was your questions. Thus, the most important thing you can do is address the questions that got you this far. Notice in the example that follows that I provide a section for each question. I first repeat my question verbatim. I do this so my reader is not forced to flip back to the front of the petition to refresh his or her memory. The very next thing I do is provide the holdings of the court of appeals so my reader is not forced to search it out in the appendix. You will find that I believe in making this an easy and pleasant experience for my reader, and you should adopt this practice as well. My next step is my discussion, where I provide my argument in a concise manner. Whenever possible, I present why the lower court is wrong or in conflict with another court. I express issues that The Supreme Court has not yet determined, and finally, I give the court the answer that I believe to be a correct resolution for my question.

REASONS TO GRANT THE WRIT

I. **[Question One] Did the panel of the Eleventh Circuit err by deciding the merit of an appeal not properly before the court to justify the denial of a certificate of appealability?**

> A. The panel improperly sidestepped the C.O.A. process by denying relief based on its view of the merits.

In reviewing the facts and circumstances of Mr. Riggs's case, the Eleventh Circuit panel "paid lip service to the principles guiding issuance of a C.O.A." *Tennard v. Dretke*, 542 U.S. 274, 283 (2004), but in actuality, the panel held Mr. Riggs to a far more stringent standard. Specifically, the Eleventh Circuit panel "sidestepped the threshold C.O.A. process by first deciding the merits of [Mr. Riggs'] appeal, and then justifying its denial of a C.O.A. based on its adjudication of the actual merits, thereby "in essence deciding an appeal without jurisdiction." *Miller-El v. Cockerll*, 537 U.S. 322 at 336-37 (2003).

As the Supreme Court held on Miller-El, the threshold nature of the C.O.A. inquiry "would mean very little if appellate review were denied because the prisoner did not convince a judge, or, for that matter, three judges, that he or she would prevail." Miller-El, 537 U.S. 322 at 337. In Mr. Riggs's case however, that is exactly what the panel did.

Mr. Riggs filed a motion in the Eleventh Circuit seeking a certificate of appealability, so that he may appeal the district court's denial of his §2255 motion. The panel however, determined that Mr. Riggs's many appointed lawyers had, indeed, provided effective assistance because they were bar members in good standing. Thus, the panel concluded that Mr. Riggs should be denied a certificate of appealability because the appeal was obviously meritless.

The panel impermissibly sidestepped the C.O.A. inquiry in this manner by denying relief because the subsequent appeal would be meritless. The panels assessment of the merits is patently wrong. The panel could not possibly resolve the merits of the appeal based solely on a motion seeking a certificate of appealability. Moreover, without the issuance of a C.O.A. and the district court's record before the panel, the panel was without jurisdiction to determine the merits of the appeal.

II.   **[Question Two] Has the Supreme Court of the United States overturned its own precedent in** *Buck v. Davis*, **137 S.Ct. 759 (2017);** *Trevino v. Thaler*, **133 S.Ct. 1911 (2013); and** *Martinez v. Ryan*, **566 U.S. 1 (2012). Where this court decided that a procedural default would not bar a claim of ineffective assistance of trial counsel; when collateral proceeding was the first place to challenge a conviction on ground of ineffective assistance.**

A.   The Eleventh Circuit of the Court of Appeals held that "Mr. Riggs was procedurally barred from raising ineffective assistance of counsel claims in his §2255 because he unsuccessfully raised the claims in direct appeal."

The Supreme Court held that a §2255 "collateral challenge may not do service for an appeal." *United States v. Frady*, 456 U.S., at 165.

In the Eleventh Circuit's de novo review, the court found that Mr. Riggs was barred by procedure because he unsuccessfully raised a claim of ineffective assistance of counsel in his direct appeal. The claim was raised in a supplemental brief filed in Pro Se after appointed counsel Brett M. Bloomston abandoned Mr. Riggs in his direct appeal. The panel, however, disregarded what The Supreme Court said in Buck, "Martinez, 566 U.S., at 9, 132 S.Ct. 1309, 182 L.Ed. 2d 272. We held that when a state formally limits the adjudication of claims of ineffective assistance of trial counsel to collateral review, a prisoner may establish cause for procedural default if (1) 'The State courts did not appoint counsel in the initial-review collateral proceeding,' or 'appointed counsel in [that] proceeding... was ineffective under the standards of *Strickland v. Washington*, 466 U.S. 668, 104 S.Ct. 2052, 80 L.Ed. 2d 674 (1984); and (2) 'the underlying... claim is a substantial one, which is to say that... the claim has some merit." Id., at 14, 132 S.Ct. 1309, 182 L.Ed. 2d 272."

The merit in Mr. Riggs's §2255 is self-evident. He made the district court aware of a conflict of interest, between he and his counsel; the court declined to appoint unconflicted counsel, forcing Mr. Riggs to represent himself at three critical stages of the criminal proceeding; the court failed to inquire into the conflict of interest; and Brett M. Bloomston was ineffective as trial and appellate counsel for failing to present the evidence, of conflict, that is obvious in the courts record.

B. The Supreme Court has not yet addressed the issue of whether the lack of counsel at the initial review collateral proceeding can qualify as cause for procedural default, in the case of a federal prisoner, concerning claims of ineffective assistance of counsel.

Under the procedural default doctrine, if a state prisoner "defaulted his federal claims in state court pursuant to an independent and adequate state procedural rule, federal habeas review of the claim is barred unless the prisoner can demonstrate cause for the default and actual prejudice as a result of the alleged violation of federal law …" *Coleman v. Thompson*, 501 U.S. 722, 750, 111 S.Ct. 2546, 115 L.Ed. 2d 640 (1991). In general, lack of an attorney and attorney error in state post-conviction proceedings do not establish cause to excuse a procedural default. Id. at 757, 111 S.Ct. at 2568.

In *Martinez*, The Supreme court announced a narrow, equitable, and non- Constitutional exception to *Coleman's* holding (that ineffective assistance of collateral counsel cannot serve as cause to excuse a procedural default) in the limited circumstances where (1) a state requires a prisoner to raise ineffective-trial-counsel claims at an initial-review collateral proceeding; (2) the prisoner failed properly to raise ineffective-trial-counsel claims in his state initial-review collateral proceedings; (3) the prisoner did not have collateral counsel or his counsel was ineffective; and (4) failing to excuse the prisoner's procedural default would cause the prisoner to lose a "substantial" ineffective-trial-counsel claim. In such a case, The Supreme Court explained that there may be "cause" to excuse the procedural default of the ineffective-trial-counsel claim. Martinez, 132 S.Ct., at 1319. Subsequently, The Supreme Court extended Martinez's rule to cases where state law technically permits ineffective-trial-counsel claims on direct appeal but state procedures make it "virtually impossible" to actually raise ineffective-trial-counsel claims on direct appeal, see Trevino, 133 S.Ct., at 1915, 1918-21.

There can be no question whether the federal criminal court system requires that ineffective assistance of counsel claims should be brought in collateral proceedings and not on direct appeal. Such claims brought on direct appeal are presumptively dismissible, and virtually all will be dismissed. The reasons for this rule are self-evident. A factual record must be developed and addressed by the district court in the first instance for effective review. Even if evidence is not necessary, at the very least counsel accused of deficient performance can explain their reasonings and actions, and the district court can render its opinion on the merits of the claim. An opinion by a district court is a valuable aid to appellate review for many reasons, not the least of which is that in most cases, the district court is familiar with the proceeding and has observed the counsel's performance, in context, firsthand. Thus, even if the record appears to need no further development; the claim will still be presented first to the district court in collateral proceedings, which should be instituted without delay, so the reviewing court can have the benefit of the district court's views. Therefore, the statutory right to appeal, which is a part of today's due process in the federal system, has been reduced to a right that no longer includes a right to appeal from Sixth Amendment I.A.C. claims.

Indigent defendants pursuing first-tier review in a §2255 proceeding are generally ill-equipped to represent themselves, for (a) a first-tier review application, forced to act in Pro Se, would face a record unreviewed by appellate counsel; and ((b) without guides keyed to a court of review. A Pro Se movant's entitlement to seek relief from ineffective assistance of trial counsel might be more a formality than a right, because navigating the criminal, appeal, and collateral process without a lawyer's assistance is a perilous endeavor for a layperson, and well beyond the competence of individuals afforded only twelve months to learn the federal process involved. Moreover, due process requires the appointment of counsel for federal defendants on direct appeal. In the average case however, the most common claim of Constitutional error is ineffective assistance of counsel. In Mr. Riggs's case it is the Eleventh Circuit, and not the United States Congress, that elected to change the reach of the United States law that granted a defendant the right to appeal his sentence when the sentence was in violation of the law, see 18 U.S.C. §3006A.

III.   **[Question Three] Does the Supreme Court decision in *Buck v. Davis* violate the equal protection of law, where it allows a different standard of review for state prisoners as compared to federal prisoners who are similarly situated.**

The Eleventh Circuit of the United States Court of Appeals failed to consider the construction of the federal review process as it is compared to the state process identified in *Martinez, Trevino, and Buck.*

Mr. Riggs claims that it is because he had no counsel during the claim preparation period in his collateral (§2255) proceeding that serves as cause for procedural default. Although he did make a claim of ineffective assistance of counsel in his §2255, the claim was weak and poorly presented because he was forced, by procedure, to rely on a jail-house-lawyer to draft his claim. Thus, it is the lack of counsel (or the ineffectiveness of §2255 counsel) that caused Mr. Riggs's claim of ineffective trial counsel to fail.

Mr. Riggs's claim is beyond the reach of direct appeal because of the federal procedure. His claim is also nearly impossible, for a layperson, to raise in a collateral proceeding where he has no right to counsel and must face a more stringent standard of review. Congress had not intended, in 1948, that a defendant be required to await the first round of collateral proceedings to raise a Constitutional error where counsel was unavailable to indigent prisoners. It is unreasonable to believe that the American Criminal Justice System would require a criminal defendant to rely, on a layperson-at-law to perfect a federal criminal appeal. This however, is exactly what the procedure requires when making the Constitutional claim that a federal defendant is deprived of the effective assistance of trial counsel.

The Supreme Court in *Martinez* held that the procedural default that occurred when *Martinez's* post-conviction counsel did not raise a claim of ineffective assistance of counsel in his state collateral proceeding would not bar his petition under 28 U.S.C. §2254, where "the state collateral proceeding was the first place to challenge his conviction on grounds of ineffective assistance." 132 S.Ct., at 1313. The Supreme Court explained that "if in the [State's] initial-review collateral proceeding, there was no counsel or counsel in that proceeding was ineffective," procedural default would not "bar a federal habeas court from hearing a substantial claim of ineffective assistance at trial." Id., at 1320 (emphasis added). In Martinez, state law required the petitioner to wait until the initial review collateral proceeding before raising such a claim. A year later, in Trevino, the Supreme Court extended Martinez's holding to cases in which the state did not require defendants to wait until the post-conviction stage, but rather to "[t]he structure and design of the [state] system in actual operation...[made] it virtually impossible for an ineffective assistance claim to be presented on direct review." 133 S.Ct, at 1915. The question is whether these holdings apply to some or all federal prisoners who bring motions for post-conviction relief under 28 U.S.C. §2255. The Seventh Circuit has already answered this question in the affirmative. In *Choice Hotels Intern., Inc. v. Grover, 792 F.*3d. 753 (7th Cir., 2015), where the panel wrote that "[a]lthough *Maples* and *Holland* [*v. Florida*, 560 U.S. 631.] were capital cases, we do not doubt that their holdings apply to all collateral litigations under 28 U.S.C. §2254 and §2255." Id., at 755 (citations omitted). A closer look at the issue should convince us that the Seventh Circuit's position is correct.

In *Massaro v. United States*, 538 U.S. 500, 123 S. Ct. 1690, 155 L. Ed. 2d 714 (2003), the Supreme Court considered the case of a man who did not raise any claim relating to the ineffectiveness of trial counsel on his direct appeal and so was trying to raise such an argument in a motion under 28 U.S.C. §2255. The United States argued that the ineffectiveness claim was procedurally defaulted because *Massaro* could have raised it on direct appeal. The Supreme court however, rejected that position and held instead that there is no procedural default for failure to raise an ineffective-assistance claim on direct appeal, even if new counsel handles the direct appeal and even if the basis for the claim is apparent from the trial record. Id., at 503-04. Indeed, the court criticized the practice of bringing these claims on direct appeal because "the issue would be raised for the first time in a forum not best suited to assess those facts." Id., at 504. All appeals courts have been critical of the practice of trying to raise claims of ineffective assistance of counsel on direct appeal, where the appointment of counsel is a statutory guarantee.

Because the federal courts have no established procedure to develop ineffective assistance claims for direct appeal, the situation of a federal petitioner is the same as the one this court described in Trevino. As a practical matter, the first opportunity to present a claim of ineffective assistance of trial or direct appellate counsel is almost always on collateral review in a motion under 28 U.S.C. §2255. Although there may be rare exceptions, as *Massaro* acknowledged, for a case in which trial counsel's ineffectiveness "is so apparent from the record" that it can be raised on direct appeal; Mr. Riggs's case is not one of those.

Neither Martinez nor Trevino suggested that, for these purposes, the difference between §2254 and §2255 was material. What does matter is the way in which ineffective assistance of counsel claims must be presented in the particular procedural system. This varies among the states and between the states and the federal system, but Mr. Riggs has already explained why, in the great majority of federal cases, ineffectiveness claims must await the first round of collateral review. Moreover, if the review were to be more restricted on either the state or the federal side, federalism concerns suggest that it would be the state side. Most of the rules that govern petitions under section 2254 are mirrored in section 2255, including, importantly, the procedure for handling second or successive petitions.

Mr. Riggs can think of no reason why Martinez, Trevino, and Buck should be read in a way that would provide different results between federal and state proceedings. The Supreme Court should intervene now to correct an egregious misapplication of settled law in an area of great public concern.

Conclusion – This section of the petition is a necessary formality. It is almost so simple that it could be left out if it were not required by the rules. If you review the examples in Chapters One and Five, you will discover that this element is very simple.

CONCLUSION

Mr. Riggs respectfully pleads that this court grant his petition for a writ of certiorari and permit briefing and argument on the issues contained herein.

CHAPTER EIGHT

HEAD START

You have ninety (90) days to complete the race that can change the rest of your life and the liberty to live it. Therefore, any head start you get is a step in the right direction. I have found that the most burdensome obstacle is that of research. Usually, a prisoner is first tasked with learning how to use a law library, learning the laws and the procedures, and then learning the controlling precedent. This book has been all about giving you a head start. It has provided the rules of the Supreme Court, the laws associated with its procedure, and now the precedent that controls the right to the issuance of a certificate of appealability.

This chapter lists the outcome and the court's position concerning the issuance of the certificate of appealability. I strongly suggest that you read these case summaries. You may very well find the issue that will win you the review you seek. Please also remember that the federal criminal justice system is a system of dollars and cents. Thus, to continue the flow of tax dollars, it only makes sense to keep you in prison as long as possible. Sometimes, just as I have learned, you must exemplify the court's conduct in the view of the public. When the voters see the corruption practiced in federal courts, then you will see them scatter like roaches. Just as the parasites they truly are. Now, on to eight very good examples:

THARPE v. SELLERS

138 S.Ct. 545
JANUARY 8, 2018

OPINION

Petitioner Keith Tharpe moved to reopen his federal habeas corpus proceedings regarding his claim that the Georgia jury that convicted him of murder included a white juror, Barney Gattie, who was biased against Tharpe because he is black, see Fed. Rule Civ. Proc. 60(b)(6). The District Court denied the motion on the ground that, among other things, Tharpe's claim was procedurally defaulted in state court. The District Court also noted that Tharpe could not overcome that procedural default because he had failed to produce any clear and convincing evidence contradicting the state court's determination at Gattie's presence on the jury did not prejudice him, see *Tharpe v. Warden*, No. 5:10-cv-433, 2017 U.S. Dist. LEXIS 161934 (MD Ga., Sept. 5, 2017).

Tharpe sought a certificate of appealability (COA). The Eleventh Circuit denied his COA application after deciding that jurists of reason could not dispute that the District Court's procedural ruling was correct, see *Tharpe v. Warden*, 2017 U.S. App. LEXIS 18735, 2017 WL 4250413, *3 (Sept. 21, 2017), The Eleventh Circuit's decision, as we read it, was based solely on its conclusion, rooted in the state court's factfinding, that Tharpe had failed to show prejudice in connection with his procedurally defaulted claim, i.e., that Tharpe had "failed to demonstrate that Barney Gattie's behavior had substantial and injurious effect of influence in determining the jury's verdict. "Ibid, (quoting *Brecht v. Abrahamson*, 507 U.S. 619, 113 S. Ct. 1710, 123 L. Ed. 2d 353 (1993)).

Our review of the record compels a different conclusion. The state court's prejudice determination rested on its finding that Gattie's vote to impose the death penalty was not based on Tharpe's race, see *Tharpe v. Warden,* no. 93-CV-144 (Super. Ct. Butts City., Ga., Dec. 1, 2008), App. F to Pet. for Cert. 102. And that factual determination is binding on federal courts, including this Court, in the absence of clear and convincing evidence to the contrary, see 28 U.S.C. §2254(e)(l). Here, however, Tharpe produced a sworn affidavit, signed by Gattie, indicating Gattie's view that "there are two types of black people: 1. Black folks and 2. Niggers"; that Tharpe, "who wasn't in the 'good' black folks category in my book, should get the electric chair for what he did"; that "Is why some of the jurors voted for death because they felt Tharpe should be an example to other blacks who kill blacks, but that wasn't my reason"; and that, "[after studying the Bible, I have wondered if black people even have souls." App. B to pet. for Cert. 15-16 (internal quotation marks omitted). Gattie's remarkable affidavit-which he never retracted- presents a strong factual basis for the argument that Tharpe's race affected Gattie's vote for a death verdict. At the very least, jurists of reason could debate whether Tharpe has shown by clear and convincing evidence that the state court's factual determination was wrong. The Eleventh Circuit erred when it concluded otherwise.

The question of prejudice-the ground on which the Eleventh Circuit chose to dispose of Tharpe's application-is not the only question relevant to the broader inquiry whether Tharpe should receive a COA. The District Court denied Tharpe's Rule 60(b) motion on several grounds not addressed by the Eleventh Circuit. We express no view of those issues here. In light of the standard for relief from judgment under Rule 60(b)(6), which is available only in '"extraordinary circumstances,' "*Gonzalez v. Crosby*, 545 U.S. 524, 536, 125 S. Ct. 2641, 162 L. Ed. 2d 480 (2005), Tharpe faces a high bar in showing that jurists of reason could disagree whether the District court abused its discretion in denying his motion. It may be that, at the end of the day, Tharpe should not receive a COA. And review of the denial of a COA is certainly not limited to grounds expressly addressed by the court whose decision is under review. But on the unusual facts of this case, the Court of Appeals' review should not have rested on the ground that it was indisputable among reasonable jurists that Gattie's service on the jury did not prejudice Tharpe.

We therefore grant Tharpe's motion to proceed *in forma pauperis*, grant the petition for certiorari, vacate the judgment of the Court of Appeals, and remand the case for further consideration of the question whether Tharpe is entitled to a COA.

It is so ordered.

LEE v. UNITED STATES
137 S. Ct. 1958
June 23, 2017

CASE SUMMARY: There was a reasonable probability that, but for counsel's erroneous advice, defendant would have rejected a guilty plea where the circumstances showed deportation was the determinative issue in his decision to accept the plea, and it was not irrational to reject the plea deal when there was some chance of avoiding deportation, however remote.

OVERVIEW: HOLDINGS: [l]-Defendant had adequately demonstrated a reasonable probability that, but for counsel's erroneous advice, he would have rejected a guilty plea where his plea colloquy and surrounding circumstances showed deportation was the determinative issue in his decision to accept the plea, and it was not irrational to reject the plea deal when there was some chance of avoiding deportation, however remote.

OUTCOME: Judgment reversed; case remanded. 6-2 Decision; 1 dissent.

SYLLABUS

Petitioner Jae Lee moved to the United States from South Korea with his parents when he was 13. In the 35 years he has spent in this country, he has never returned to South Korea, nor has he become a U.S. citizen, living instead as a lawful permanent resident. In 2008, federal officials received a tip from a confidential informant that Lee had sold the informant ecstasy and marijuana. After obtaining a warrant, the officials searched Lee's house, where they found drugs, cash, and a loaded rifle. Lee admitted that the drugs were his, and a grand jury indicted him on one count of possessing ecstasy with intent to distribute. Lee retained counsel and entered into plea discussions with the Government. During the plea process, Lee repeatedly asked his attorney whether he would face deportation; his attorney assured him that he would not be deported as a result of pleading guilty. Based on that assurance, Lee accepted a plea and was sentenced to a year and a day in prison. Lee had in fact pleaded guilty to an "aggravated felony" under the Immigration and Nationality Act, 8 U.S.C. §1101(a)(43)(B), so he was, contrary to his attorney's advice, subject to mandatory deportation as a result of that plea, see §1227(a)(2)(A)(iii). When Lee learned of this consequence, he filed a motion to vacate his conviction and sentence, arguing that his attorney had provided constitutionally ineffective assistance. At an evidentiary hearing, both Lee and his plea-stage counsel testified that "deportation was the determinative issue" to Lee in deciding whether to accept a plea, and Lee's counsel acknowledged that although Lee's defense to the charge was weak if he had known Lee would be deported upon pleading guilty, he would have advised him to go to trial. A Magistrate Judge recommended that Lee's plea be set aside and his conviction vacated. The District Court, however, denied relief, and the Sixth Circuit affirmed. Applying the two-part test for ineffective assistance claims from *Strickland v. Washington*, 466 U.S. 668, 104 S. Ct. 2052, 80 L. Ed. 2d 674, the Sixth Circuit concluded that, while the Government conceded that Lee's counsel had performed deficiently, Lee could not show that he was prejudiced by his attorney's erroneous advice.

HELD: Lee has demonstrated that he was prejudiced by his counsel's erroneous advice. Pp. 5-13.

a) When a defendant claims that his counsel's deficient performance deprived him of a trial by causing him to accept a plea, the defendant can show prejudice by demonstrating a "reasonable probability that, but for counsel's errors, he would not have pleaded guilty and would have insisted on going to trial." *Hill v. Lockhart*, 474 U.S. 52, 59, 106 S. Ct. 366, 88 L. Ed. 2d 203.

Lee contends that he can make this showing because he never would have accepted a guilty plea had he known the result would be deportation. The Government contends that Lee cannot show prejudice by accepting a plea where his only hope at trial was that something unexpected and unpredictable might occur that would lead to acquittal. Pp. 5-8.

b) The Government makes two errors in urging the adoption of a per se rule that a defendant with no viable defense cannot show prejudice from the denial of his right to trial. First, it forgets that categorical rules are ill-suited to an inquiry that demands a "case-by-case examination" of the "totality of the evidence." *Williams v. Taylor*, 529 U.S. 362, 391, 120 S. Ct. 1495, 146 L. Ed. 2d 389 (internal quotation marks omitted); Strickland, 466 U.S., at 695, 104 S. Ct. 2052, 80 L. Ed. 2d 674. More fundamentally, it overlooks that the *Hill v. Lockhart* inquiry focuses on a defendant's decision-making, which may not turn solely on the likelihood of conviction after trial.

The Decision whether to plead guilty also involves assessing the respective consequences of a conviction after trial and by plea, see *INS v. St. Cyr*, 533 U.S. 289, 322-323, 121 S. Ct. 2271, 150 L. Ed. 2d 347. When those consequences are, from the defendant's perspective, similarly dire, even the smallest chance of success at trial may look attractive. For Lee, deportation after some time in prison was not meaningfully different from deportation after somewhat less time; he says he accordingly would have rejected any plea leading to deportation in favor of throwing a "Hail Mary" at trial. Pointing to Strickland, the Government urges that "[a] defendant has no entitlement to the luck of a lawless decisionmaker." 466 U.S., at 695, 104 S. Ct. 2052, 80 L. Ed. 2d 674. That statement, however, was made in the context of discussing the presumption of reliability applied to judicial proceedings, which has no place where, as here, a defendant was deprived of a proceeding altogether. When the inquiry is focused on what an individual defendant would have done, the possibility of even a highly improbable result may be pertinent to the extent it would have affected the defendant's decision-making. Pp. 8-10.

c) Courts should not upset a plea solely because of post hoc assertions from a defendant about how he would have pleaded but for his attorney's deficiencies. Rather, they should look to contemporaneous evidence to substantiate a defendant's expressed preferences. In the unusual circumstances of this case, Lee has adequately demonstrated a reasonable probability that he would have rejected the plea had he known that it would lead to mandatory deportation: Both Lee and his attorney testified that "deportation was the determinative issue" to Lee; his responses during his plea colloquy confirmed the importance he placed on deportation; and he had strong connections to the United States, while he had no ties to South Korea.

The government argues that Lee cannot "convince the court that a decision to reject the plea bargain would have been rational under the circumstances" *Padilla v. Kentucky*, 559 U.S. 356, 372, 130 S. Ct. 1473, 176 L. Ed. 2d 284, since deportation would almost certainly result from a trial. Unlike the Government, this Court cannot say that it would be irrational for someone in Lee's position to risk additional prison time in exchange for holding on to some chance of avoiding deportation. Pp. 10-13.

825 F. 3d 311, reversed and remanded.

BUCK v. DAVIS
137 S. Ct. 759
February 22, 2017

DECISION: Where Federal Court of Appeals denied certificate of appealability (COA) for review of claim of ineffective assistance of trial counsel, (1) Court of Appeals exceeded scope of COA analysis; (2) accused demonstrated ineffective assistance; and (3) Federal District court abused discretion by denying motion for relief under Rule 60(b)(6) of Federal Rules of Civil Procedure.

CASE SUMMARY: It was error to deny a prisoner a COA to pursue his Sixth Amendment claims on appeal where he demonstrated ineffective assistance when his attorney called an expert who testified about a connection between his race and the likelihood of violence, and that error entitled him to relief under Fed. R. Civ. P. 60(b)(6).

OVERVIEW: HOLDINGS: (1) – Because a reviewing court inverted the statutory order of operations by deciding the merits of an appeal and then denying the COA based on adjudication of the actual merits, it placed too heavy a burden on the prisoner at the COA stage; (2) – For Sixth Amendment purposes, the prisoner demonstrated prejudice during the sentencing phase where his attorney called an expert who testified about a connection between his race and the likelihood of violence and it was reasonably probable that the death sentence would not have been imposed otherwise; (3) – Denying a Fed. R. Civ. P. 60(b)(6) motion was error where it was clear that the prisoner may have been sentenced to death due to his race, the State had admitted that sentencing based on race considerations was error in other cases, and it was inappropriate to consider race no matter how it was injected into the proceeding.

OUTCOME: Judgement reversed; case remanded. 6-2 Decision; 1 Dissent.

HELD:

1. The Fifth Circuit exceeded the limited scope of the COA analysis. The COA statute sets forth a two-step process: an initial determination whether a claim is reasonably debatable, and, if so, an appeal in the normal course. 28 U.S.C. §2253. At the first stage, the only question is whether the applicant has shown that "jurists of reason could disagree with the district court's resolution of his constitutional claims or— could conclude the issues presented are adequate to deserve encouragement to proceed further." *Miller-El v. Cockrell*, 537 U.S. 322, 327, 123 S. Ct. 1029, 154 L. Ed. 2d 931. Here, the Fifth Circuit phrased its determination in proper terms. But it reached its conclusion only after essentially deciding the circumstances. The question for the Court of Appeals was not whether Buck had shown that his case is extraordinary; it was whether jurists of reason could debate that issue. The State points to the Fifth Circuit's thorough

consideration of the merits to defend that court's approach, but this hurts rather than helps its case.

Pp.___-___197 L. Ed. 2d, at 16-18.

2. Buck has demonstrated ineffective assistance of counsel under Strickland.

Pp.-   197 L. Ed. 2d, at 18-20.

(a) To satisfy Strickland, a defendant must first show that counsel performed deficiently. 466 U.S., at 687, 104 S. Ct. 2052, 80 L. Ed. 2d 674. Buck's trial counsel knew that Dr. Quijano's report reflected the view that Buck's race predisposed him to violent conduct and that the principal point of dispute during the penalty phase was Buck's future dangerousness. Counsel nevertheless called Dr. Quijano to the stand, specifically elicited testimony about the connection between race and violence, and put Dr. Quijano's report into evidence. No competent defense attorney would introduce evidence that his client is liable to be a future danger because of his race. Pp. ____ - ___197 L. Ed. 2d, at 18-19.

(b) Strickland further requires a defendant to demonstrate prejudice—"a reasonable probability that, but for counsel's unprofessional errors, the result of the proceeding would have been different. 466 U.S., at 694, 104 S. Ct. 2052, 80 L. Ed. 674. It is reasonably probable that without Dr. Quijano's testimony on race and violence, at least one juror would have harbored a reasonable doubt on the question of Buck's future dangerousness. This issue required the jury to make a predictive judgment inevitably entailing a degree of speculation. But Buck's race was not subject to speculation, and according to Dr. Quijano, that immutable characteristic carried with it an increased probability of future violence. Dr. Quijano's testimony appealed to a powerful racial stereotype and might well have been valued by jurors as the opinion of a medical expert bearing the court's imprimatur. For these reasons, the District Court's conclusion that any mention of race during the penalty phase was de mimimis is rejected. So is the State's argument that Buck was not prejudiced by Dr. Quijano's testimony because it was introduce by his own counsel, rather than the prosecution. Jurors understand that prosecutors seek convictions and may reasonably be expected to evaluate the government's evidence in light of its motivations. When damaging evidence is introduced by a defendant's own lawyer, it is in the nature of an admission against interest, more likely to be taken at face value. Pp.____,____197 L. Ed. 2d, at 19-20.

3. The District Court's denial of Buck's rule 60(b)(6) motion was an abuse of discretion.
Pp.,___-___197 L. Ed. 2d, at 21-24.

(a) Relief under Rule 60(b)(6) is available only in "extraordinary circumstances. Gonzalez, 545 U.S., at 535, 125 S. Ct. 2641, 162 L. Ed. 2d 480. Determining whether such circumstances are present may include consideration of a wide range of factors, including "the risk of injustice to the parties" and "the risk of undermining the public's confidence in the judicial process." *Liljeberg v. Health Services Acquisition Corp.*, 486 U.S.

847, 863-864, 108 S. Ct. 2194, 100 L. Ed. 2d 855. The District Court's denial of Buck's motion rested largely on its determination that race played only a de minimis role in his sentencing. But there is a reasonable probability that Buck was sentenced to death in part because of his race. This is a disturbing departure from the basic premise that our criminal law punishes people for what they do, not who they are. That it concerned race amplifies the problem. Relying on race to impose a criminal sanction "poisons public confidence" in the judicial process, *Davis v. Ayala*, 576 U.S. _____, _____, 135 S. Ct. 2187, 192 L. Ed. 2d 323, a concern that supports Rule 60(b)(6) relief. The extraordinary nature of this case is confirmed by the remarkable steps the state itself took in response to Dr. Quijano's testimony in other cases. Although the State attempts to justify its decision to treat Buck differently from the other five defendants identified in the Attorney General's public statement, its explanations for distinguishing Buck's case from Saldano have nothing to do with the Attorney General's stated reasons for confessing error in that case. Pp._____-_____, 197 L. Ed. 2d, at 21-23.

(b) Unless Martinez and Trevino, rather than Coleman, would govern Buck's case were it re-opened, his claim would remain unreviewable and Rule 60(b)(6) relief would be inappropriate. The state argues that Martinez and Trevino would not govern Buck's case because they announced a new rule under *Teague v. Lane*, 489 U.S. 288, 109 S. Ct. 1060, 103 L. Ed. 2d 334, that does not apply retroactively to cases (like Buck's) on collateral review. This argument, however, has been waived: the State failed to advance it in District Court, before the Fifth Circuit, or in its brief in opposition to Buck's petition for certiorari. Pp._____-_____, 197 L. Ed. 2d, at 23-24.

623 Fed. Appx. 668, reversed and remanded.

WELCH v. UNITED STATES
136 S. Ct. 1257
April 18, 2016

DECISION: Holding in *Johnson v. United States* (2015 US) 135 S. Ct. 2551, 192 L. Ed. 2d 569, 2015 U.S. LEXIS 4251 – that increased sentence under 18 U.S.C.S. §924(e)(2)(B)'s residual clause violated due process under Federal Constitution's Fifth Amendment—announced new substantive rule that applied retroactively.

CASE SUMMARY: *Johnson v. United States*, which held that the residual clause of the Armed Career Criminal Act, 18 U.S.C.S. §924(e)(2)(B)(ii), was void for vagueness, was a substantive decision that applied retroactively to a prisoner's case on collateral review; it affected the reach of the Act rather than the judicial procedures by which the Act was applied.

OVERVIEW: ISSUE: Whether *Johnson v. United States*, which held that the residual clause of the Armed Career Criminal Act of 1984, 18 U.S.C.S. §924 (e)(2)(B)(ii), was void for vagueness, was a substantive decision that applied retroactively to a prisoner's case on collateral review. HOLDINGS: [l]-Johnson changed the substantive reach of the Act and was therefore a substantive decision. It was not a procedural decision, as it affected the reach of the underlying statute rather than the judicial procedures by which the statue was applied; [2]-The Teague balance did not depend on whether the underlying constitutional guarantee was procedural or substantive, but instead on whether the new rule itself had a procedural or substantive function; [3]-It was not necessary for the new rule to limit Congress's power in order to be substantive.

OUTCOME: Judgment vacated and case remanded. 7-1 Decision; 1 Dissent.

SYLLABUS

Federal law makes the possession of a firearm by a felon a crime punishable by a prison term of up to 10 years, 18 U.S.C. §§922(g), 924(a)(2), but the Armed Career Criminal Act of 1984 increases that sentence to a mandatory 15 years to life if the offender has three or more prior convictions for a "serious drug offense" or a "violent felony," §924(e)(l). The definition of "violent felony" includes the so-called residual clause, covering any felony that "otherwise involves conduct that presents a serious potential risk of physical injury to another." §924(e)(2)(B)(ii). In *Johnson v. United States*, 576 U.S.__, 135 S. Ct. 2551, 192 L. Ed. 2d 569, this Court held that clause unconstitutional under the void-for-vagueness doctrine.

Petitioner Welch was sentenced under the Armed Career Criminal Act before Johnson was decided. On direct review, the Eleventh Circuit affirmed his sentence, holding that Welch's prior Florida conviction for robbery qualified as a "violent felony" under the residual clause. After his conviction became final, Welch sought collateral relief under 28 U.S.C. §2255, which the District denied. The Eleventh Circuit then denied Welch a certificate of appealability. Three weeks later, this Court decided Johnson. Welch now seeks the retroactive application of Johnson to his case.

HELD: Johnson announced a new substantive rule that has retroactive effect in cases on collateral review. Pp. ____-____194 L. Ed. 2d, at 398-404.

a) An applicant seeking a certificate of appealability in a §2255 proceeding must make "a substantial showing of the denial of a constitutional right." §2255(c)(2). That standard is met when "reasonable jurists could debate whether... the petition should have been resolved in a different manner." *Slack v. McDaniel*, 529 U.S. 473. 484, 120 S. Ct. 1595, 146 L. Ed. 2d 542. The question whether Welch met that standard implicates a broader legal issue: whether Johnson is a substantive decision with retroactive effect in cases on collateral review. If so, then on the present record reasonable jurists could at least debate whether Welch should obtain relief in his collateral challenge to his sentence. Pp.____-____, 194 L. Ed. 2d, at 398-399.

b) New constitutional rules of criminal procedure generally do not apply retroactively. *Teague v. Lane*, 489 U.S. 288, 310, 109 S. Ct. 1060, 103, L. Ed. 2d 442. Substantive rules alter "the range of conduct or the class of persons that the law punishes," id., at 353, 124 S. Ct. 2519, 159 L. Ed. 2d 442. Procedural rules, by contrast "regulate only the manner of determining the defendant's culpability." Ibid. Under this framework, Johnson is substantive. Before Johnson, the residual clause could cause an offender to face a prison sentence of at least 15 years instead of at most 10. Since Johnson made the clause invalid, it can no longer mandate or authorize any sentence. By the same logic, Johnson is not procedural, since it had nothing to do with the range of permissible methods a court might use to determine whether a defendant should be sentenced under the Act, see Schiro, supra, at 353, 124 S. Ct. 2519, 159 L. Ed. 2d 442. Pp. - 194 L. Ed. 2d, at 399-400.

c) The counterarguments made by Court-appointed amicus are unpersuasive. She contends that Johnson is a procedural decision because the void-for- vagueness doctrine is based on procedural due process. But the Teague framework turns on whether the function of the rule is substantive or procedural, not on the rule's underlying constitutional source. Amicus' approach would lead to results that cannot be squared with prior precedent. Precedent also does not support amicus' claim that a rule must limit Congress' power to be substantive, see, e.g., *Bousley v. United States*, 523 U.S. 614, 118 S. Ct. 1604, 140 L. Ed.

2d 828, or her claim that statutory construction cases are an ad hoc exception to that principle and are substantive only because they implement the intent of Congress. The separation-of-powers argument raised by amicus is also misplaced, for regardless of whether a decision involves statutory interpretation or statutory invalidation, a court lacks the power to exact a penalty that has not been authorized by any valid criminal statute. Pp.____,____ 194 L. Ed. 2d, at 400-404.

Vacated and remanded.

CHRISTESON v. ROPER
135 S. Ct. 891
January 20, 2015

DECISION: Federal habeas corpus petition whose appointed attorneys missed tiling deadline held entitled to substitute counsel under 18 U.S.C.S. §3599(e) to argue for equitable tolling.

CASE SUMMARY: A motion to substitute habeas counsel was improperly denied where petitioner's appointed attorneys missed the filing deadline for filing a habeas petition, the best argument for equitably tolling was the attorneys' own failure, and thus, there was a significant conflict of interest entitling petitioner to new counsel under 18 U.S.C.S. §3599(e).

OVERVIEW: HOLDINGS: [l]-Petitioner's motion to substitute habeas counsel was improperly denied where his appointed attorneys had missed the filing deadline for filing his first habeas petition, petitioner's best argument for equitably tolling the limitations period was the attorneys' own failure to satisfy the AEDPA's statute of limitations, and thus, there was a significant conflict of interest that entitled petitioner to new counsel under 18 U.S.C.S. §3599(e).

OUTCOME: Petition for certiorari granted; judgment reversed and case remanded. Unanimous decision, 1 dissent (based on lack of briefing and argument).

TREVINO v. THALER
133 S. Ct. 1911
May 28, 2013

DECISION: Procedural default held not to bar federal habeas corpus court from hearing substantial claim of ineffective assistance of counsel at trial, where state procedural framework typically made meaningful opportunity to raise ineffective-assistance claim on direct appeal highly unlikely.

CASE SUMMARY: PROCEDURAL POSTURE: A Texas court found petitioner death row inmate's ineffective assistance of trial counsel (IATC) claim was procedurally defaulted for failure to raise it in initial state postconviction proceedings. On the inmate's federal habeas petition, the district court held the procedural default was an independent and adequate state ground barring federal review. The U.S. Court of Appeals for the Fifth Circuit affirmed. Certiorari was granted. Because in Texas it was highly unlikely an inmate had a meaningful opportunity to raise an ineffective assistance of trial counsel claim on direct appeal, procedural default did not bar a federal habeas court from hearing it if, in initial-review collateral proceedings, there was no counsel or counsel in that proceeding was ineffective.

OVERVIEW: Texas did not expressly require IATC claims to be raised on initial collateral review. Texas law on its face appeared to permit (but not require) that the claim be raised on direct appeal. But Texas procedure made it virtually impossible for appellate counsel to adequately present an IATC claim on direct review, as the trial record often failed to contain the necessary substantiating information. A motion-for-new-trial was often inadequate because of time constraints and the lack of the trial record being transcribed at that point. In Texas, a writ of habeas corpus issued in state collateral proceedings ordinarily was essential to gathering the facts necessary to evaluate IATC claims. As a systematic matter, Texas did not afford meaningful review of an IATC claim. Where a state procedural framework, by reason of its design and operation, made it highly unlikely in a typical case that a defendant would have a meaningful opportunity to raise an IATC claim on direct appeal, a procedural default would not bar a federal habeas court from hearing a substantial IATC claim if, in the initial-review collateral proceeding, there was no counsel or counsel in that proceeding was ineffective.

OUTCOME: The Fifth Circuit's judgment finding that procedural default of the ineffective assistance of trial counsel claim was an independent adequate state ground barring the federal review was vacated and the case was remanded for further proceedings. 5-4 Decision; 2 Dissents.

SYLLABUS

In *Martinez v. Ryan*, 566 U.S. 1, 17, 132 S. Ct. 1309, 182 L. Ed. 2d 272, 278, 288 this Court held that "a procedural default will not bar a federal habeas court from hearing a substantial claim of ineffective assistance at trial if, in the [State's] initial-review collateral proceeding, there was no counsel or counsel in that proceeding was ineffective." Martinez regarded a prisoner from Arizona, where state procedural law required the prisoner to raise the claim during his first state collateral review proceeding. Ibid. This case regards a prisoner from Texas, where state procedural law does not require a defendant to raise his ineffective-assistance-of-trial-counsel claim on collateral review. Rather, Texas law appears to permit a prisoner to raise such a claim on direct review, but the structure and design of the Texas system make it virtually impossible for a prisoner to do so. The question presented in this case is whether, despite this difference, the rule set out in Martinez applies in Texas.

Petitioner Trevino was convicted of capital murder in Texas state court and sentenced to death after the jury found insufficient mitigating circumstances to warrant a life sentence. Neither new counsel appointed for his direct appeal nor new counsel appointed for state collateral review raised the claim that Trevino's trial counsel provided ineffective assistance during the penalty phase by failing to adequately investigate and present mitigating circumstances. When that claim was initially raised in Trevino's federal habeas petition, the District Court stayed the proceedings so Trevino could raise it in state court. The state court found the claim procedurally defaulted because of Trevino's failure to raise it in his initial state postconviction proceedings, and the federal court then concluded that this failure was an independent and adequate state ground barring the federal courts from considering the claim. The Fifth Circuit affirmed. Its decision predated Martinez, but that court has since concluded that Martinez does not apply in Texas because Martinez's good-cause exception applies only where state law says that a defendant must initially raise his ineffective-assistance-of-trial-counsel claim in initial state collateral review proceedings, while Texas law appears to permit a defendant to raise that claim on direct appeal.

HELD: Where, as here, a State's procedural framework, by reason of its design and operation, makes it highly unlikely in a typical case that a defendant will have a meaningful opportunity to raise an ineffective-assistance- of-trial-counsel claim on direct appeal, the exception recognized in Martinez applies. Pp. 421-429, 185 L. Ed. 2d, at 1051-1057.

(a) A finding that a defendant's state law "procedural default" rests on "an independent and adequate state ground" ordinarily prevents a federal habeas court from considering the defendant's federal constitutional claim. *Coleman v. Thompson*, 501 U.S. 722, 729-730, 111 S. Ct. 2546, 115 L. Ed. 2d 640. However, a "prisoner may obtain federal review of a defaulted claim by showing cause for the default and prejudice from a violation of federal law." Martinez, supra, at 10, 132 S. Ct. 1309, 182 L. Ed. 2d 272, 278, 282. That exception allows a federal habeas court to find "cause" to excuse such default where (1) the ineffective-assistance-of-trial-counsel claim was a "substantial" claim; (2) the "cause" consisted of there being "no counsel" or only "ineffective" counsel during the state collateral review proceeding; (3) the state collateral review proceeding was the "initial" review proceeding in respect to the "ineffective-assistance-of-trial-counsel claim"; and (4) state law requires that the claim "be raised in an initial- review collateral proceeding." Id., at 14, 132 S. Ct. 1309, 182 L. Ed. 2d 272, 288, Pp. 421-423, 185 L. Ed. 2d, at 1051-1053.

(b) The difference between the Texas law—which in theory grants permission to bring an ineffective-assistance-of-trial-counsel claim on direct appeal but in practice denies a meaningful opportunity to do so — and the Arizona law at issue in Martinez—which required the claim to be raised in an initial collateral review proceeding — does not matter in respect to the application of Martinez. Pp. 423-429, 185 L. Ed. 2d, at 1053-1057.

(1) This conclusion is supported by two characteristics of Texas' procedures. First, Texas procedures make it nearly impossible for an ineffective- assistance-of-trial-counsel claim to be presented on direct review. The nature of an ineffective-assistance claim means that the trial record is likely to be insufficient to support the claim. And a motion for a new trial to develop the record is usually inadequate because of Texas rules regarding time limits on the filing, and the disposal, of such motions and the availability of trial transcripts. Thus, a writ of habeas corpus is normally needed to gather the facts necessary for evaluating these claims in Texas. Second, where Martinez not to apply, the Texas procedural system would create significant unfairness because Texas courts in effect have directed defendants to raise ineffective-assistance-of-trial-counsel claims on collateral, rather than on direct, review. Texas can point to only a few cases in which a defendant has used the motion-for-a-new-trial mechanism to expand the record on appeal. Texas suggests that there are other mechanisms by which a prisoner can expand the record on appeal, but these mechanisms seem special and limited in their application, and cannot overcome the Texas courts' own well-supported determination that collateral review normally is the preferred procedural route for raising an ineffective-assistance-of-trial-counsel claim. Respondent also argues that there is no equitable problem here, where appellate counsel's failure to bring a substantial ineffective-assistance claim on direct appeal may constitute cause to excuse the procedural default, but respondent points to no case in which such a failure by appellate counsel has been deemed constitutionally ineffective. Pp. 423-428, 185 L. Ed. 2d, at 1053-1056.

(2) The very facts that led this Court to create a narrow exception to Coleman in Martinez similarly argue for applying that exception here. The right involved—adequate assistance of trial counsel—is similarly and critically important. In both instances practical considerations—the need for a new lawyer, the need to expand the trial court record, and the need for sufficient time to develop the claim—argue strongly for initial consideration of the claim during collateral, not on direct, review, see Martinez, 566 U.S., at 13, 132 S. Ct. 1309, 182 L. Ed. 2d 272, 277. In both instances failure to consider a lawyer's "ineffectiveness" during an initial-review collateral proceeding as a potential "cause" for excusing a procedural default will deprive the defense of any opportunity for review of an ineffective-assistance-of-trial-counsel claim, see id., at 11, 132 S. Ct. 1309, 182 L. Ed. 2d 272. Thus, for present purposes, a distinction between (1) a State that denies permission to raise the claim on direct appeal and (2) a State that grants permission but denies a fair, meaningful opportunity to develop the claim is a distinction without a difference. Pp. 428-429, 185 L. Ed. 2d, at 1056-1057. 449 Fed. Appx. 415, vacated and remanded.

McQUIGGIN v. PERKINS
133 S. Ct. 1924
May 28, 2013

DECISION: Actual innocence, if proved, held to be gateway through which state prisoner petitioning for federal habeas corpus relief might pass, regardless of whether impeded by procedural bar or expiration of 28 U.S.C.S. §2244(d)(l)'s limitations period.

CASE SUMMARY

PROCEDURAL POSTURE: Respondent state inmate filed a petition for a writ of habeas corpus, seeking federal district court review of his conviction of first-degree murder. The district court dismissed the petition; however, the U.S. Court of Appeals for the Sixth Circuit reversed and remanded. The U.S. Supreme Court granted certiorari to resolve a conflict amount the circuits on whether 28 U.S.C.S. §2244(d)(1) could be overcome by showing of actual innocence. Although state inmate who sought habeas relief in federal court six years after he obtained the last of three affidavits which supported his claim that he did not commit murder was not barred by 28 U.S.C.S. §2244(d)(1) from seeking review, court of appeals erred to extent it eliminated timing as a factor relevant to evaluating inmate's affidavits.

OVERVIEW: The inmate filed a petition for a writ of habeas corpus in 2008, more than eleven years after his conviction for first-degree murder became final, claiming that he was innocent and received ineffective assistance of counsel during his trial, and he submitted three affidavits signed by witnesses that supported his claim. The district court found that even if the affidavits could be characterized as newly discovered evidence, the inmate was not entitled to relief because he obtained the last affidavit in 2002 but did not file his petition until 2008. Although the Sixth Circuit found that the inmate's petition was untimely under 28 U.S.C.S. §2241(d)(1), it held that his claim of actual-innocence allowed him to pursue his habeas petition as if it had been filed on time. The Supreme Court vacated the Sixth Circuit's decision and remanded the case. While the court rejected the State's argument that habeas petitioners who asserted convincing actual-innocence claims had to prove diligence to cross a federal court's threshold, it found that the Sixth Circuit erred to the extent that it eliminated timing as a factor relevant in evaluating the reliability of the affidavits.

OUTCOME: The Supreme Court vacated the Sixth Circuit's decision and remanded the case. 5-4 Decision; 1 dissent.

MARTINEZ v. RYAN
132 S. Ct. 1309
March 20, 2012

DECISION: State prisoner's failure to raise ineffective-assistance-of-trial-counsel claims in only proceeding-initial-review collateral proceeding-in which state allowed such claims held not to bar federal habeas corpus court from hearing claims, if prisoner had no, or ineffective, counsel in proceeding.

SUMMARY

PROCEDURAL POSTURE: A district court denied petitioner inmate's habeas claim of ineffective assistance of trial counsel, ruling that Ariz. Rule Crim. P. 32.2(a)(3) was an adequate and independent state-law ground to bar federal review and no case was shown to excuse the procedural default since post-conviction counsel's errors did not qualify as cause for a default. The U.S. Court of Appeals for the Ninth Circuit affirmed. Certiorari was granted.

OVERVIEW: Where under state law, claims of ineffective assistance (IA) of trial counsel had to be raised in an initial-review collateral proceeding (IRCP), a procedural default would not bar a federal habeas court from hearing a substantial claim of IA at trial if, in the IRCP, there was no counsel or counsel in that proceeding was ineffective. The inmate's attorney in the IRCP filed a notice akin to an Anders brief, in effect conceding a lack of any meritorious claim, including a claim of IA at trial, which the inmate argued was IA. The Ninth Circuit did not decide if it was. Rather, it held that because he did not have a right to an attorney in the IRCP, the attorney's errors in the IRCP could not establish cause for the failure to comply with the State's rules. Thus, the Ninth Circuit did not determine if the attorney in the IRCP was ineffective or whether the claim of IA of trial counsel was substantial. Nor was prejudice addressed. Those issues remained open for a decision on remand. While 28 U.S.C.S. §2254(i) precluded relying on IA of a postconviction attorney as a "ground for relief," it did not stop its use to establish "cause" to excuse procedural default.

OUTCOME: The judgment upholding the denial of habeas relief was reversed, and the case was remanded for further proceedings. 7-2 decision; 1 opinion, 1 dissent.

SYLLABUS

Arizona prisoners may raise claims of ineffective assistance of trial counsel only in state collateral proceedings, not on direct review. In petitioner Martinez's first state collateral proceeding, his counsel did not raise such a claim. On federal habeas review with new counsel, Martinez argued that he received ineffective assistance both at trial and in his first state collateral proceeding. He also claimed that he had a constitutional right to an effective attorney in the collateral proceeding because it was the first place to raise his claim of ineffective assistance at trial. The District Court denied the petition, finding that Arizona's preclusion rule was an adequate and independent state-law ground barring federal review, and that under *Coleman v. Thompson*, 501 U.S. 722, 111 S. Ct. 2546, 115 L. Ed. 2d 640, the attorney's errors in the post-conviction proceeding did not qualify as cause to excuse the procedural default. The court of Appeals for the Ninth Circuit affirmed.

Held: 1. Where, under state law, ineffective-assistance-of-trial-counsel claims must be raised in an initial-review collateral proceeding, a procedural default will not bar a federal habeas court from hearing those claims if, in the initial-review collateral proceeding, there was no counsel or counsel in that proceeding was ineffective. Pp. _____-_____, 182 L. Ed. 2d, at 282-288.

a) Given that the precise question here is whether ineffective assistance in an initial-review collateral proceeding on an ineffective-assistance- at-trial claim may provide cause for a procedural default in a federal habeas proceeding, this is not the case to resolve the question left open in Coleman: whether a prisoner has a constitutional right to effective counsel in initial-review collateral proceedings. However, to protect prisoners with potentially legitimate ineffective-assistance claims, it is necessary to recognize a narrow exception to Coleman's unqualified statement that an attorney's ignorance or inadvertence in a post-conviction proceeding does not qualify as cause to excuse a procedural default, namely, that inadequate assistance of counsel at initial-review collateral proceedings may establish cause. P. 182 L. Ed. 2d, at 282.

b) A federal court can hear Martinez's ineffective-assistance claim only if he can establish cause to excuse the procedural default and prejudice from a violation of federal law. Coleman held that a post-conviction attorney's negligence does not qualify as 'cause,' because "the attorney is the prisoner's agent," and "the principal bears the risk of" his agent's negligent conduct. *Maples v. Thomas*, ante, at 132 S. Ct. 912, 181 L. Ed. 2d 807. However, in Coleman, counsel's alleged error was on appeal from an initial- review collateral proceeding. Thus, his claims had been addressed by the state habeas trial court. This marks a key difference between initial-review collateral proceedings and other collateral proceedings. Here, where the initial-review collateral proceeding is the first designated proceeding for a prisoner to raise the ineffective-assistance claim, the collateral proceeding is the equivalent of a prisoner's direct appeal as to that claim because the state habeas court decides the claim's merits, no other court has addressed the claim, and defendants "are generally ill-equipped to represent themselves" where they have no brief from counsel and no court opinion addressing their claim. *Halbert v. Michigan*, 545 U.S. 605, 617, 125 S. Ct. 2582, 162 L. Ed. 2d 552. An attorney's errors during an appeal on direct review may provide cause to excuse a procedural default; for if the attorney appointed by the State is ineffective, the prisoner has been denied fair process and the opportunity to comply with the State's procedures and obtain an adjudication on the merits of his claim. Without adequate representation in an initial-review collateral proceeding, a prisoner will have similar difficulties vindicating a substantial ineffective-assistance-at-trial claim. The same would be true if the State did not appoint an attorney for the initial-review collateral proceeding. A prisoner's inability to present an ineffective-assistance claim is of particular concern because the right to effective trial counsel is a bedrock principle in this Nation's justice system.

Allowing a federal habeas court to hear a claim of ineffective assistance at trial when an attorney's errors (or an attorney's absence) caused a procedural default in an initial-review collateral proceeding acknowledges, as an equitable matter, that a collateral proceeding, if proper consideration was given to a substantial claim. It thus follows that when a State requires a prisoner to raise a claim of ineffective assistance at trial in a collateral proceeding, a prisoner may establish cause for a procedural default of such claim in two circumstances: where the state courts did not appoint counsel in the initial-review collateral proceeding for an ineffective-assistance-at-trial claim; and where appointed counsel in the initial-review collateral proceeding, where that claim should have been raised, was ineffective under *Strickland v. Washington*, 466 U.S. 668, 104 S. Ct. 2052, 80 L. Ed. 2d 674. To overcome the default, a prisoner must also demonstrate that the underlying ineffective-assistance-at-trial claim is substantial. Most jurisdictions have procedures to ensure counsel is appointed for substantial ineffective-assistance claims. It is likely that such attorneys are qualified to perform, and do perform, according to prevailing professional norms. And where that is so. States may enforce a procedural default in federal habeas proceedings. Pp.____,____ 182 L.Ed. 2d, at 282-286.

c) This limited qualification to Coleman does not implicate stare decisis concerns. Coleman's holding remains true except as to initial-review collateral proceedings for claims of ineffective assistance at trial. The holding in this case should not put a significant strain on state resources. A State facing the question of cause for an apparent default may answer that the ineffective-assistance-of-trial-counsel claim is insubstantial. The limited circumstances recognized here also reflect the importance of the right to effective assistance at trial. Other claims may not implicate the same fundamentals of the adversary system. The Antiterrorism and Effective Death Penalty Act of 1996 does not speak to the question presented here, and thus does not bar Martinez from asserting attorney error as cause for procedural default. Pp.____,____182 L. Ed. 2d, at 286-288.

2. Whether Martinez's attorney in his first collateral proceeding was ineffective and whether his ineffective-assistance-at-trial claim is substantial, as well as the question of prejudice, are questions that remain open for a decision on remand, P. ____,____182 L. Ed. 2d, at 288.

623 F.3d 731, reversed and remanded.

CONCLUSION

You are now armed with an understanding that cannot be obtained from anywhere else. But, even with this advancement, you are not guaranteed review. If you fail in this effort, meaning you are summarily denied a writ of certiorari, that is not to say that you don't deserve relief. A quest to seek post-conviction relief is not an easy one, and only those who persevere will find justice. Thus, I encourage you to continue your fight. It's only when martyrs and patriots fight against tyranny that liberty prevails.

The petition for a writ of certiorari is often considered a formality rather than a form of relief. I however disagree. In looking at the history of litigation against the Armed Career Criminal Act, you find that it crumbled under the constant pressure of the people. I, therefore, encourage you to exercise every step of the process. It's only through constant effort that the American people, like us, can fight against the injustice that plagues our nation. No different than the fight against slavery in the 1800's, we too must fight the fight against mass-incarceration. This fight does not end on the steps of The Supreme Court. To know what's coming as your next step, stay in touch with Freebird Publishers, watch for their release of *Post-Conviction Relief: Second Last Chance*.

A preview of

Post-Conviction Relief: Second Last Chance

By: Kelly Patrick Riggs

Published by
Freebird Publishers

With the certiorari process soon to be behind you, it's important to know that it is not the end of the road. The Supreme Court's decision has nothing to do with the merits of your case. What you must prepare for is your 'second last chance'. It's unfortunate but the post-conviction process is quite similar to the criminal justice process. It, too, must be followed to its fullest extent for the bar members involved to maximize its fullest financial potential. The people who operate the Criminal Justice System are compensated for every step of the process that they exercise. That is why district courts ordinarily do not grant §2255 and §2254 motions until ordered by the court of appeals to do so. Likewise, the Court of Appeals grants only a small number of certificates of appealability for the sole purpose of maintaining the illusion of being fair. Most of which are granted only to litigants who can afford counsel.

For those of us who are required to present our own case, as Pro Se litigants, we are doomed to exercise the secondary process in our post-conviction relief effort. Regardless of how meritorious our claims are. The next book, *Post-Conviction Relief: Second Last Chance*, covers the secondary process in great detail. The filing that follows is just one of the many examples you will find contained in this next book.

KELLY PATRICK RIGGS

INTRODUCTION

The process of post-conviction relief is much like any other battle. You have, at a minimum, two opposing parties and a field on which to fight. In the criminal justice system, this battle is identified by an American citizen who seeks justice, a federal judge who seeks to maintain the finality of the conviction (of a modern-day slave) and the processes of federal law that represent the battlefield. The disturbing part is that the American citizen is out-numbered and out-matched. He is most often untrained in law fighting against the judge, the prosecutor, and his own criminal defense lawyer who are now, as they always have been, working together to perpetuate mass-incarceration.

When I first heard someone say words much like these, I was shocked. I couldn't believe that the government, which I supported for so many years, would use our criminal justice system to funnel tax dollars into privately held companies. And at the expense of someone's liberty. It wasn't until I witnessed blind men convicted of seeing and fishermen sentenced to prison for throwing the small ones back into the ocean that I opened my eyes. It's only now, as I watch a federal judge try to conceal her own culpability in the murders of DeAndre Washington and Gary "Sambo" Hazelrigg, that I realize how broken our criminal justice system really is.

It's because of the foregoing that it is important to share more of the federal procedure with the prisoners of war who seek justice in America.

UNITED STATES DISTRICT COURT
NORTHERN DISTRICT OF ALABAMA
SOUTHERN DIVISION

Kelly Patrick Riggs	
v.	Case No.:
	2:15-cv-8043-KOB
United States of America	[2:12-cr-297-KOB-JEO]

MOTION FOR RELIEF FROM FINAL JUDGEMENT IN §2255 PROCEEDING PURSUANT TO FED. R. CIV. P., RULE 60(b)(6)

Mr. Riggs moves this court to relieve him from the final judgement, to deny his §2255, because the court failed to address all his grounds for relief as required by *Clisby v. Jones*, 960 F.2d 925 (11th Cir. 1992)(*en banc*).

JURISDICTION

The district court has exclusive authority, under Fed. R. Civ. P., Rule 60(b)(6), to relieve Mr. Riggs from its final judgement because it failed to reach the merit of the claims raised in ground three of this amended §2255. Pursuant to Rule 60(b), a district court may relieve a party from a final judgement, order, or proceeding on certain grounds, including any reason that justifies relief. Fed. R. Civ. P., Rule 60(b). A Rule 60(b) motion should be treated as a successive habeas petition if it "seeks to add a new ground for relief" or "attacks the federal court's previous resolution of a claim on the merits." *Gonzales v. Crosby*, 545 U.S. 525, 532, 125 S.Ct. 2641, 2648, 162 L. Ed. 2d 480 (2005). But when the Rule 60(b) motion attacks "some defect in the integrity of the federal habeas proceedings," and not a merit issue, it is not an impermissible successive motion.

STATEMENT OF THE CASE

On or about November 11, 2015, Mr. Riggs submitted an instant motion seeking post-conviction relief pursuant to 28 U.S.C. §2255. His primary claims - although poorly particularized because of his ignorance of law - were based on four basic events: 1) he and his defense counsel, Glennon F. Threatt, Jr., suffered from two distinct and separate conflicts of interests; 2) that he had been outright denied counsel at a critical, pre-guilt, stage of the criminal proceeding; 3) he suffered from a constructive denial of counsel at a critical stage; and 4) he had been abandoned by counsel on direct appeal. After years of delay in the United States district court, Mr. Riggs was granted leave to amend and/or clarify his §2255.

In the amended §2255, Mr. Riggs concisely presented four grounds for relief: 1) his guilty plea was not intelligent, knowing, and voluntary; 2) Counsel was ineffective because he had a conflict of interest; 3) that he had been deprived of counsel in his criminal case; and 4) he is actually innocent.

On may 2, 2018, the district court denied Mr. Riggs's §2255 motion based on three of his four grounds, "(l) his guilty plea was not intelligent, knowing, and voluntary; (2) counsel was ineffective because he had a conflict of interest; and (3) he is actually innocent.

ARGUMENT

Mr. Riggs was deprived of his right to due process in his §2255 proceeding, because the court failed to reach the merits of the third ground in his amended motion. The Eleventh Circuit of the United States court of appeals has routinely held that "when a district court fails to address the claims presented in a §2255 habeas petition, we vacate without prejudice and remand the case for consideration of all the remaining claims. *Clisby v. Jones*, 960 F.2d 925, 936 (11th Cir. 1992)(*en banc*). In Clisby, the district court dismissed thirteen of the petitioner's claims, granted habeas relief on one claim, and reserved judgment on the remaining five claims. Id at 935. In response, we expressed concern over the 'growing number of cases in which [we were] forced to remand for consideration of issues, the district court chose not to resolve'." Id at 935-36. We acknowledged the disruptive effect that such 'piecemeal litigation' had on a state's criminal justice system. Id. at 935. Accordingly, in an effort to streamline habeas procedure, we exercise our supervisory authority and instructed district courts to resolve all claims for relief raised in a petition for writ of habeas corpus pursuant to §2254, 'regardless of whether habeas relief is granted or denied' Id. at 936. We have defined a 'claim for relief' as 'any allegation of a Constitutional violation'.

In Mr. Riggs's §2255 proceeding the district court failed to address an entire ground for relief. Ground three in Mr. Riggs amended §2255 raised three separate claims of outright denial of counsel. The district court did however state in a footnote, on page 8 of its memorandum that "the record confirms that Mr. Riggs was represented by counsel at every stage of his criminal proceeding." Although, mentioned in a footnote the district court failed to mention, let alone address, a single issue of merit in Mr. Riggs ground three.

In a second footnote, on page 8 of the courts memorandum, the court expressed that Mr. Riggs, "attempts to assert a claim of ineffective assistance about Ms. Barnett's actions …" In this the district court outright lies. Mr. Riggs, in his ground three, did not claim that Ms. Barnett (an assistant Federal Public defender) had provided ineffective assistance of counsel. Mr. Riggs accused Ms. Barnett and Glennon F. Threatt, Jr. of ATTEMPTED MURDER and conspiracy to murder a federal informant, Mr. Riggs. Moreover, Mr. Riggs's ground three particularizes several claims against defense counsel Brett M. Bloomston as providing ineffective assistance of trial counsel. But yet the district court failed to even acknowledge Mr. Bloomston as trial counsel at all.

Finally, the district court discusses Mr. Riggs' arguments concerning how the federal defender's office helped to conceal evidence and testimony in DeAndre Washington's murder. What the district court leaves out, however, is that Mr. Riggs specifically named United States District Judge Karon Owen Bowdre as the official who received not only the report about DeAndre Washington's murder but also a threat to murder Sambo Hazelrigg, who was subsequently murdered in 2015.

It is likely because Mr. Riggs accused District Judge Karon Owen Bowdre of being an accessory after the fact in DeAndre Washington's murder, and a facilitator in Sambo Hazelrigg murder, that she has refused to address the merit in Mr. Riggs case. Moreover, Judge Bowdre must continue to deny Mr. Riggs any review on the merits of his claims to maintain her own credibility. In the event Judge Bowdre were to rule in the interest of justice, in Mr. Riggs's case, it would lend credence to Mr. Riggs' claim that she is indeed culpable in three murder investigations. Thus, an equitable ruling on Mr. Riggs's ground three would shatter Judge Bowdre's public reputation and the people's confidence in the district court's ability to reach the ends of justice in the Northern District of Alabama.

CONCLUSION

Wherefore, Mr. Riggs moves this court to grant him relief from the final judgment in his §2255 proceeding, so it may determine the merit of ground three in his amended §2255. In the alternative, Mr. Riggs asks that Judge Bowdre recuse herself due to her personal interest in the outcome of this case. This motion will be, as all others in this proceeding have been, made available for public opinion in Mr. Riggs's books, the Post-Conviction Relief Series available on Amazon.com.

Amazon.com/author/KellyPatrickRiggs

Submitted on April 1, 2019, by:

X_____
Kelly Patrick Riggs, Pro Se

Reg. Number

Address

CERTIFICATE OF SERVICE

This motion has been served on all parties as required by rule and law.

Submitted on April 1, 2019, by:

X_____
Kelly Patrick Riggs, Pro Se

Reg. Number

Address

FREEBIRD PUBLISHERS

Thanks for your interest in Freebird Publishers!

We value our customers and would love to hear from you! Reviews are an important part in bringing you quality publications. We love hearing from our readers-rather it's good or bad (though we strive for the best)!

If you could take the time to review/rate any publication you've purchased with Freebird Publishers we would appreciate it!

If your loved one uses Amazon, have them post your review on the books you've read. This will help us tremendously, in providing future publications that are even more useful to our readers and growing our business.

Amazon works off of a 5 star rating system. When having your loved one rate us be sure to give them your chosen star number as well as a written review. Though written reviews aren't required, we truly appreciate hearing from you.

Sample Review Received on Inmate Shopper

poeticsunshine

★★★★★ **Truly a guide**

Reviewed in the United States on June 29, 2023

Verified Purchase

This book is a powerhouse of information. My son had to calm/ground himself to prioritize where to start.

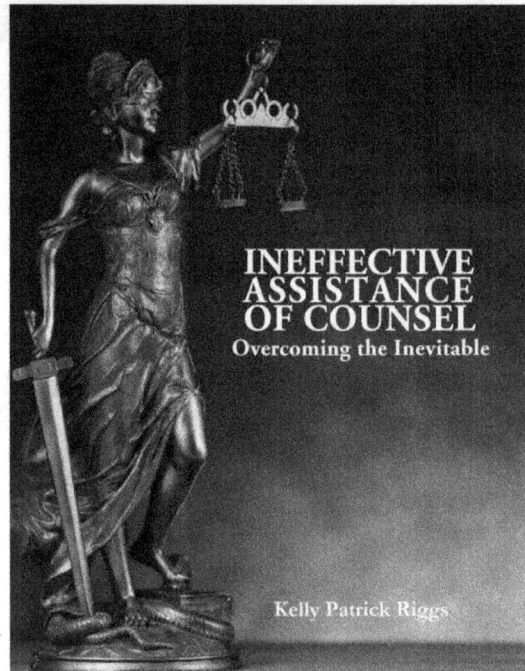

The image is an advertisement covering essentially the entire page.

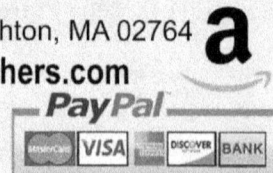

GRAPHIC IS ONE IMAGE OF OUR BOOK COVERS. NOT THUMBNAIL PHOTOS

Freebird Publishers

CURRENT FULL COLOR CATALOG
98 Pages filled with books, gifts and services for prisoners

We have created four different versions of our new catalog A: Complete B:No Pen Pal Content C:No Sexy Photo Content D:No Pen Pal and Sexy Content. Available in full Color or B&W (please specify) please make sure you order the correct catalog based on your prison mail room regulations. We are not responsible for rejected or lost in the mail catalogs. Send SASE for info on stamp options.

Freebird Publishers Book Selection Includes:

- Ask. Believe. Receive.: Our Power to Create Our Own Destiny
- Celebrity Female Star Power
- Cell Chef 1 & 2
- Cellpreneur: The Millionaire Prisoner's Guidebook
- Chapter 7 Bankruptcy: Seven Steps to Financial Freedom
- Convicted Creations Cookbook
- Cooking With Hot Water
- DIY for Prisoners
- Federal Rules of Criminal Procedures Pocket Guide
- Federal Rules of Evidence Pocket Guide
- Fine Dining Cookbook 1, 2, 3
- Freebird Publisher's Gift Look Book
- Get Money: Self Educate, Get Rich. & Enjoy Life (3 book series)
- Habeas Corpus Manual
- Hobo Pete and the Ghost Train
- Hot Girl Safari: Non-Nude Photo Book
- How to Write a Good Letter From Prison
- Ineffective Assistance of Counsel
- Inmate Shopper
- Inmate Shopper Censored
- Introduction to Financial Success
- Kitty Kat: Adult Entertainment Resource Book
- Life With a Record
- Locked Down Cookin'
- Locked Up Love Letters: Becoming the Perfect Pen Pal
- Parent to Parent: Raising Children from Prison
- Penacon Presents: The Prisoners Guide to Being a Perfect Pen Pal
- Pen Pal Success: The Ultimate Guide to Getting & Keeping Pen Pals
- Pen Pals: A Personal Guide for Prisoners
- Pillow Talk: Adult Non-Nude Photo Book
- Post-Conviction Relief Series (Books 1-7)
- Prison Health Handbook
- Prison Legal Guide
- Prison Picasso
- Prisoner's Communication Guidelines for Navigating in Prison
- Prisonyland Adult Coloring Book
- Pro Se Guide to Legal Research & Writing
- Pro Se Prisoner: How to Buy Stocks and Bitcoin
- Pro Se Section 1983 Manual
- Section 2254 Pro Se Guide to Winning Federal Relief
- Soft Shots: Adult Non-Nude Photo Book
- The Best 500 Non-Profit Organizations for Prisoners & Their Families
- Weight Loss Unlocked
- Write & Get Paid

CATALOG ONLY $5 - SHIPS BY FIRST CLASS MAIL
ADDITIONAL OPTION: add $5 for Shipping and Handling with Tracking

NO ORDER FORM NEEDED CLEARLY WRITE ON PAPER & SEND PAYMENT TO:
FREEBIRD PUBLISHERS 221 Pearl St., Ste. 541, North Dighton, MA 02764
www.FreebirdPublishers.com Diane@FreebirdPublishers.com Text/Phone: 774-406-8682
We accept all forms of payment. Plus Venmo & CashApp! Venmo: @FreebirdPublishers CashApp: $FreebirdPublishers

www.ingramcontent.com/pod-product-compliance
Lightning Source LLC
Chambersburg PA
CBHW081501200326
41518CB00015B/2344